THEMES AND VARIATIONS

THE SOCIETY OF BIBLICAL LITERATURE
SEMEIA STUDIES
Edward L. Greenstein, Editor

THEMES AND VARIATIONS
A Study of Action
in Biblical Narrative

by
Robert C. Culley

Scholars Press
Atlanta, Georgia

THEMES AND VARIATIONS

© 1992
The Society of Biblical Literature

Library of Congress Cataloging in Publication Data

Culley, Robert C.
    Themes and variations : a study of action in biblical narrative /
    by Robert C. Culley.
    p. cm. — (The Society of Biblical Literature Semeia studies)
    Includes bibliographical references and indexes.
    ISBN 1-55540-757-9 (cloth : alk. paper). — ISBN 1-55540-758-7
    (pbk.)
    1. Narration in the Bible. I. Title. II. Series: Semeia
studies.
BS521.7.C857 1992
220.6'6—dc20   92-26201
                                                  CIP

Printed in the United States of America
on acid-free paper

Contents

Preface

My discussion of story patterns goes back to 1974. What I present here has been developed gradually since then and tried out in a number of articles. Much of what appears here has been read in the form of papers at meetings of various learned societies. Three previously published articles have been used in a revised form: an article on Genesis 18–19, "Analyse alttestamentlicher Erzählungen—Erträge der jüngsten Method-endiscussion," *Biblische Notizen* (1978), pp. 27–39; "Action Sequences in Gen 2–3," *Semeia* (1980), pp. 25–33; and "Stories of the Conquest: Joshua 2, 6, 7, and 8," *Hebrew Annual Review* (1985), pp. 25–44. Many have helped along the way. The Faculty of Religious Studies, McGill University, has offered a congenial setting for teaching and research. My colleagues, the office and library staff, and the students have provided a stimulating atmosphere in which to carry on my work. I would like to thank Roland Boer, a doctoral candidate in biblical studies, who read the manuscript finding many a slip, and also Elizabeth Brown, a research assistant, who helped with the checking of the manuscript. The sharp eye and mind of Edward Greenstein, the editor of *Semeia Studies*, caught many matters of form and substance which I had to correct or reconsider.

The final drafts of the Introduction were written while I was supported by a research grant from the Social Sciences and Humanities Research council of Canada, to which I express by gratitude.

Appreciation is due to Scholars Press, especially for the watchful diligence of Darwin Melnyk and the patient attention of Dennis Ford.

Finally, my thanks to Sasha, Cynthia, Shelagh, and Ian. Their weird sense of humor (a happy genetic malfunction which has affected our whole family) has taught me not to take myself too seriously.

Introduction

By using the terms "themes" and "variations," I am trying to capture the particular feature of action in biblical narrative that I wish to study in this monograph, namely, the phenomenon of repeated yet variable patterns. For example, stories about a punishment are rather common in the Bible and appear to have the same pattern of a wrong leading to a punishment. If this story pattern of punishment may be considered a "theme," then the individual stories about punishments may be seen as the "variations," in that they play out and explore the possibilities of the theme. While the phrase "themes and variations" comes from music, I do not want to suggest a close analogy between what happens in music and in biblical narrative. It is simply that the musical phrase evokes the double nature of the phenomenon of repeated yet varied patterns in biblical narrative which will be the subject of this study. The phenomenon is double in nature in that our attention may be drawn now to the common pattern apparently shared by a number of stories and now to the particular and unique articulation of that pattern in a given story.

The recognition of repeated but varied patterns in biblical narrative is not novel. The Book of Judges provides a striking example of the recognition of a repeated pattern shared by a group of stories. Here a collector of stories about the judges actually states a pattern right at the beginning of his collection (Judges 2 and 3) which, he suggests, is reflected in the stories, different though they be from one another individually. In this particular case, the pattern discovered is really two patterns set together, a compound of punishment and rescue. The people do wrong and are punished; they cry out for help and God sends a rescuer who delivers them. I will discuss this in more detail below.

In addition to this example from the biblical period, one can point to a number of scholars in recent times who have in one way or another dealt with repetitions and variations in narrative. The Russian folklorist, Vladimir Propp, is perhaps the best known and most frequently cited scholar on this topic. In his study of one hundred Russian tales he argued that all the tales shared a single overall pattern even though the stories all differed in varying degrees one from the other. Then, too, in his study of the Bible, Northrop Frye describes the narrative pattern in the Book of Judges as a U-shaped pattern (apostasy, disaster and bondage, repentance, deliverance) and finds this pattern repeated in different ways throughout biblical narrative (1982:169–71). Finally, in the study of oral narrative, where stories exist as varied versions in performances, Albert Bates Lord uses the term "multiformity" to describe the kind of stability and variation characteristic of oral narrative (1960:99–123). Lord comments that the notion of song must be thought of in two ways: the song as a particular story that can be recognized from performance to performance and the song as a particular performance that is different from all other performances.

The patterns in biblical narrative which I will be examining have to do with action, with the sequence of events, with what happens in the stories. A thorough examination of action in narrative would call for a full and complete description of how action works at all levels in narrative, a "grammar" of narrative action so to speak. But I have not set out to do this, even though this study will certainly touch on the complex issue of how one traces the movement of the action in narrative. My approach will be somewhat selective and a bit haphazard. Most of the discussion of patterns will be devoted to sets of examples that can be identified in terms of content, like rescue stories and punishment stories, even though this will entail a certain amount of wavering back and forth between more general and more specific notions of patterns.

For example, many have pointed to a basic movement in narrative that runs from tension to resolution, and this seems to function in a great many stories. It is possible to state this general movement in more specific terms; for example, from wrong to punishment, or from difficult situation to rescue. Patterns about punishment and rescue seem to be quite common and easily recognized, especially in the biblical material, not only within smaller stories but also in larger stretches of text consisting of different kinds of material, such as the story of the exodus from Egypt.

While the subject of biblical narrative has been a popular topic recently, there has been little specific discussion of narrative action, even though it would seem to be an obvious issue. Action is a prominent feature of narrative, almost by definition, since most narrative leads readers through a series of events or happenings, and this is certainly true of biblical stories. There are, of course, other significant features of narrative, such as character and point of view, which are often mentioned alongside action as key characteristics of narrative. Actions in stories do not occur by themselves but are performed by actors. Stories are recounted by a narrator who manipulates the perspective or point of view through which the events and persons in the narrative are presented. Both character and point of view have received careful attention from biblical scholars. In her book, *Poetics and Interpretation of Biblical Narrative*, Adele Berlin includes chapters on both characterization and point of view, although not on narrative action. Robert Polzin's study, *Moses and the Deuteronomist*, makes point of view the central element in his analysis of the composition of the Deuteronomistic History (18). My study will be an attempt to explore some aspects of action in biblical narrative.

In the following chapters the exploration of patterns and variations in biblical narrative is carried out in three stages. The first chapter provides a general orientation by indicating briefly the notions of text and criticism that lie behind my study of patterns. The second chapter seeks to describe and explain in some detail what I mean by patterns of action and illustrate this with examples from the biblical text. This amounts to the identification of some "themes," or basic patterns of action, that recur. The last chapter applies this discussion of patterns to a selection of more complex texts in which common patterns appear to be repeated in many different forms, and so attention is devoted to the "variations."

CHAPTER ONE

Developing an Approach

Biblical Narrative and Biblical Studies

In making a study of repeated and varied patterns in Hebrew narrative, I am entering an area that has received relatively little attention. The study of the Bible and of its narratives in particular has proliferated so in recent years that it may not be out of place to explain how my own approach has evolved and where my work fits into the larger picture. Over the past few decades a much wider range of approaches has been and are being explored. For the last hundred years or so, historical criticism has been, and indeed probably continues to be, the major force in biblical studies. Even this approach has changed over the years, however, as may be seen, for example, in the way that it has been expanded and modified by the introduction of sociological analysis, which I would include, for purposes of this discussion, among the bundle of analytical procedures that make up historical criticism. On the other hand, literary approaches, embodying a whole range of analytical methods and strategies of reading, have come upon the scene rather recently and offered another angle from which to view the biblical text. Then, too, there is the question of the Bible as scripture, as a religious book, whether this is understood historically to refer to its role as scripture for ancient Israel or theologically to mean its function as scripture for both Judaism and Christianity. This perspective, actually the oldest way of reading the Bible, has emerged again recently in the form of discussion about the idea of canon. This may be seen in the work of Brevard Childs, who has sought to make the notion of the Bible as scripture the starting point for his work of interpretation (1984).

The scene is becoming even more complex. In addition to the three approaches just noted, one currently encounters a number of perspectives (stances, strategies, critical practices, whatever might be the term most apt to describe them) that take a different turn. Among them are those variously identified as ideological criticism (political and feminist readings, for example), deconstruction, poststructuralist criticism, and postmodern readings (see *Semeia* 51). Some forms of these approaches, like ideological criticism, can, but need not, work within or in conjunction with the more familiar approaches just mentioned. These newer perspectives are often understood as radical critiques of current historical, literary, and religious/theological study of the biblical text, challenging how these texts have been read and calling in to question the underlying epistemological and metaphysical assumptions about text and interpretation of the more commonly used approaches. Furthermore, some of these newer approaches, like the political and feminist, have a sharp political edge since they can be and are employed as instruments of change in society and its institutions, both social and religious.

The current, complex situation in biblical studies has developed so rapidly within the past few years that it is no easy task to keep abreast of developments across the widened spectrum of criticism, with older, more familiar approaches changing and redefining themselves and newer methods challenging common assumptions and perspectives. While the turmoil in the discipline makes for exciting times, it certainly leaves me, at least, operating with a less certain grasp of the practice of biblical studies than I have had heretofore, or, should I say, than I thought I had. This may be all to the good. The current situation calls our attention again, and in a dramatic way, to what we all know, namely, that we always have been and always will be working with presumptions and suppositions that are far more tentative than we like to admit.

As I have already indicated, I cannot here respond to the whole range of approaches that face any contemporary biblical scholar. I can only describe some features of biblical narrative that lie in the background of my study of patterns and relate them in limited ways to the larger context of biblical studies. But before moving to these matters and the question of biblical narrative, I would make two general observations, one related to the term *biblical* and one related to the term *narrative*. This will mean a short comment on what kind of document the Hebrew Bible is and a brief indication of some ways in which the study of narrative in general has influenced my work.

The Bible needs to be treated as a special case. It is not a text like all other texts, at least not like many other texts. This is so because the Bible exhibits a combination of features rarely found together, and here I am thinking of three characteristics in particular. First, the Bible is an ancient collection of many different kinds of material, coming from a people who belonged to an ancient civilization in the Near East. Second, the Bible is in large part story and poetry, although it contains other kinds of literature such as law; and it has achieved the status of a secular, literary classic in contemporary Western civilization. Third, the Bible has served as scripture not only for ancient Israel but in succeeding centuries for two contemporary, religious communities, the Jewish and the Christian. I am not trying to make a case for the absolute uniqueness of the Bible; but I am indicating that there are few comparable texts—ancient collections that have played a similar role as secular classics for a dominant civilization and sacred scripture for major religious communities.

Understandably, these three aspects of the Bible have each elicited strong responses from readers. Indeed it would seem important to consider historical questions, remain sensitive to literary issues, and be ready to explore the question of the Bible as scripture. In other words, the essential concerns of the three critical approaches mentioned above flow from features in the writings themselves. It is appropriate for historical criticism to give weight to the fact that the Bible is an ancient text. It is equally fitting for literary approaches to explore the implications of the fact that the Bible is text, language, composed largely of narrative and poetry. It is also relevant to reflect on the Bible as a book that has functioned and continues to function within a religious community. Consequently, in the following study, I will try to remain open to, and on occasion feel free to adopt, the language of historical criticism, literary studies, and religious approaches where it appears helpful to do so. However, to be prepared to look in all three directions implies that each perspective has its limitations in explaining the Hebrew Bible and that no one approach taken alone appears adequate to explore the richness and diversity of the biblical material.

Scholars are certainly aware of the existence of historical, literary, and religious approaches to the text and many, perhaps most, work with more than one of them. It has not been unusual for biblical scholars to recognize the importance of all three. This can be illustrated simply by referring briefly to the work of four rather different scholars. James Barr has striven to keep all three of these aspects before him, as may be seen from his discussions of the historical, theological, and literary in *The Bible in the Modern World* (see also Barr, 1980a, 1981, and Barton: 198–211). Meir Steinberg has sought to take account of historical, literary, and religious or theological aspects by defining biblical narrative in such a way that the three principles of historiography, aesthetics, and ideology are seen to be inextricably intertwined with one another in the narrative discourse of the Bible. Norman Gottwald, in the last chapter of his textbook, *The Hebrew Bible: A Socio-Literary Introduction,* has noted briefly the interrelationship of social, literary, and theological elements in the study of the Bible (but see the comments of Jobling, 1987). In a study of Judges 4 and 5, Mieke Bal (1988) has employed the semiotic concept of codes. Of the many available codes she has selected four for special study: historical, theological, anthropological, and literary. This is another way of recognizing and discussing different aspects of the biblical text.

Even if the Bible is a special kind of text, it can still be treated as a text and subjected to the kinds of questions raised by such newer approaches as the ideological, poststructuralist, and postmodern, which frequently challenge commonly accepted notions about text and criticism. In my study of patterns, I will not be directly exploring any of these approaches. Indeed, I would confess that my understanding of them at the moment is more passive than active. One might say that they function in what I do as an absent presence. Thus, I will continue to employ current critical language familiar to biblical scholars because it makes sense to do this in a study of patterns. This language will be used, however, in a "certain way," that is, with an awareness of challenges that have been posed and with an increased sensitivity to the tentative and incomplete nature of any discourse about texts.

My expressed inclination to try to remain open both to older and newer critical stances does not necessarily mean that I do so within a clearly defined or perceived framework. I have no larger theory that can embrace and interrelate all the approaches to text discussed in this chapter. Nor am I sure that a global theory is necessary or desirable. I am operating more on a hunch. The biblical text is remarkably complex, and I am positing as a practical measure the use and application of different approaches and strategies concurrently or serially where it appears helpful. Each approach or strategy works in different ways and attends to different textual features. In any event, my provisional openness is an attempt to come to terms with our current, fluid situation by working pragmatically and, needless to say, cautiously. While I am conscious of the range of approaches and perspectives in use, in practice I will limit myself to a few that seem to be helpful or important in pursuing the specific subject at hand, the investigation of repeated and varied patterns in biblical narrative.

The Study of Narrative in General

Although I have been discussing the study of the Bible, criticism of texts takes place, of course, on a grand scale outside biblical studies, and this work regularly influences what biblical scholars do. Current ideological, poststructuralist, and postmodern readings of the biblical text have been stimulated by writers in other fields. This is nothing new. Appropriation of approaches, perspectives, and textual strategies developed in other disciplines has long been a common practice of biblical scholars.

My own familiarity with the world of narrative study is limited, random, and rather anecdotal. Yet, because the partial picture I have gained has had some influence on the way I have developed an approach to the present study, I will give some brief indication of what in the general study of narrative has contributed to my own reflections on the biblical story. The effect of general narrative research on my own work has been largely indirect. It has led me to ask questions that I would not have otherwise asked and to raise possibilities that I might otherwise have ignored. However, as will be seen below, my study of patterns has been directly stimulated by one particular brand of narrative analysis and one particular scholar, Vladimir Propp.

Even a slight acquaintance with narrative studies reveals two things. First, the study of narrative exhibits a remarkable variety of approaches. Second, it is evident that this variety is spread through a number of major disciplines with significant exchange taking place among them. The same names crop up in the bibliographies of books and articles in different fields and areas. The study of narrative in general has become a rich and complex network of discussion.

Some of the most important contributions to the study of narrative have come from literary theory. *The Nature of Narrative* by Robert Scholes and Robert Kellogg, which appeared in 1966, intrigued me by its contention that the discussion of narrative should be broadened to include oral tradition, works influenced by oral tradition, and early written narrative, as well as the novel. Within this wider perspective, texts like the Bible automatically become part of the general discussion. I will return to the notion of tradition below.

This study represents only one of many possible approaches to narrative offered by literary theory, and a 1983 survey of issues in narrative by Shlomith Rimmon-Kenan, *Narrative Fiction: Contemporary Poetics*, illustrates this well. She mentions a number of treatments of narrative which were but specific applications of more general literary approaches including, for example, New Criticism, Russian Formalism, French Structuralism, the Tel-Aviv School of Poetics, and the Phenomenology of Reading. Now one could add further examples—post-structuralist and deconstructionist contributions as well as Marxist and feminist readings, not to mention other perspectives like speech act theory, all discussed in a recent book, *Contemporary Literary Theory* edited by G. Douglas Atkins and Laura Morrow (1989). Or one could turn to the fascinating collection of interviews of critics by Imre Salusinszky (Derrida, Frye, Bloom, Hartman, Kermode, Said, Johnson, Lentricchia, and Miller), which appeared in 1987 as *Criticism in Society*. It may be added that Seymour Chatman's book of 1978, *Story and Discourse: Narrative Structure in Fiction and Film*, had already pointed out, as the title suggests, that the study of narrative may be extended beyond the strictly "literary" to other media like film.

While vaguely aware of the broad expanse of literary theory, I was most influenced in my work on narrative by anthropology and folklore, particularly some structuralist analysis. I would cite in particular the work of the anthropologist Claude Lévi-Strauss and the folklorist Vladimir Propp, both of whom played roles in a wide range of disciplines. In Lévi-Strauss's famous essay, "The Structural Study of Myth," he analyzes myths in terms of bundles of relations and organizes them paradigmatically according to basic bi-polar oppositions. The message emerges from what happens among stories rather than from individual stories themselves. Little attention is paid to the movement of action in the narrative. Myths should be studied in groups, it is argued, because a myth consists of all its variants. My own work does not directly apply this kind of analysis, but the idea of groups and variations has led me to consider placing similar narrative patterns in groups and examining them in terms of a common pattern and its variations (see my article on themes and variations, 1975).

Vladimir Propp's method has had a more direct influence on my study of patterns. This folklorist gained wide recognition for his book, *Morphology of the Folktale*, originally published in 1928 (see Milne, 1988, for a summary and assessment). In his study of one hundred Russian folktales, Propp came to the conclusion that even though the tales differed considerably in content, they followed the same underlying scheme of action. He divided this generalized action pattern into units called functions, which defined major stages in the story. It was argued that these functions always appeared in the same order. Propp's attribution of a central role to narrative action contrasts sharply with the work of Lévi-Strauss where it is hardly taken into account at all. My analysis does not apply Propp's set of functions to biblical narrative; but it works with smaller movements of action, which are similar to the links Propp made between some of these functions.

Even though Propp and Lévi-Strauss differ significantly in their approach, they have both remained important to the development of structuralist analysis of texts. The two approaches are, in effect, combined in the work of A.J. Greimas. This is evident in work in which his model is applied in biblical studies (see, e.g., Groupe d'Intrevernes).

Linguistics has gained significance in the study of narrative, especially in the area of discourse analysis, or text linguistics as some prefer to call it. Here grammar is explored in units of language larger than the sentence. My study of patterns does not employ this kind of analysis, but I have been informed by it perceptibly. As early as 1975 *The Thread of Discourse* by Joseph E. Grimes showed clearly that linguists interested in discourse were investigating many features of narrative that had long been part of the study of narrative in literary criticism. These features include events, participants, setting, cohesion, and viewpoint. More recently, the linguist Robert E. Longacre has developed a form of discourse analysis on the basis of tagmemic theory and has applied it to two biblical texts, the flood story and the story of Joseph. Longacre's work will be cited when these stories are discussed below.

Finally, I would mention the influence of Paul Ricoeur, a major contemporary philosopher, who has long shown an interest in the interpretation of texts, and particularly in questions of narrative. I have found especially helpful his insistence upon a communication structure as the fundamental feature of discourse—someone saying something to someone about something (e.g., 1981:138); his discussions of the world of the text (e.g., 1981:140); and his interest in the importance of emplotment for narrative (1984–1988). Within his philosophical enterprise he has devoted a significant portion of his writings over the years to questions that touch on narrative. The interdisciplinary nature of the study of narrative is well illustrated in the second volume of his trilogy, *Time and Narrative*, in which he refers to such varied critics as Northrop Frye, Frank Kermode, Roland Barthes, Vladimir Propp, Claude Bremond, A. J. Greimas, Gérard Genette, Boris Uspensky, and Mikhail Bakhtin.

Biblical Narrative

I will concentrate on four features of biblical narrative in order give some account of the understanding of text and criticism that underlies my study of repeated and varied patterns. While my remarks have until now pertained to the Bible, generally I will now refer only to narrative. In reducing the scope of the discussion from the Bible as a whole to a particular section of it, the narrative writings, I will continue to discuss questions of text and criticism on the basis of this part of the whole. The narrative material is not simply a scattered collection. It constitutes a major block from Genesis to Kings and forms a continuous history, even though not all the narrative material in the Bible is included in it. Biblical narrative can be viewed as a composite, traditional, and religious text. Accordingly, I will treat the narrative material under three headings: composite and traditional, text, and the religious dimension.

1. Composite and Traditional

In general, these two terms should be kept separate because a traditional text need not be composite nor a composite text traditional. However, in biblical narrative the two are, in my view, closely related.

A. Composite. I treat biblical narrative as composite in the way historical critics have usually understood it, as an amalgam of different sources and traditions. The assumption of the composite nature of the Bible has long played a major role in historical criticism; indeed, the exhaustive exploration of the composite nature of the biblical text must be seen as one of the most significant contributions of historical critics. Of course, historical criticism involves much more than the idea of a composite text. Along with the search for sources comes an equally strong interest in linking these components to the historical and social contexts in which they originated. It is these contexts within which the sources are understood and interpreted. The project of historical criticism entails an astonishing array of approaches connected with the study of the past, especially now that social sciences like sociology, anthropology, and folklore are being employed on a significant scale, at least to the extent that they can be applied to the ancient world (but see the comments of Gottwald, 1983:27, 1985:32–34).

Historical critics have made their point well. Numerous gaps and tensions can be identified throughout the narrative material, and it seems reasonable to explain many of these as traces of the different sources and traditions from which the text has been composed (see Tigay). But it is one thing to recognize the composite nature of the text and quite another to pursue the full enterprise of historical criticism and reconstruct in detail how the text has evolved into its present form. It is a delicate art and remains a matter of considerable controversy even among historical critics. It is a legitimate enterprise. Nevertheless, one can recognize the composite nature of the narrative material without necessarily having to determine precisely and in detail how it is composite.

In observing the composite nature of biblical narrative, I do not so much seek to gain a precise identification of sources and an adequate description of exactly how all the parts came together. I view the composite nature of the text as a feature or characteristic of the narrative material as such, something that attentive readers experience when they encounter gaps, recognize tensions, and become aware of different voices in the narration. If biblical narrative is by its very nature composite, it would seem to me important to find ways of incorporating this fact into one's understanding of text. While others should be free to divide the text into its constituent sources and traditions, I would prefer to find ways of recognizing and taking into account tensions and discontinuities as part of a whole. As I will note below, historical criticism does not, in the main, work this way because historical scholars have not been inclined to work with a notion of a composite *text*, a single text that happens to be composite.

I refer briefly to three scholars, spanning about a century, in order to illustrate what I have been saying: Julius Wellhausen, who antedates the turn of the century; Martin Noth, who developed his theories about fifty years ago; and John Van Seters, who is still fully engaged in his work on the narrative material.

Wellhausen, a remarkable scholar, played a significant role in defining how the composite nature of the biblical text was to be understood; his influence remains considerable (see, *Semeia* 25 edited by Douglas Knight). To describe his approach I use the term "source criticism" instead of "literary criticism" simply to avoid confusion with the literary perspective to be referred to below. The fact that the term "literary criticism" has been applied to Wellhausen's method shows that this kind of analysis has been viewed as an appropriate a way of dealing with ancient literature. Wellhausen's identification of source documents was based on clues discovered in the text by means of careful reading in which close attention was paid to contradictions, changes in style, and the presence in the text of different perspectives or tendencies that might signal the work of different authors. In other words, and this may be something of an oversimplification, a text was taken to be a work produced by a single author, that is, a unit having the kind of consistency and coherence Wellhausen would expect from a single author.

Source criticism, then, seeks written texts and authors, although this also entails identifying the work of editors and glossators. While Wellhausen's work was the culmination of a long period of literary analysis involving numerous scholars, his analysis of the Pentateuch yielded the classic statement of the Documentary Hypothesis (see his *Prolegomena*) according to which four major sources representing four major authors arose over a period of several centuries: J (ninth century), E (eighth century), D (seventh century), and P (fifth century). Although Wellhausen assumed that oral traditions lay behind many of the narratives of the Pentateuch, he did not believe it was effective to try to identify and recover oral sources.

One might add that this kind of text analysis implied a specific strategy of interpretation in that a source, or text, was read within its presumed original, historical context. Historical reconstruction of the political and religious history behind the documents was produced largely on the basis of information found in the texts, and the reconstruction in turn became the framework within which texts were analyzed into sources and dated, and in the light of which they were read. Scholars show their awareness of the circular nature of this process and the inherent difficulty associated with the historical reconstruction of the ancient world, but there is little choice.

Martin Noth assumed the kind of source criticism proposed by Wellhausen but expanded its scope under the influence of the work of Gunkel and his followers. Because Noth, like Wellhausen, had a keen interest in history and even produced a history of Israel, he took for granted that a careful analysis of the biblical texts into sources was essential for his historical reconstruction. At the same time, he wrote commentaries and other textual studies in which he saw his task as exposition of the biblical text. Noth was interested not only in documents but in all stages of transmission of traditions so that, linking Wellhausen and Gunkel so to speak, he proposed that the history of tradition (*Überliefer-ungsgeschichte*) meant tracing the growth of tradition from its earliest beginnings to the form of the present text (1981:1). In other words, Noth's approach reconstructs a lengthy process that takes into account source criticism (written sources), form criticism (oral sources), and the final form of the text (the work of final historians, editors, and redactors).

Noth's view of text was thus more complex than Wellhausen's in that he tried to deal with written documents and unwritten traditions. Even so he was inclined to understand a text as a written document produced by a single author. His view of authors can be seen in his studies of the Deuteronomistic History and the Pentateuch. As far as the Deuteron-omistic historical work is concerned, he argued that the final collector, the Deuteronomist, was not simply a redactor but a genuine author who planned and ordered his material with thought and care, even though he often left the wording of his sources in the form in which he received it (1981:10). It is interesting that Noth would allow that a work might consist of an author's words as well as large amounts of material produced by others and included with very little change. The Pentateuch for Noth was different. The main written sources of the Pentateuch (J, E, and P) were regarded as the work of authors along the lines of the Deuteronomist. However, because Noth understood the final stage of the Pentateuch to be the result of the purely mechanical task of putting written sources together (1972:250–51), he would not speak of the Pentateuch's author. In Noth's view, the process of joining literary sources did not lead to a whole that was greater than its parts. The Priestly and the Yahwist traditions were simply set side by side and left unhindered to display their different perceptions of the faith of Israel without any attempt at synthesis. For Noth, then, the Deuteronomistic history was a literary work and the Pentateuch was not because, while a work may contain much that is not from its author, its final form must have been shaped by the author.

Nevertheless, at the end of his book on the Pentateuch, Noth does offer a hint that authorship and work need not be so closely related. He concedes that in rare instances some new unity may be achieved when sources are brought together, and he cites the two creation stories at the beginning of Genesis as an example. Here, J and P stand in tension because they display different perceptions of humanity; yet, each says things that need to be said. As Noth puts it: "Both of these views...

simultaneously constitute the reality of man as he lives in this world at all times" (251). He leaves it at this. But his comments do evoke the notion of author and text, especially where he sees a new unity arising from a juxtaposition of sources.

The approach of John Van Seters represents, in many ways, a return to Wellhausen and his exclusive concern with authors and documents, although Van Seters introduces some significant insights of his own. He is one of several scholars who are currently rethinking the problem of the Pentateuch (see the review of Whybray). Van Seters begins his study of the Yahwist by noting with approval the claim of Wellhausen that the Yahwist's work was a history book (1986:37). He flatly rejects the notion of a long process of tradition of the sort proposed by Noth and others. However, he departs quite radically from Wellhausen at one point, the date of the Yahwist, which, as far as Van Seters is concerned, must lie in the exilic period (1975:309–12). Van Seters argues that the narrative traditions of the Hebrew Bible are best understood as historiography produced by individuals in the later period of Israel's history. The Deuteronomist and the Yahwist were historians, literary figures, who, while they performed the important task of collecting past traditions, produced historical works (1975, 1983, 1986:37–55, 1987). Like Wellhausen, he sees a close relationship between author and work.

Van Seters' own understanding of ancient authors and the works they produced is worth noting, especially as he has expressed it in his article on the Yahwist (1986, also 1987). Here he argues that the structure of the Yahwist's work can only be properly understood if it is seen as the product of an ancient historian, using the works of early Greek historians as examples of what this kind of writing might be. His analogy for what a work is in terms of unity and coherence comes from ancient literature and not modern. According to Van Seters, while the ancient historians play a dominant role in shaping their work, they make liberal use of older sources. A critic, he argues, must function with a different notion of unity from one that might be expected in modern works produced by a single author. A critic must search "for certain editorial structures and connective devices that appear to make sense out of the whole or at least out of the larger units within it" (54). It may be noted in passing that Whybray is prepared to make a similar statement about the Pentateuch as a whole (242).

In sum, then, historical critics were right to stress the composite nature of the Bible's narrative material; but, by tying the notions of author and work so closely together that a work was conceived only as the product of a single author, they limited the idea of what could be considered a work. Nevertheless, the descriptions of the nature of ancient texts by Noth and more especially by Van Seters point to a more complex notion of author and work, which in turn could entail a more complex process of reading. This brings us to the notion of traditional.

B. Traditional. Biblical narrative is traditional. Because this term is broad and can be applied to many different things, let me indicate how I mean it in the context of the present discussion. I use the term to refer to the ways in which ancient writings often differ from modern texts. There is no need to exaggerate the differences and posit a qualitative distinction between ancient literature and modern literature, but there does seem to be sufficient dissimilarity to warrant attention. The term "traditional" has often been applied to certain literary texts from the past, like the Bible and the epics of Homer; but it may also be applied to texts from contemporary societies in which writing is not commonly used for producing and transmitting literature. Thus, while the question of the traditional is to some extent historical, and a function of the historical distance, between modern and ancient texts, the more germane issue here lies in how traditional texts may differ from other kinds of texts.

To say, then, that biblical narrative is traditional is to align it with a certain kind of literature. On the basis of a wide range of studies on orality and literacy, Walter Ong has proposed that we consider three broad periods to mark the changes that have taken place in the development of literature: oral, manuscript, and print. In the western world these stages have succeeded one another over a long period of time. The distinction among oral, manuscript, and print stages does not simply reflect the fact that literature has been produced and conserved through different media (speech, writing, and printing press). The three types of literature may display different characteristics as a result of the different media in which they are conveyed and the nature of the corresponding cultures in which they function.

Biblical narrative was written down in a period that might be fairly described as manuscript or scribal, that is, in a time when writing was used but probably in a more limited and specialized way than it is today. A stage of oral tradition may have preceded the scribal one, making a significant impact on the literature of the subsequent scribal one in that oral forms and styles may persist to a substantial degree well into a period characterized by writing. If so, the narrative of the scribal period would continue to display a measure of oral style and retain characteristics associated with an oral period alongside newer features developed in association with writing (for fuller discussion, see Culley, 1976a, 1976b, 1986; Ong: 78–116; but note the critique of Ben-Amos, 36). Thus, while biblical narrative is not merely transcribed folklore or oral literature, it may not at all be inappropriate, because of the Bible's scribal nature, to compare it to material collected by folklorists and students of oral literature as well as to texts from the earlier Greek period and the Middle Ages in the West and to texts from scribal periods in other cultures.

It will be helpful for the sake of illustration to discuss in brief the work of some scholars who have described biblical narrative as traditional. Following that we shall look at three features that may characterize scribal or traditional literature.

Within biblical studies, Hermann Gunkel was certainly one of the most prominent figures to have attributed the differences between biblical and modern literature to the origins of Hebrew narrative in an oral society. Furthermore, he proposed a critical approach, *Gattungsgeschichte* (or as it has been translated in English, Form Criticism), which sought to discern and describe these differences. He assumed that much of the literature of ancient Israel had been influenced by types of stories and poems current in a period of oral tradition in early Israel. In his view, these types, along with the language and forms in which they were expressed, became so firmly rooted in an oral period that even later authors who composed in writing betrayed the influence of tradition to such an extent that they continued to follow the established patterns (1963:2–3). What struck Gunkel particularly was the weight of tradition in ancient societies.

While Gunkel's precise understanding of what happens in an oral society and his perception of the nature of oral literature are no longer adequate in the light of recent research, he did take significant steps toward defining Israelite literature as traditional. His discussion of literary types or forms (*Gattungen*) became immensely important in subsequent biblical studies. Gunkel accepted the results of Wellhausen's source analysis but, in contrast to Wellhausen, he assumed that oral forms were still sufficiently evident in the written sources that they could be studied on their own. In the Pentateuch, for example, Gunkel found evidence of a long literary process that began with individual legends and small collections circulating orally and culminating in Wellhausen's J and E, which Gunkel was inclined to consider collections put down in writing (1963:22). Gunkel's conclusions served as the foundation on which Noth built in his studies of the Deuteronomist and the Pentateuch. Gunkel's notion of authorship thus included not only writers of large documents as understood by Wellhausen but also vast numbers of oral poets and storytellers whose traditions contributed to these larger documents. Since at the stage of oral tradition there could be no question of identifying documents and authors, Gunkel saw his task as identifying traditional literary patterns (in the case of narrative, types of stories like myth and legend), which at one time functioned in settings in the life of the community (ceremonies, and other kinds of repeated occasions).

It may be added in passing that Gunkel's fascination with literary forms had a distinct historical orientation. His ambition was to write a history of Israelite literature that would review the literary forms that Israel had produced (Klatt: 166–92). A brief attempt at this may be found in *Die Israelitische Literatur* (1963 from the second edition of 1925; first edition 1906). It consists in placing the various literary types of the Hebrew Bible in historical order.

Since the time of Gunkel, much more information has become available about oral literature from field studies by folklorists and students of oral tradition. This work is substantial, as may be seen by the bibliographies in the journal, *Oral Tradition*. (For a review of some of the earlier work relevant to the study of the Hebrew Bible, see Culley, 1976a, 1986). One of the best known studies of oral narrative is *The Singer of Tales* by Albert Bates Lord. While the type of narrative he studied was poetry, he raised a number of issues that have wider relevance. For example, he argues that the term "traditional" is critical for the kind of poetry he studied since the poets were passing on well-known stories. On the one hand, because these poems were created afresh in each performance, the artists enjoyed the latitude continually to produce change. On the other hand, because the poems were familiar to both poets and audience, a high degree of stability was maintained. This stability, or traditionality, consists in a high level of repeated material, both in the form of repeated, or formulaic, language and in the form of repeated narrative patterns and structures (Lord: 120, 220–21).

Some biblical scholars, too, have explored a possible background of the Pentateuch in a poetic tradition. Drawing on a proposal of Frank Cross that goes back to W. F. Albright, Ronald Hendel suggests that it is plausible to consider the Jacob cycle as "a variant literary form of an older, fully elaborated epic cycle with roots in the traditional forms of West Semitic oral narrative" (31).

It was noted above that Scholes and Kellogg, in *The Nature of Narrative*, included in the western tradition the whole range of narrative from early myth and folktale to the modern novel. For them, this vast body of material constitutes "a real tradition of narrative literature in the Western world" that should be studied as a whole (4). However, in the light of the work of Lord and others, they treated the earliest stage of this narrative corpus (myths, folktales, and oral epics, including the Hebrew Bible) as traditional in a special sense. They spoke of traditional story, traditional plot, and traditional narrative. What they meant by traditional narrative comes out most clearly in their discussion of Icelandic literature. The sagas are identified as traditional prose narratives because they bear "the formal and rhetorical stigmata of oral composition" (50); that is, they display characteristics such as the presence of highly stylized diction, conventional structure, and an authoritative and reliable narrator. This is said even though the sagas may have been composed in writing. The style of the sagas may have been established by oral tradition.

Let us turn to the ways that oral tradition works and by which oral style can affect scribal activity. In an analysis of oral tradition based on a small selection of field studies, I found that the oral transmission of prose is similar to the process described by Lord for oral narrative poetry (Culley, 1976b: 31; see also Gunn, 1978). There appears to be a continual re-creation of traditional stories in performance, a process involving both change and stability. It seemed reasonable to suggest that the main traditional building block of narrative was something variously described as a stock scene, incident, episode, or core plot. This is rather similar to the "theme" that Lord identified in oral narrative poetry and in Homer. These repeated elements seemed to be sufficiently flexible that they could be expanded, adapted, elaborated, and linked together in a variety of ways. I discussed nine examples of similar stories and episodes in biblical narrative and concluded that many of the examples appeared to be similar to the stock or traditional episode characteristic of oral prose. This need not be interpreted as direct evidence of oral transmission, but it may be evidence of a traditional oral style continuing in a scribal period close to the time when oral tradition was active (see also Alter, 1981: 47–62, who has more recently discussed some of these repeated elements under the label "type scenes").

In a recent study, Susan Niditch has portrayed biblical narrative as traditional. Her book, *Underdogs and Tricksters: A Prelude to Biblical Folklore*, examines a selection of biblical stories about such stock folktale figures as underdogs and tricksters. She describes her aim as resuming and carrying forward the interest in folklore that had played a significant role in the research of Gunkel. Biblical literature, she comments, "is traditional literature having more in common with Homer's *Odyssey* than a

Faulkner novel, with a Child ballad than a Robert Lowell poem, with a Zande ritual drama than a Sam Shepard play" (xiii). To recognize biblical material as traditional means "to notice its repeated patterns of thought, content, and language, traceable to no single originator, recurring within individual works, in different works of the same period, and in works of varying periods" (xiii). Niditch does not argue that the Bible in its present form is simply oral tradition but rather that it is traditional, at least to some extent, in the way that oral literature is traditional. This is why she seeks to exploit the work of folklorists in her examination of biblical narrative.

In order to maintain a strong sense of the gap between modern and ancient literature, Niditch seeks quite deliberately "to speak of cultural and literary assumptions shared by composers and intended audiences" (xiii). In this respect, her approach would support the usual concerns of historical criticism such as its interest in sociological and historical settings (16). Nonetheless, in her view an application of folklore to biblical studies would call for some rethinking of source and redaction criticism as well as tradition history. Thus Niditch's desire to explore text and setting from a social science perspective, particularly through anthropology and sociology, offers a different slant on historical critical research (see also the comments on the sociology of storytelling in Overholt: 314–21).

Even though the application of the term "traditional" to the Bible, and in particular biblical narrative, still requires much further reflection and refinement, I think that it points in a helpful direction. By assuming the traditionality of biblical narrative, I can identify three related issues that have played a certain role in my own analysis of repeated and varied patterns: literary type, anonymity, and repetition.

(1) Literary type. Folklorists present rich and varied classifications of the types of oral prose (see, e.g., Jason: 15–55); legend is surely one of the important types commonly found among many different peoples and cultures. Without getting involved in detailed questions of genre, I would suggest that a great deal of biblical material is like legend. Like legend, biblical narrative moves on the human plane and involves presumed historical figures; but like legend, it also has a divine or supernatural plane that intersects the human one, either by means of dramatic intervention or merely through subtle influence. It is hardly ever totally absent. In the ensuing study of biblical narrative patterns I will frequently ask how the divine and human planes are interrelated.

(2) Anonymity. In biblical narrative, authors are not identified. This is so not only at the level of individual narratives but also at the level of

larger collections like the Deuteronomistic History, the Pentateuchal sources such as J and P, or the Pentateuch itself. This consistent lack of attribution strengthens one's perception that the material is traditional. It does not mean that there was no creative person who shaped and controlled the form we now have. It may mean, however, that "authors" are to be thought of as they appear to have been in oral societies, and perhaps in manuscript societies: primarily as persons who performed or passed on the old, familiar stories in the old, familiar way. In other words, the production of texts in a scribal period may involve both stability and change, a mixture of established tradition and new creation, similar to the process found in oral tradition. If my description of the process as a mix of stability and change is accurate, the, "authors" of biblical narrative may be viewed as custodians of the tradition. They were dealing with givens. They told what they knew and what everyone knew. This perception of them does not trivialize their role as artists or their ability to set their own stamp on material but only suggests that they were creative in the service of the traditions they shared with their audiences.

I have used the oral performer as a partial model for scribal authors because the persistence of anonymity in biblical narrative suggests to me that this notion of "author" seems to have continued into the manuscript or scribal stage of Israelite tradition. In his study, *Did the Greeks Believe in their Myths?*, the classics scholar Paul Veyne has remarked on the wide gulf that separates modern and ancient conceptions of history (6–7). Even when ancient Greek historians set their names to their works, history was still viewed as tradition, and, "even had they been able to, they would not have sought to rework this tradition but only to improve it" (7).

(3) Repetition. All literature is to some extent conventional and so contains a significant degree of repetition. This kind of repetition includes features like generic and story patterns. If we follow a clue from the study of oral narrative, we find that traditional narrative has a level of repetition higher than the conventional. Repetition is hard to measure in a text like the Bible because it contains a limited corpus of material (for discussion, see Culley, 1976b:30–32,64–67; Gunn, 1974, 1976; Alter, 1981:47–62). Nonetheless, since this study will be considering repeated patterns, the relationship of redundancy to traditional literature is worth keeping in mind.

Concluding comments on composite and traditional. I suggested above that it would be useful to keep the notions of composite and traditional in tandem in the case of biblical narrative. This would mean that the composite nature of biblical narrative, the placing of traditions and documents together in a scribal period, may in a real sense reflect the continuation of a traditional style that has its roots in oral tradition and continues to display stability and change. Even the apparently simple act of placing documents side by side not only preserves traditional material but can convey something new by means of the tensions created through placing the earlier and later material together.

2. Text

If biblical narrative is composite and traditional, in what sense can it be considered a text? In what way can it be treated as a whole? As we have seen, historical critics have been inclined to stress that the Bible is composite and have, in some ways on account of that, had less to say about it as a text. Scholars who adopt a literary perspective, however, have shown a strong interest in the Bible as a text or work. It is therefore to the work of these scholars that we turn for examples of how the reading of a composite text can be achieved.

Before proceeding, however, we may note that the question of what constitutes a "literary" approach is not at all clear. The term "literary" cannot be used without qualification. Those who pursue a literary approach to the Bible differ in their understanding of the term. In my comments above on the study of narrative in general, I gave some indication of the remarkable range of approaches (modes of analysis, stances, and strategies) that can be gathered under the heading of literary studies. Some of this variety is mirrored in discussions of the Bible.

With regard to the Bible, and particularly biblical narrative, as a work or text one can distinguish three perceptions that deserve comment here. First, there are those who argue that we need to work with the assumption that the biblical text is a unity. Second, there are those who want to find some way of taking into account the composite nature of the biblical text. And third, there are those who believe that the text is problematic in a number of ways, demanding special strategies of reading. In the light of what I have said above, my view will lean in the direction of those who explore the question of composite text. However, in order to place my view in its proper context it will be important to take stock of what has been said about the text as a unity and the text as problematic. Before considering these three perspectives, I offer two preliminary comments: one on the term "literary" and another on some previous work by some biblical scholars on literary questions.

I will be using the term "literary" in a descriptive sense simply to refer to the kinds of approaches found within departments of literature and in journals devoted to the study of literature. In this use of the term, literary could well, and often does, include historical criticism, which is clearly one way of studying texts. The writers I shall mention in regard to the literary study of the Bible will not only be biblical scholars who have explicitly adopted a literary approach but also literary critics who have for one reason or another turned to the Bible. Many of these authors see themselves doing something quite distinct from the kind of historical criticism commonly done in biblical studies.

Posing literary questions to the biblical text has not been foreign to biblical studies. Examples of a literary interest in the biblical text have long existed, although much of this work has functioned in close conjunction with historical criticism and has employed, or implied, a notion of the Bible as a composite akin to that generally held by historical critics. For example, James Muilenburg developed the approach known in North America as rhetorical criticism, and this has been continued by many of his students (see Jackson and Kessler). Similarly, stylistic analysis has been pursued in many countries and in many different ways; the writings of Luis Alonso Schökel may be cited as an example (1961). That much stylistic analysis of this type remains quite evidently within the framework of historical criticism may be seen from Sean McEvenue's grammatical and stylistic analysis of some narratives attributed to the Priestly writer. Because McEvenue means by "style" those features produced in a text by an individual, he has selected for his study historical narratives that are "presumably the work of one author-editor toward the end of the exile period" (19).

A thoroughgoing attempt to establish a literary approach to the Bible has been proposed by Wolfgang Richter in his book *Exegese als Literaturwissenschaft*. Richter argues that the Bible is literature and that as a consequence biblical studies should be understood first and foremost as the study of literature. Consequently, historical questions must be postponed to a later stage of research (12). In order to develop a model for literary analysis he urges that careful attention be paid to the nature of biblical material, which is significantly different from contemporary, western literature. The literary forms of the Hebrew Bible have more in common with folk literature. Authors are not identified. Texts are composite, exhibiting stages of growth. Oral tradition has played a significant role both in its form and content. Thus, while Richter agrees that we must be open to the contribution of literary studies in other fields, the

special nature of the biblical text requires that the study of biblical literature gain its shape and direction from careful attention to the nature of
the biblical material (25).

I agree with Richter for the most part, as one would gather from what
I have said above. However, Richter is inclined to work with the notion
of composite text that is characteristic of historical criticism. Thus, he
continues to use terms and concepts found in earlier biblical studies such
as literary criticism (source analysis), form, genre (*Gattung*), tradition
criticism, and redaction criticism, even though he redefines these terms
carefully to apply to formal features perceived at different levels of the
text and to exclude matters of content and history. At the level of form,
he performs a thorough syntactical analysis not only of individual
clauses but also of the relationship between clauses. Literary criticism
(identifying sources) is used to establish the basic unit or text. In
Richter's work, as we have noted with regard to historical criticism generally, it would appear that sources and traditions are identified and
defined in terms of their inner consistency. Each subsequent stage of
development is determined in the same way whether it be the work of
another author or editor. Richter's method assumes that a text can be
properly studied only when the contribution of each separate author,
traditionist, or editor has been identified and separated out. Further
applications of Richter's approach have been carried out by a number of
his students and colleagues and have issued in several studies of narrative texts over the years (for example, Gross, Schweizer, Vanoni, and
Floss).

Having made these two preliminary comments, we may now consider
the three issues just identified.

A. Reading the text as a unity. There are scholars, both biblical and
others, who argue for a unified or holistic view of the text, often in
explicit opposition to the kind of composite view usually found among
historical critics. Studying the text as a unified whole has produced
meaningful results. This is not surprising since for many centuries the
Bible was treated as a single text or book. The narrative traditions display
a remarkable degree of coherence.

There are, however, different ways of treating the question of unity.
Three brief examples illustrate this. In his book, *The Bible from Within*,
Meir Weiss follows the lead of the New Criticism and *Werkinterpretation*
and proposes what he calls a "total interpretation" in which the verbal
expression itself becomes the center of attention rather than the content

or ideas (e.g., theme, plot). One moves from a consideration of each word, to the order of words, the structure of sentences, and so on, right up to the structure of the work as a whole in order to show how all the parts come together to produce a unified sense. Similarly, structuralist analysis also assumes that texts are unified structures of language that must therefore be treated as wholes (see Culley, 1985a:173–78, for the earlier work of Polzin, Jobling, and CADIR [Centre pour l'Analyse du Discours Religieux]; more recently Jobling:10–12, and 89–92).

In her book on narrative, *Poetics and Interpretation*, Adele Berlin displays a more nuanced perception. While she adopts a poetics perspective in which the present text is viewed as a unity (112), Berlin does not deny the presence of sources and layers of tradition, although she is cautious about identifying them. While books like Genesis appear to be made up of originally separate stories, she prefers to treat the present conglomerate as the reflection of a special mode of composition, a way of ordering or arranging stories to form a larger whole.

Finally, David Gunn offers still another angle on the unity of the text in *The Fate of King Saul*. Sensitive to the presence of tensions in the text due to sources and traditions, he seeks to establish a unified view of the composite text by treating authorship in broad terms apart from any notion of the authorial intention that is normally attributed to a single author. Thus, Gunn describes the author as "a kind of super-ego . . . linked to all who have left their mark on the story" (1980:15).

I shall pursue the question of the unified text further by commenting more fully on the work of: Northrop Frye, Meir Sternberg, and Robert Polzin. Although these three scholars adopt rather different approaches to the biblical text, all three propose to read the text in a unified way. They all accept the composite nature of the text but do not grant this feature of the text a significant place in the work of interpretation.

Northrop Frye's views on the Bible have been summed up conveniently in *The Great Code: The Bible and Literature* (see also Robertson for a somewhat similar view). Frye is of particular interest to me here because of the importance he gives to narrative patterns and to their role in producing coherence in the text (see also his discussion of the world of the text, e.g., 1963). Frye approaches the Bible strictly from the point of view of a literary critic (xi), and for him the Bible always means the Christian Bible, both Old and New Testaments. He does not dispute what historical critics have claimed, granting that the Bible is "the end product of a long and complex editorial process" (xvii). As a mosaic composed of many and varied elements set one beside the other, the biblical text hardly shows the kind of ordering a single author would produce (206). However, Frye grants little importance to the question of authorship in the Bible, since he believes that one can no longer distinguish between the early and later contributions to the text. He observes that "the editors are too much for us: they have pulverized the Bible until almost all sense of individuality has been stamped out of it" (203). Thus he finds good reasons for studying the end product, the final text, as a whole in and for itself.

The very fact that the Bible has been read for so many centuries as a unity also suggests to Frye that there must be substantial grounds in the text itself for studying it as a whole. Since he rejects a concept of unity related to authorship, he takes the Bible as an imaginative unity in which the major constituents cohere. Thus, the biblical text can be regarded as a unified structure from the point of view of two major categories, narrative and imagery, and it is in this sense that the Bible can be treated as a whole (1982: xiii). The parts which make up this whole are then narrative patterns and images. The unity of the whole is experienced in two ways: as the narratives come together into one great narrative (or myth) and as the images join in one great complex of metaphor. The interplay of these two dimensions gives the unity of the whole both a dynamic (narrative) and a static (metaphoric) aspect (62–65).

In his discussion of biblical narrative, Frye draws attention to what he calls a "U-shaped pattern" in the book of Judges: apostasy, descent into disaster and bondage, and then the rise again through deliverance (169). Because this reflects, according to Frye, the pattern of comedy that occurs in literature generally, he claims that the entire Christian Bible may be perceived as a divine comedy in that a major movement from loss to restoration runs from Genesis through Revelation. What is more, the U-shaped pattern repeats itself on a smaller scale throughout the Bible. This is especially striking in the historical books, where the fortunes of Israel rise and fall in a series of repeated U-shaped patterns that are related not only sequentially but also paradigmatically in the sense that the high point and low points of all the patterns are related to each other metaphorically (170–98; see also Exum and Whedbee). My study of repeated action sequences will deal with these kinds of patterns. In other words, I will be dealing with the same phenomenon but in a rather different way.

In *The Poetics of Biblical Narrative*, Meir Sternberg treats the narrative as a whole. His examination of poetics is both lengthy and complex, and his view of biblical narrative is quite elaborate. While Sternberg assumes that the Bible is a work of literature, he wants to distance himself from labels such as "the Bible as literature" and "the literary approach to the Bible." He calls for a wider view of the biblical text which, as I noted earlier, tries to take into account the historical, literary, and religious dimensions of biblical narrative. It is this multiple perspective that is of interest to me. Sternberg describes biblical narrative as a "multifunctional discourse" regulated by "three principles: ideological, historiographic, and aesthetic" (41). Recognizing these three as rivals, at least in theory, Sternberg nevertheless sees them bound together in "relations of tense complementarity" which move toward "operating as a system, a three-in-one, a unity in variety" (44), although the system functions by the procedures of artistic communication (48). Because communication is a critical concept for Sternberg, he adopts a rhetorical slant, describing narrative as: "a functional structure, a means to a communicative end, a transaction between a narrator and an audience on whom he wishes to produce an effect" (1).

While he appears to accept the possibility of sources in theory, in practice he does not indicate any that he needs to deal with. His reading strategy does not entail looking for sources. On the one hand, Sternberg accepts the search for real authors and the desire to place material in its historical context as legitimate and even valid sources to inform biblical poetics (64). He has nothing, he declares, against historical criticism. On the other hand, he characterizes source criticism as a will-o'-the-wisp. Since, in his view, almost nothing is known about biblical writers, and since their identity will likely remain beyond recovery, a shift is required from "composition as *genesis* to composition as *poesis*" (68). From the point of view of poetics, the narrator may then be described as a construct of the reader produced "to make sense of the work as an ordered design of meaning and effect" (75). Sternberg argues that in biblical narrative the storyteller, the persona as opposed to the historical writer, is a constant. As far as Sternberg is concerned, poetics can assume, for all practical purposes, a single narrator and a single narrative model for most of biblical narrative, although it still remains possible to explain tensions in the text by employing a genetic approach rather than a poetic one. In this way, like Frye, he finds himself in a position to treat biblical narrative as a single body.

Robert Polzin's view of the biblical text, as set out in *Moses and the Deuteronomist*, differs from Frye's and Sternberg's in that while he takes the text as a whole, he looks for certain kinds of dissonance within this whole. The differences he notices are not the sources and traditions of historical criticism. His perception of text follows a compositional approach derived to a large extent from the work of two Russian literary critics, Mikhail Bakhtin and Boris Uspensky. A remarkable feature of this compositional, or perspectival, approach is that it acknowledges the possibility that different points of view may exist in one and the same text. Accordingly, Polzin seeks to read the text in such a way as to identify these different points of view, or voices. Thus his view of the text as a whole involves the idea that the different points of view form the basic components in the compositional structure of the unified text. To be sure, Polzin agrees that the biblical text must have had a complicated prehistory involving editorial activity that probably accounts for many of the changes in perspective encountered there. Nevertheless, he claims that "whether the present text is the product either of a single mind or of a long and complicated editorial process, we are still responsible for making sense of the present text by assuming that the present text, in more cases than previously realized, does make sense" (17).

His work on the Deuteronomistic History illustrates his point. Polzin starts from the assumption that this text is "a unified literary work" (18). The "Deuteronomist" represents the one person or several persons who produced the final form of the text, "that imagined personification of a combination of literary features that seem to constitute the literary composition of the Deuteronomistic History" (18). Since this personification must be created or constructed from the text, Polzin employs the term "implied author." In the end, he affirms the notion of textual unity in that he identifies one point of view as the "ultimate semantic authority" (the text's basic ideological perspective and so the implied author's point of view) in the light of which other points of view are to be understood (20).

Frye, Sternberg, and Polzin each hold that whatever its past history, the text's present blend manifests a strong measure of coherence, and it is to this whole that primary attention should be paid. In other words, it is not only fruitful but appropriate to view a composite document like the Bible as a whole and, with some adjustments, read it as one would other texts. This is a strong claim, and I would agree in large measure. I stressed above, however, that the biblical text is *traditional* as well as *composite*. I would ask whether one might give serious consideration to both the coherence and the tensions and discontinuities in the text? Polzin's view of text does involve the presence of different voices within it providing an opening in this direction.

B. Reading the text as a composite. As we have seen, historical critics have been inclined to look for and underscore differences but seemed reluctant to pursue a view of text as a whole. The literary critics just discussed have looked for and lent importance to features that suggest coherence, but they were less inclined to explore differences. As many have recognized, historical and literary perspectives, as critical approaches, can have different agendas and may often head in different directions. Even so, both base their work on careful reading and appeal to features of the text to support their readings whether it be clues to its composite nature or signs of its coherence. As I have indicated, I would consider both these features and come to the study of biblical narrative and the examination of its patterns prepared to explore the idea that we are dealing with a text that has substantial coherence but that is also composite and traditional. I have, however, no simple suggestion as to how to deal with both of these features at the same time.

In this present study, I will take only two steps in the direction of investigating this double idea of text further. In my discussion of repeated and varied patterns below I will comment on some specific examples of composite texts. Second, I will refer here to four scholars who in different ways and in varying degrees have acknowledged the importance of recognizing the composite nature of the biblical text: Robert Alter, David Damrosch, Edward Greenstein, and David Jobling. Taking these two steps will not solve the problem of how to deal with texts that are composite and traditional. It will, I hope, lend support to my suggestion that the idea is worth examining.

In the *The Art of Biblical Narrative*, Robert Alter adopts a literary approach that is also sensitive to religious and historical dimensions of biblical narrative, which he describes as "a complete interfusion of literary art with theological, moral, or historiosophical vision . . ." (1981:19). From the point of view of literary studies, Alter comes to the Bible as he would any other text, giving attention to several levels: single words, relationships between blocks of material within stories or between stories, the use of dialogue in rendering narrative action, and the role of the narrator who is both all-knowing and reliable. However, he also insists that one recognize the fact that the Bible is an ancient text. The gap between the biblical period and our own day poses a methodological dilemma (1983:116). Either we modernize the ancient text by treating it like contemporary literature, or we shun a literary perspective and become bogged down in philological and historical details. Alter's strategy stems from the following principles. As an ancient text, the Bible has its own particular set of narrative procedures, but it may be possible to recover some understanding of these conventions. His examination of type-scenes as narrative conventions represents one of his attempts to do this.

According to Alter, one of the major difficulties facing an attempt to regain the literary art of the Bible is its composite nature, which with its tensions does not mesh with a modern sense of literary unity (1981:131–54). His judgment is that biblical writers and redactors have a perception of unity that differs in some respects from our own. In an attempt to recapture something of this he posits the notion of "composite artistry." Composite texts require a literary analysis that attempts to deal fruitfully with the phenomenon of layers of tradition woven together or set side by side. At the end of a discussion of some duplications in the Joseph story, he comments that "the biblical author, dealing as he often did in the editing and splicing and artful montage of antecedent literary materials, would appear to have reached for this effect of multifaceted truth by setting in sequence two different versions that brought into focus two different dimensions of his subject" (140). He points out that many literary theorists have noted that literary texts "involve a condensation of meanings, a kind of thickening of discourse, in which multiple and even mutually contradictory perceptions of the same object can be fused within a single linguistic structure" (153).

In *The Narrative Covenant*, David Damrosch responds to the complex nature of the biblical text by making a deliberate attempt to bring together literary and historical analysis. His purpose is "to explore the origins and growth of biblical narrative" (1). To accomplish this he considers topics like the historical setting of the material in the Near East, employs the results of source criticism, and raises questions of origin and growth, all of which play an important role in historical criticism. In order to account for the rich prose tradition of the Hebrew Bible, Damrosch proposes that it must have resulted from a substantial transformation of Mesopotamian genres.

Having argued that "a close conjunction of literary and historical criticism is needed for a full understanding of the origins and growth of biblical literature" (298), Damrosch must face the problem of how to read a composite text, and to this problem he devotes his conclusion. Since both early and late stages coexist in the present form of the biblical text and indeed often stand opposed, this mixture of sources and traditions poses "unusual problems for anyone who wishes to take them into account while focusing on the text as a whole" (299). While Alter's discussion of composite artistry provides an interesting slant on the problem, it does not satisfy Damrosch because of what he takes to be Alter's ambiguous position on historical criticism. For his part, Damrosch argues that the issue of composite texts is quite complex, and so he offers four analogies of composites that may help in reflecting on composite artistry in the Bible. An example of appropriation of older material with little or no change is cited from Mesopotamia. A reworking of older material from the past involving the juxtaposition of sharp contrasts is noted in Icelandic sagas. A composite text produced by one author is pointed to in the *Essais* of Montaigne. Finally, Damrosch mentions perspectival assembly in *Thousand and One Nights* with its multiple compositional principles and causal explanations that challenge the reader to take account of several different perspectives at once.

Rejecting the choice "between the 'confused textual patchwork' of historical criticism and the 'purposeful pattern' sought by literary analysis," Damrosch believes that an integration of literary and historical study yields what he calls a "purposeful patchwork" (325). In order to capture the dynamics of biblical narrative, Damrosch argues that we need to be able to read passages in several different ways at the same time, which means in practice following in turn the various authors identified by historical criticism. This may confuse matters for those seeking to articulate a precise link between each author and a historical setting but "for most readers an awareness of the multiplicity of biblical narrative should enrich the reading process it " (325; but see the evaluation of Greenstein, 1988:352).

Another scholar who has written on the composite nature of the biblical text is Edward Greenstein. In a study of Gen 37:18–36 and 39:1 he explored the famous problem of the two versions of how Joseph got to Egypt. As most do, Greenstein identifies two narrative sequences: one where the brothers put Joseph in a pit intending to kill him but, at Judah's request, sell him to Ishmaelites; and one where the brothers put Joseph in a pit and, in spite of Reuben's plan to rescue him, Midianites take him away. Greenstein's strategy is to deal with these two versions from the perspective of text as a unity ("a work of art is a systematic whole in which every part functions within the system," 116). All the parts are to be explained as participating in the whole. Therefore, one must be open to the possibility that the redactor had an intention in setting the two sequences alongside one another, the point being to read the biblical stories "*as they are told*" (117). The two sequences match in part and conflict in part so that each "reaches for the reader's acceptance" (121). The matching produces a clear reading but the conflicting areas create a blur. In the end, the goal is "to expose the multiplicity of readings within the text and the design of the literary arrangement" (124).

David Jobling also has a pertinent comment on the composite nature of the biblical text and the need for criticism to recognize this as a significant feature of the text. Speaking from the point of view of structural analysis, he suggests that the notion of final form "has become something of a fetish for structuralists" (90). One needs, he argues, to accept the obviously composite nature of the biblical text. Since all sorts of tensions reside in the text and therefore belong to it, they are relevant to structural analysis and must be described in structural terms (90–91).

The views of Alter, Damrosch, Greenstein, and Jobling are important, in my mind, because they argue that there is potential value in attending to the composite character of the text of biblical narrative, even though they do not agree on how exactly to go about doing this. In various ways, they seek to give weight both to the idea of *text* and to the quality of *composite*, which I have discussed above and linked with *traditional*. Tensions in biblical narrative material are seen less as problems and more as invitations to explore richer readings.

C. The text as problematic and strategies of reading. This rather vague heading represents an attempt to acknowledge some of the current developments in biblical studies, stances like the political and feminist and strategies like the deconstructionist, post-structuralist, and postmodernist, which I referred to above as trends in recent literary theory that have just begun to have some impact on the study of Hebrew narrative. They do not form a homogeneous group by any means. Still, if one were to risk a generalization, it may not be far from the mark to say that they all seem to view the text as problematic in one way or another, and they appear to understand reading as a strategy necessary in order to confront the problematic nature of the text. As I indicated above, I will not be dealing directly with any of these stances and strategies in my study of patterns but will be trying only to preserve an awareness of challenges they pose. At least by assuming that biblical narrative is traditional and composite, I will be sensitive to some signs of difference in the biblical text, which, while displaying substantial coherence, also exhibit tensions, diverse perspectives, and an interplay of various voices.

Thus, in order to recognize the kind of challenge to the biblical text and its criticism that these approaches offer, and in order to say at least something about the role given to reading strategies, I will make brief mention of deconstructionist and feminist readings of biblical narrative. It is interesting that, in the *Literary Guide to the Bible*, Robert Alter and Frank Kermode identify deconstructionists and some feminist critics as those "who seek to demonstrate that the text is necessarily divided against itself" (6, and commented on in Greenstein 1989a). Certainly, uncovering difference in texts has become an important issue in these two perspectives and, in conjunction with this, the act of reading has gained remarkable prominence, as may be seen from recent discussion of the role of the reader in literary theory (see Tompkins). Commenting on one of the implications of reader-oriented theory in biblical studies, David Gunn has remarked that it "legitimizes the relativity of different readings and thus threatens to unnerve conventional understandings of biblical authority" (1987:69). Approaches related to readers and reading have been picked up and employed much more by New Testament scholars than by those who study the Hebrew Bible (e.g., Fowler, 1985), and this interest in the reader has led some critics into a discussion of post-modernism (Fowler, 1989; Moore, 1989; and the literature cited in these articles).

Deconstruction is rather new to narrative research of the Hebrew Bible, but it has begun to show some influence. For example, Peter D. Miscall, who has employed an eclectic approach in his commentary on 1 Samuel, acknowledges that an interest in deconstruction accounts for his leanings toward indeterminacy and ambiguity and leads to his refusal to argue for a single interpretation of 1 Samuel (xx–xxv). The fullest discussion of deconstruction and biblical narrative so far is the article "Deconstruction and Biblical Narrative," by Edward L. Greenstein. He tackles sympathetically "one of the most radical and difficult expressions of postpositivist thinking" (43) and seeks to indicate its implications, both positive and negative, for reading biblical narrative. Raising questions about the various assumptions of unity made when reading the biblical text, Greenstein suggests that employing perspectives like deconstruction "would by not presuming unity reveal internal division and instability within texts" (44). For him, this is a positive step. At the very least, it would help shake our normal and accepted ways of reading the biblical text and, like many feminist readings, shock us into the awareness of obvious but frequently unnoticed features of the text. After struggling with a notoriously difficult text, the narrative in Lev 10:1–5 on the death of Aaron's sons, Greenstein raises, for the sake of argument, the possibility that the story of Nadab and Abihu may challenge or subvert "the scrutability of the divine retribution" (61) and the simple acquiescence in the applicability of a punishment pattern to all cases (see my discussion of punishment stories in Chapter Three, section A, where I also raise the problematic nature of punishment). He argues that deconstruction can be used as a way of "remystifying the text, insisting on the unknown as we grope for the known" (62).

Feminist discussions of biblical narrative have been appearing for some time (see, e.g., the volume edited by Adela Yarbro Collins and *Semeia* 42 edited by J. Cheryl Exum and Johanna W. H. Bos). Feminist perspectives reflect a wide range of opinion and a variety of strategies. For example, Danna Nolan Fewell has suggested that a feminist reading that challenges the text not only helps to expose its patriarchy but may also display how this same patriarchy breaks down within it (82). She recognizes the usefulness of deconstructive criticism and comments: "any reading that produces a text with complete thematic unity (which every reading inevitably does) is a misreading" (82). On the other hand, Pamela Milne has argued that the biblical texts themselves are at the deepest levels so fundamentally patriarchal that they are beyond rescue as scripture (1989:34).

Mieke Bal's *Lethal Love: Feminist Literary Readings of Biblical Love Stories* brings together literary theory, feminism, and narratology. Her interest lies not so much in the Bible as scripture but in the status of the Bible as "one of the most influential mythical and literary documents of our culture" (1), since the Bible is a remarkable example of how language and literature have power over culture, especially with regard to questions of gender. Bal's strategy involves paying attention to different readings of biblical texts, both popular and scholarly, not to establish the correct reading of any particular text but to uncover the relatively arbitrary nature of all readings and what guides them. In Bal's view, the use of a whole range of reading strategies, hermeneutical frameworks, concepts, and methods can serve to demonstrate not only their value and potential but also their limitations and shortcomings (9). If literary analysis can show that there is no truth, then "where truth is absent, women can creep in, and rewrite themselves back into the history of ideology" (132).

Concluding comments on text. In this section I have sought to balance my discussion of the traditional and composite text above with a consideration of text that was not simply derived from the idea of the composite nature of the biblical text. This meant turning to studies by literary critics who evince a strong impression of coherence in the Bible, and placing these beside the work of historical critics with their compelling perception of difference. When these two perceptions are set alongside one another, coherence and difference seem less to be signs of different critical approaches to the biblical text—historical criticism as opposed to literary criticism—than important characteristics of the biblical text that warrant attention in any critical discussion. In this present study, I am stipulating that this will be a helpful way to view the text and that this is the view that I will work with in studying patterns in biblical narrative. In support of this preference, I have cited the example of some biblical scholars who in one way or another attempt to take account of the composite nature of the text, endeavoring to note both coherence and difference. It has also become apparent, in reviewing some recent readings of the biblical text, that the perception of difference represents a much deeper issue for some critics than that of dealing with a composite text. In fact, one senses a sharper division between literary scholars who stress the unity of the text and those who find the text problematic than the division between historical and literary perspectives.

3. The Religious Dimension

So far I have mentioned two aspects of Hebrew narrative and suggested that it is important to see these writings not only as composite and traditional but also as text. The third and last characteristic to be mentioned is the religious dimension. This is a large issue, and I do not intend to pursue it very far. I will only proceed indirectly and in a limited area in order to give some brief indication of how I would relate the study of repeated and varied patterns in biblical narrative to the religious dimension of the text. I will offer two comments and then refer to the work of three scholars. The first general comment will be simply to suggest how, in my view, some of the patterns to be identified may play a role in the text's religious aspect. The second comment will concern a specific issue, the portrayal of the relationship between the divine and the human in biblical narrative, because I will be making some observations on this topic from time to time in the examination of patterns in specific texts. In making these comments, I shall reduce discussion of the religious dimension of the text to just one issue, the relationship between text and community. My reason is that religious texts frequently function within a religious community, and this is certainly true of the Hebrew Bible, which does so in more than one religious community. The Bible arose out of ancient Israel, and it is likely that some of the biblical writings functioned as special texts during the latter part of the history of this community. Since then the Hebrew Bible has functioned as scripture within the Jewish community and, as part of Christian Bible, for the Christian community.

When I use the term "religious," I mean to include in it two ways of regarding biblical narrative. One is a perspective that might be used in the study of religion in general: the way outsiders would view a text that functions as scripture in a religious community to which they do not belong. The second is a perception that could be called theological: the way persons within a religious community understand, explain, and use their own religious texts. In either case, when I speak of how a religious text "functions" in a community, I am thinking of how it can provide a common vision, a way of looking at reality.

To the outsider, a religious text such as the Hebrew Bible consists of the kind of literature from which a believing community may construct a world view or vision of reality, a perception of the way things ought to be or indeed really are behind the vagaries of experience. It is from such a vision that members of a religious community work out what to believe, what to do, and what to hope. They also find in this vision a basis for ritual activity and ethical decisions.

For insiders, such as members of Jewish and Christian communities, the Bible is not accepted as scripture because of its function but functions as scripture because it has been received as a special book (for a helpful discussion of the Bible as a document of communities, see Barr, 1980c). The community believes that the text represents, however this may be understood and expressed, a word of God, and this defines its special nature. Even so, the community itself plays an important and special role since its members usually see themselves as ones addressed by the text and thus especially competent to read their scripture correctly. Thus, the community participates very actively in the process of reading, interpreting, and making decisions about what the writings mean.

But the matter is more complicated than this. I have spoken of a vision of reality presented by the text and constructed by the community. It would be more accurate to say visions of reality, for, if the Bible is a text that is traditional and composite, then it displays both a level of coherence that suggests an overall vision and a measure of difference that permits, and even encourages, alternative readings. Similarly, since the community is itself diverse, different readings and interpretations of the text continually arise, producing a wide range of opinion on many different matters, even on fundamental issues like theories about what it means to say that the Bible is scripture, word of God, and how it should be read.

In any case, it is in the light of this notion of the interrelationship of text and community, and especially a shared but complex vision that I understand the religious dimension of biblical narrative. It is this perception that will provide the context for my comments on the possible contribution of repeated and varied patterns to the religious dimension of narrative. For example, patterns like those I refer to as rescue and punishment may be important elements in the complex vision that the community elaborates through its encounter with its scripture. I make this general comment only to indicate why I think that some of the patterns to be examined may have importance beyond whatever historical and literary significance they may have as reflections of ancient Israel or textual structures.

Apart from this general suggestion about the socio-religious function of patterns, there is one particular element that will play a role in my investigation of specific narrative texts in Chapter Three, namely, how biblical narrative portrays the relationship between divine and human. I would view this particular relationship as part of the world view or vision of reality of a religious community. Of course, the way biblical narrative presents the divine and the human may be, and has been, analyzed and discussed within many different frameworks apart from the study of narrative patterns (see, e.g., Amit and the references there). This relationship can also be studied from a number of different angles. From a historical perspective, one could ask how the documents reflect religious or theological perspectives of ancient Israel—how ancient Israelites, or some of them at least, perceived the interaction of divine and human in their view of reality. From a literary perspective, the relationship of the divine and human can be interpreted as part of the world of the text, the vision or picture of reality embodied in Hebrew narrative which any reader encounters and enters by engaging with the text. These two perspectives are not unrelated to each other, nor are they unrelated to the visions articulated by the religious communities in their study of scripture.

In order to comment further on what I have just said, I will refer to the work of three scholars who present different slants on the Bible as scripture, although they each touch on one or more of the issues just discussed. They all read the Bible from a Christian perspective, and this necessarily restricts the scope to the extent that Jewish views will not be heard. Reading the Bible as scripture was the way that the Bible was studied at the beginning of the common era and for several centuries thereafter. During this time, both Christian and Jewish communities developed various ways of reading the biblical text appropriate to its function as Scripture. With the rise of historical criticism, a significant shift occurred. The Bible was also read in an academic community where it was treated as a book like other books and investigated by means of critical and historical approaches just as any other ancient text might be. The more recent use of literary perspectives has taken place by and large within the academic community. Readers within religious communities have had to decide whether or not, and how, to relate historical and literary approaches to their study of scripture.

For many who adopted historical-critical analysis, this perspective became the necessary starting point for all readings, religious included. An example of a treatment of the religious dimension of the Bible through historical criticism may be seen in the writings of Krister Stendahl. In his article on biblical theology in the *Interpreter's Dictionary of the Bible*, he argued that biblical theology is a historical discipline and must be a purely descriptive undertaking that seeks only to determine what the texts meant in their own time and setting, that is, when they were first spoken or written. Historical criticism, then, becomes the first stage of investigation and is employed to describe in a historical way the various theologies that came together in the biblical tradition. Only after one has determined what the texts *meant* in their earliest setting can one take a second and separate step in order to ask what the texts *mean* now as sacred texts for modern religious communities. This hermeneutical move may involve a translation of what the text meant in the ancient world into an appropriate modern idiom, as in the case of Bultmann, for example. Or, within the historical framework of biblical thought one might propose with Stendahl "a systematic theology where the bridge between the centuries of biblical events and our own time was found in the actual history of the church as still ongoing sacred history of God's people" (428). This would give a key role to the religious community.

Alternatively, it may be argued that one best comes to the Bible as a religious book through a literary perspective. This suggestion, again from a Christian perspective, can be illustrated by referring to David Clines, "Story and Poem: The Old Testament as Literature and as Scripture." The Old Testament, he asserts, is largely imaginative literature, both story and poetry. If this is so, it follows that the Christian Church should develop a way of reading scripture appropriate to this fact. Clines goes further: the Bible can *only* be perceived as Scripture when it is read as literature. Using a literary approach similar in many ways to that of Frye, Clines argues that to view the Old Testament as literature means looking for its unity. In the Pentateuch, for example, Clines finds the unifying factor in the theme of the triple promise of descendants, land, and relationship with God (122). A literary reading avoids the problem of the gap between ancient and modern mentioned by Stendahl. Imaginative literature, like the story and poem of the Bible, proffers alternative worlds. When the worlds presented in the Bible are chosen as visions to be valued and striven for in life, the biblical text assumes a religious function as Scripture. In this view, the world of the text has been given a significant role.

The writings of Brevard Childs are of relevant interest for several reasons. Above all, his is a full-scale attempt to treat the Bible in a religious perspective and he makes this his starting point for studying the text. Thus, he begins with the assumption that the appropriate way to read the Bible is from a religious point of view, that is, in terms of its role as scripture for a community. For him this means that one does not start with historical criticism, as did Stendahl, nor with a literary approach, as did Clines, but with the perception of the Bible as a religious book. Childs describes this as a canonical approach (for others who use the notion of canon, see e.g., Sanders, 1984, and Sheppard, 1982). He proposes two ways that this can be done. One is a confessional approach in which the Christian community reads its own canonical scripture. Childs, as part of this community, would adopt this kind of reading for himself. But there is also, he suggests, a different approach that does not set out within a confessional framework but seeks to examine how ancient Israel as a religious community treated its own special writings.

Childs' confessional approach was outlined in an article written in partial response to the views of Stendahl just described (1964, see also 1986). Here Childs defined biblical theology as a task carried out within a specific theological or confessional framework, in his case that of the Christian faith. The Bible, both Old and New Testaments, is scripture for Christians, the word of God, the witness to revelation. How, he asks, should members of this community of faith read their own canonical text? Not by beginning with the stance of historical criticism. Old Testament theology is, according to Childs' definition, a Christian enterprise in which Christians seek to read the Old Testament as part of their own scripture in a dialectical relationship with the New Testament. Of course, the Hebrew Bible read as Jewish scripture by the Jewish community would need to be defined differently.

In proposing this kind of reading, Childs quite consciously tries to resume the earlier ecclesiastical tradition of reading the Bible as scripture and to explore what this might mean in the modern period. In order to do this Childs resorts to the traditional Christian concept of *sensus literalis*, and he is aware that the meaning of this phrase is far from self-evident (1977, see also Frei, 1986). Indeed, for him, one of the critical issues of contemporary Christian theology "lies in a search to recover a new understanding of the *sensus literalis* of Scripture" (92). The religious or theological nature of the biblical text must be the starting point for study and the governing perspective for reading. Historical criticism should be performed no less rigorously, but it must be subordinated to the primary task of grasping the significance of the Hebrew Bible as a religious text.

Childs' second, non-confessional approach may be found in his *Introduction to the Old Testament as Scripture* (1979). Here, for the purposes of writing a canonical introduction, Childs brackets the framework of faith that obtains in contemporary communities, specifically his own Christian perspective, and seeks to view the Hebrew Bible in its context in ancient Israel. He still argues that the religious nature of the material must be given priority because from early on much of the material functioned as scripture in the religious community with the result that the final form is due to shaping within that community. The description of this process in ancient Israel and its final product can be achieved by anyone trained in the task regardless of one's confessional or non-confessional stance.

Childs declares his aim in this book: "to describe the form and function of the Hebrew Bible in its role as sacred scripture for Israel" (16). The relationship between the text and the religious community is of critical importance. The texts emerged within and were shaped by the community (73); yet, as normative texts, they in turn shaped the community. The text is viewed as composite, just as historical critics describe it. Still, in spite of the validity of historical criticism the text is not read as composite. When Childs seeks a historical reading of the text (71) this means taking account of a "force" that operated within the community, generated by the religious function of the text by virtue of the normative role it played in the community's life. Yet, while recognizing that canon is a process, he also insists that it is a product, the end result of the process, and it is to this product, the final form of the text, that a canonical approach must turn (73).

For Childs, it is within the framework of the final form of the text that the various elements and layers uncovered by historical criticism are to be interpreted. For example, the book of Exodus is to be discussed as a whole in its present form since this book is more than the sum of its parts, the sources of its prehistory, for "the decisive canonical witness is often found in the manner by which the parts of have been combined" (176–77). Thus, the message of the book of Exodus is not to be sought in its original units but in the book as a whole and in the meaning these original units gain in this context. Still, he is prepared to listen to the individual sources such as J and P and, in a way, he treats the sources as parts of the whole.

As for literary criticism, while conceding a certain common interest in the final form of the text between some kinds of literary approaches and his own, Childs declines to take advantage of any kind of literary perspective. As he puts it: "the canonical is concerned to understand the nature of the theological shape of the text rather than to recover an original literary or aesthetic unity" (74). A book that is fundamentally religious in nature, origin, and function needs to described in terms of its form and function as scripture for a religious community (1979:74).

The views of Childs have remained controversial (see, e.g., Barr, 1983, and Barton, 1984). Many issues require further discussion. For example, a literary approach would appear to many to be a next logical step given Childs' view of the text as a whole. Nor is it clear how one can define a "religious" or "theological" reading apart from the literary nature of the biblical text, which relates the past through genres like story and poem. Still, the linking of text and community is an important issue, whether or not one agrees with the precise way Childs has worked it out.

Summary on the religious dimension. Rather than begin with the notion of the Bible as a religious book in the sense I have described above, I attempt to view the religious dimension as one aspect among, and related to, other aspects of text like the historical and the literary. The concept "religious text" was expressed in terms of how the text functions within its religious community in providing a vision of reality. Narrative patterns like rescue and punishment may play a role in this dynamic, and so may the relationship of the divine and human as depicted in narrative.

A Concluding Comment

If the Hebrew Bible is viewed as a text that is traditional and composite along the lines that I have described it in this chapter, then it is clear that the meaning of the term *text* has to remain fluid because in a way we are dealing with texts within texts within texts. The Hebrew Bible has sufficient coherence as a whole that it can be treated as a text, but the same is also true of many of its parts. This would be so of several of the units into which the Bible is presently divided: chapters like Job 28, groups of chapters like the Joseph story, books like Genesis, groups of books like the Pentateuch. The same could be said, as I have argued, for a generic category like the narrative material. Similarly, some of the sources and traditions that historical critics have proposed and that appear to have gained some general acceptance could be treated as texts: the Deuteronomistic historical work, the work of the Yahwist, and so on. At the same time, all are parts of the larger whole, the Bible, and parts of the smaller divisions of the whole just mentioned. These texts are never completely independent from their surroundings, and many form important elements in larger groupings.

In the detailed study of patterns to follow, I will not be dealing with this whole range of possibilities. The narrative material will be treated generally as a text within which patterns are repeated and varied. Within this, I will treat units of various sizes as texts, simply calling them stories and assuming that they contain enough coherence to be read as such. Some of the longer stories will contain the differences, tensions, and discontinuities that may suggest earlier sources and traditions; these will be discussed when appropriate. Thus, units the size of a few verses like the story of Elisha and the poison pot (1 Kgs 4:38–41) as well as units the size of the exodus account will be examined as texts.

With so fluid a view of text as this, one must agree that readers have a choice. They may read at any or all levels and do this from different perspectives, such as the ones discussed earlier—historical, literary, or religious. Readers have tended in the past and will continue in the future, to indicate their preference, and may even insist upon it. It may be argued, too, that one should only call a text what appears by virtue of its coherence and style to be the product of a single author. Or it could be maintained that a text should be read as a unity in which all the parts must be seen to fit harmoniously into the whole. Or it may be asserted that one must read the final form of the text and work out some concept of unity at that level. Or it can be proposed that reading a text must give a preference to uncovering differences in order to uncover fundamental tensions that exist in all texts. My choice is rather pragmatic. For the purpose of identifying patterns I will think of the narrative material as a whole as a text but will deal with units that run anywhere from a few verses to fourteen chapters. I will endeavor to take account of both coherence and difference in order to capture as much of the richness and diversity of the text as possible.

Speaking generally about the question of text in a public lecture at McGill University a few years ago, Hillis Miller commented to the effect that the metaphor used to describe "text" is important because the image one has of "text" affects how one reads and studies it. I have no simple metaphor or analogy to offer that would indicate how one might picture a text that is traditional and composite, in which both coherence and tension are important features. Since some interesting metaphors or analogies have been suggested, it may be useful to consider some of them at this point.

In speaking of the complexity of the Talmud, Neusner (39) has proposed the metaphor of the web of a loom, a model that could be applied to the biblical text as well. It evokes the image of a single fabric with a warp and woof of variously colored and differently textured threads. Greenstein has compared the composite text of biblical narrative to a braid with strands of different colors intertwined (1989b:38). I once heard Martin Noth use the analogy of a European church built over of several centuries uniting in the one building sections in Romanesque, Gothic, and Baroque styles. Rather than a medieval cathedral, Josipovici prefers the analogy of the Centre Pompidou: "a huge and imposing edifice whose skeleton is quite visible and to which more parts can be added without altering the basic structure" (68, but see also his comments on the Gothic cathedral, 302). Barr has noted, more as a comment than a formal analogy, that the "Bible is more like a battlefield, in which different traditions strive against one another" (1980b:115). Blum has described the final form of the Pentateuch as a landscape that in its relief presents its history (1990:382, also 17 and 72). It may be added that metaphors have also been used to picture scholarly approaches to the Bible, as in Flanagan's use of the metaphor of the hologram to describe the relationship of such critical approaches as the literary and historical, or in Greenstein's use of the blind men and the elephant (1990).

While no such metaphor captures exactly what I want to say, there is a comparison that I find helpful. In reflecting on the concept of a text that is composite, traditional, and religious, my mind has turned to a religious community, although the similarities are probably not sufficiently close to propose it as a proper metaphor for the biblical narrative. Yet, a superficial consideration at least offers some useful points of comparison.

Religious communities regularly divide into different groups holding diverse views of their commonly-held religious tradition, and one may think of the branches, denominations, and sects to be found in Christianity, Judaism, and Islam. The presence of major parties or streams within a single religious community may involve mutual recognition and cooperation to a certain degree and on many issues while allowing sharp disagreement on other, sometimes quite fundamental issues. Smaller groups on the fringe may enjoy little recognition or be virtually excluded by the rest of the community. To be attentive to the community as a whole—to all groups attempting to express the one tradition—means to listen to different voices that present at the same time an impression of coherence (all belong to the same tradition) and of tensions (different voices express this tradition in various ways). This may suggest something of the way in which biblical narrative may be viewed as a traditional and composite and text. The biblical text did arise out of and still reflects an ancient religious community, or at least some elements of it, evolving over time, and this fact touches on the way I have sought to describe the religious dimension of the text.

CHAPTER TWO

The Themes

This chapter turns to the central issue of this study: repeated yet varied patterns of action in biblical narrative. This description of the topic highlights the linkage of the two important features which are to be explored in relationship to each other: repetition and variation. Both of these aspects must be explored. It is not enough simply to identify repeated patterns; it is also necessary to recognize that the individual examples of a given repeated pattern differ from each other. The task of this chapter will be to consider what I have identified in the title as the *themes*, that is, the repeated patterns. Once the recurrent patterns have been identified, it will be possible in the next chapter to consider how these constants are varied.

I suggested at the outset that what I mean by repeated patterns of action is something fairly obvious. Time after time in biblical narrative a person, or a group, in a difficult situation is rescued. Similarly, a person, or group, committing a wrong is punished. This kind of repetition is easily recognized by most readers, or can be, once attention is drawn to it. Yet, even though repeated patterns of action are easily spotted, the task of identifying and describing them in some systematic and economic way is, as often happens with obvious features in texts, a rather complex task involving a good deal of detailed analysis.

In the following discussion of patterns, the aim will be to present an orderly description which will illustrate the phenomenon, at least to the degree necessary for the purposes of this study. Care must be taken to arrange the material and interpret it along the way. Nevertheless, because the main goal remains the consideration of the phenomenon of repeated patterns, the development of a method for describing them is important only to the extent of its pragmatic value in affording a means of presenting the material. Although the procedure used in this chapter to analyze the patterns appears to be adequate for the task at hand, it is not without problems, and some inconsistencies will be apparent in the description. With respect to the study of narrative, this is a very limited investigation. Among the various features of narrative only action will be considered. And with regard to action, only repeated and varied patterns will receive attention.

A modest language of description will be necessary. The phenomenon being investigated, repeated patterns in biblical narrative, dictates the nature of the language of description. The repeated patterns will simply be described in terms broad enough to apply to the biblical material being considered. The description, then, does not have to be framed in terms of a general theory of action that might apply to all narrative, although there seem to be many ways in which my analysis is both related and relevant to other narrative traditions, as well as to the study of narrative in general.

In fact, as I indicated in the preceding chapter, my own work began by reading what others had done in the study of narrative, in particular Propp's *Morphology of the Folktale*. Even though Propp examined a limited set of Russian fairy tales and did not appear to be concerned about a general model for narrative analysis, his study became remarkably influential in narrative studies, suggesting that despite the limited scope of his investigation, he has identified some characteristics of narrative in general. At first glance, it may not seem that the long list of functions that Propp found in his stories could be directly relevant to biblical narrative, nor should one anticipate that this should be so (for a full discussion of this problem, see Milne, 1988). Nevertheless, what Propp sought to do, broadly stated, was to identify a narrative pattern common to a given group of stories. Thus, it seemed to me worthwhile to follow Propp at least to this extent and to see what patterns might be found in biblical narrative when groups of similar stories were examined. After working along these lines for a number of years, I returned to Propp and discovered that the patterns I had found in biblical narrative were more closely related to Propp's analysis than I had thought. While no particular correspondence between biblical stories and the full pattern of thirty-one functions was apparent, Propp's full pattern was made up of smaller elements, a number of paired functions that identified movements much like the ones I have been talking about: a difficult situation leads to a rescue or a wrong leads to a punishment.

Since the present study flows directly from my earlier work but contains some modifications of definition and description, it will be useful to review briefly what I have done so far. My earliest attempts appeared in "Structural Analysis: Is It Done With Mirrors?" (1974) and in the last section of *Studies in the Structure of Hebrew Narrative* (1976b). In these writings attention was directed to groups of similar stories, the groups being created on the basis of a common feature such as a miracle, a punishment, or a deception. It was proposed that, by comparing stories that could be grouped on the basis of a shared feature, common structures might come to light. In forming groups, the shortest possible stories were selected on the assumption that narrative structure would appear in its simplest form in such brief stories. Comparison would then be facilitated. The common structure of a group of stories was then described in terms of three stages, which were intended to identify important phases in the action. For example, stories involving a miracle were described as follows: (1) a party with a problem brings this to the attention of someone with power to help; (2) the helper responds; (3) the miraculous result is indicated (1976b).

In later studies I devoted more attention to describing the movement of the action, and a simpler statement of this was proposed (See e.g., 1978, 1980a, 1980b). The movement in a pattern was now defined in terms of two stages rather than three: an initial stage that posed a complication or tension and a final stage that presented a resolution. This two-stage, or two-phase, pattern was called an *action sequence*. Now, instead of grouping stories according to whether they contained a miracle or a deception, action sequences were identified and labelled in such a way as to describe the kind of narrative action they display. In a story about a punishment, for example, an action sequence was identified as a *wrong/wrong punished* sequence in order to indicate that the narrative action begins with someone committing a wrong and ends with the perpetrator being punished for the wrong.

No simple relationship exists between story and sequence. While some very brief stories seemed to consist of a single action sequence, most narratives were found to be more complex, composed of two or more action sequences combined in various ways. Yet, even in these more complex narratives, a single action sequence often appeared to stand out and form the central movement in a given story so that it was possible to label narratives as punishment stories, miracle stories, and so on.

The Action Sequence

Up to this point, I have spoken generally of narrative patterns, but from now on I will use the more exact term *action sequence*. The word *pattern* has been useful because it is widely used and readily understood. But precisely because it is so general, some advantage may be gained in employing a term more descriptive of the feature being investigated. *Action sequence* has been used before in the study of narrative (e.g., Gülich and Raible: 197–232), although I am not deliberately trying to link my use of the phrase to the way others have employed it. The term makes clear that the kinds of patterns I am interested in have to do not just with action but with sequences of action. The rest of this chapter will discuss the action sequence and identify some repeated sequences found in biblical narrative. Examples from biblical narrative will be provided at each step of the way.

In this study, then, the term *action sequence* will refer to a movement within a story which goes from the arousal of an expectation to the fulfillment of that expectation. I might have said from complication to resolution, since it is widely accepted that most stories trace just such a movement, usually referred to as plot. However, an action sequence is not really identical with plot, since, as I have just indicated, more than one action sequence (movements from expectation to fulfillment) may be present in a given story. In fact, almost all the biblical stories to be discussed below have more than one action sequence, and sometimes several. Beyond this, groups of stories are sometimes linked by action sequences. Identifying action sequences provides a useful means of tracing movements of action at various levels of narrative, not only within single stories and episodes but also within larger sections of narrative that have been produced by bringing stories and episodes together.

Action sequences are not formally marked on the surface of the text and do not seem to be signaled by any particular arrangement of words, clauses, or even groupings of clauses within individual stories. Since such patterns of action appear to function below the surface of a given text, identifying patterns is not a matter of engaging in close analysis of clauses and paragraphs, features of style like the use of words and phrases, structural elements like episodes and scenes, or the like, in individual stories. To be sure, these features are important in the study of narrative, but they do not seem to be critical in the identification and description of the kind of repeated movements of action that I am exploring in this study. Action sequences show themselves when similar stories are brought together and compared.

With regard to narrative action, one might argue that action sequences are building blocks of narrative. They are linked together in different ways to form stories. Stories may be expanded and elaborated into richer and more complex entities by joining action sequences together in various ways. This line of discussion leads naturally to a consideration of narrative structure in general, if one begins to reflect on the role sequences might play in the organization of narrative texts as such. While this subject certainly interests me, I will not pursue it, because the primary interest of this study lies in repeated and varied patterns of action in biblical narrative texts rather than in all texts.

While all sequences reflect a movement from expectation to fulfillment, I will attempt to work at a more specific level of description and to identify action sequences according to a more precise definition of the actions they describe, specifying those that move from wrong to punishment, difficulty to rescue, and so on. This permits a rough kind of grouping so that different kinds of action sequences can be distinguished and similar material brought together. A movement from a wrong to a punishment will be identified as a *punishment sequence* and a movement from a difficult situation to a rescue will be identified as a *rescue sequence*. Labels such as *wrong/punished* or *difficulty/rescued*, which I will be using to identify action sequences, imply both the more general and more specific dimensions of the narrative sequence. The slash indicates the more general structure of the movement from expectation to fulfillment. Yet the terms used, for example "difficulty" and "rescued," reflect the more specific way in which this more general structure is realized. The use of specific terms like "wrong" or "rescued," simply means that sequences are described on the basis of repeated actions in biblical narrative that appear to share the same pattern. The level of description remains related to the material being studied, biblical narrative, and how actions in that material may be grouped.

Since one particular sequence quite often appears to stand out as the main sequence of the story around which others may be gathered or within which they may be set, stories will frequently be identified in terms of their prominent sequence. For example, if a punishment sequence seems to be the main sequence in a story, the story will be called a punishment story.

It was suggested earlier that action sequences might be considered building blocks of narrative. However, repeated action sequences in biblical narrative may constitute building blocks in another way. As recurring elements in the composite text of biblical narrative, repeated action sequences, say of punishment and rescue, produce a redundancy that may help create a sense of coherence in composite material.

In choosing to concentrate on movements of action in narrative, it is clear that action has been given priority over character. This is an arbitrary choice but not an unreasonable one. In stories, actions and actors are necessarily interrelated because most actions that happen in stories are performed by a character. Since action sequences identify and describe key narrative actions at a certain degree of abstraction, it would also be quite appropriate to identify and describe actors in abstract terms according to the roles characters play as Propp did. In a punishment story, a story with a dominant *wrong/punished* sequence, it is usually possible to identify a character who commits a wrong, the wrongdoer, and a character who is wronged and who subsequently becomes the punisher of the wrongdoer. However, I have decided not to venture very far into the exploration of characters and roles, apart from some attention to the role of the deity and a few comments on character roles in the Joseph story. Reference to the participation of the deity will come up in connection with discussion of the divine-human dimensions of the biblical material.

Action sequences identify a movement between two stages or phases of narrative, one that presents the opening situation of an action and one that relates the closing situation. These two phases reflect the general movement from expectation to fulfillment which, as I have just explained, will be expressed in more specific terms. For example, if a sequence is labelled *wrong/punished*, this means that the first phase consists of an action in which one party (a person or a group) performs an act that wrongs another party (a person or group), although in biblical stories such an action is usually a wrong against the deity. The second phase consists of an action in which the wronged party punishes the party doing the wrong. A very brief example may be found in 2 Kgs 2:23–25. When some little boys make fun of the prophet Elisha, he curses them and two she-bears attack the boys.

The two phases of a sequence are related to each other in a specific way, and this has been implied by describing the movement they express as one from expectation to fulfillment. In other words, the two phases are related to each other by what may be called a "narrative logic." A sequence involves a progression in which the opening action leads logically to the closing action, which in turn is seen as the logical result of the opening action. The action identified in the first phase (say, a wrong against the deity) is the cause of the action of the second phase (the punishment of the wrongdoer by the deity). This may seem rather obvious, and so it should, but it is important to be clear about this relationship between the phases of an action sequence when one faces the practical problem of identifying action sequences. For example, an action in a story is identified as a wrong not so much because it appears to us to be a reprehensible act but rather because it is an action that actually leads to a punishment in the story. In other words, the causal structure of an action sequence helps determine which of the many actions in a given punishment story can be identified as the wrong.

As a matter of fact, there are many kinds of smaller paired actions in narrative texts related by cause and effect, but these will not be included in my listing of action sequences. Such actions would include an instruction given and obeyed, a question posed and answered, and a request made and accepted. In a real sense, stories move forward on the basis of this kind of paired action, a fact that has been noted by others. Conroy has given some attention to this aspect of narrative texts in his study of 2 Samuel 13–20. There he speaks of microtextual patterns that help shape the text by acting as minor points of narrative tension (93–95) and lists such pairs as command/execution, request/granting, news or message/reaction, and question/answer. Such patterns are indeed pervasive in narrative texts, but they do not often exhibit the kind of movement from expectation to fulfillment that would permit them to stand as an autonomous story or carry the main action of a story, and Conroy appears to recognize this when he calls them microtextual. What I call an action sequence identifies a pair of actions that could function as the main action in a story, even though such pairs often function as subordinate movements within stories. The distinction between action sequences and smaller paired actions in texts may not always be clear, although I think that there is a sufficient difference between them to be able to bracket out the smaller patterns from the discussion of action sequences.

Biblical scholars have noticed narrative movements like those I call action sequences. Westermann, for example, has defined a narrative in terms of an arc of tension that moves from tension to resolution ("von einer Spannung zu einer Lösung," 1981:33, although the English translation says "through climax to resolution," 1985:45). In an earlier study he claimed that the main stories in Genesis 1–11 belong to a narrative type featuring a movement from tension to resolution involving crime and punishment of which the purest example is Genesis 2–3 (1980:44–45). He divided the structure of these Genesis stories into three stages: (1) a transgression, (2) statement of punishment or of an intention to punish, and (3) an act of punishment (49–50; see also Clines, 1978:62–63).

A number of other scholars have made similar suggestions. Aware of Westermann's notion of an arc of tension, de Pury sought to apply it to the Jacob narrative in order to test whether or not this cycle was simply a collection of individual stories or a narrative in itself (2:475). In his discussion, de Pury also refers to the way Propp marked out lines of tension in stories, especially the movement from the recognition of the lack of something to the elimination of that lack (2:481). Long has found a three-stage pattern in some stories of the prophets in 1 and 2 Kings: situation/crisis; divine oracle; fulfillment/resolution of crisis (1973). Brevard Childs has identified two patterns in the wilderness traditions of Exodus and Numbers (1974:258; see my comments in 1976b:112). His first pattern involves need, complaint, intercession, intervention. The second consists of complaint, anger and punishment, intercession, and reprieve. The description of plot by Aitken as a movement from problem to solution should also be noted, especially since he uses the term "action sequences" for the three elements in this movement (8).

In addition to Conroy's aforementioned discussion of small sets of paired actions in narrative, he also deals with similar movements at a higher level. In the first stage of his analysis (narrative as process), he treats plot, or action. He identifies structural building blocks beneath the surface of the text, small-scale narrative patterns that underlie the specific content of the text (10) and so may be common to many stories even when they differ in content. He mentions specifically a movement that runs from a state of desire to a state in which the desire is satisfied. In his view, the drive toward satisfying a desire directs the narrative action through encounters with obstacles to activities that remove the obstacles

(18). This kind of movement is very close to what I mean by action sequence.

A number of scholars have applied various kinds of structural analysis to biblical texts (Culley, 1985a) and this often involves attention to movements of action. Several have attempted to use elements of Propp's approach (for a review of such work see Milne, 1988:125–175). The most extensive investigation to date of the use of Propp's method in the analysis of biblical texts may be found in *Vladimir Propp and the Study of Structure in Hebrew Narrative* by Pamela J. Milne. After an examination of Propp's approach and a critical review of those who have applied it to biblical texts, Milne tests the approach on the stories in Daniel 1–6. She uses Propp's model as a heuristic device and with a clear understanding that, as a fairy tale model, it will not account for all the features of the Daniel tales. Since these tales are limited in number, Milne does not try to develop a new model for narrative analysis on the basis of this small group. Her interest lies in using Propp to garner clues to tale structure and to genre in the Daniel stories. She concludes that the use of Propp highlights enough structural features to permit the suggestion that three genres are involved: (1) Daniel 1–2 and 5; (2) Daniel 3 and 6; and (3) Daniel 4. The interest in genre, which implies the need for fuller tale models, has taken Milne in a different direction from my use of action sequences.

Another kind of structural analysis has been adopted by the Groupe d'Entrevernes., whose work is based on the approach of A. J. Greimas. The method proposed by Greimas takes into account the level at which Propp worked by identifying narrative programs at one stage of text analysis, although this amounts to only one level in a very complex model of narrative analysis (Culley, 1985a:175–77). The approach is briefly illustrated by an analysis of Genesis 11 by the Groupe d'Entrevernes (171–72). This kind of investigation aims at a complete analysis of all features of narrative and so goes far beyond what I am attempting here.

In the folklore approach to narrative developed by Niditch, to which I make reference in the previous chapter, she employs a set of overlays that apply to four levels of the text: generic, specific, typological, and individual. At the most general level, the generic, the action in a story is stated in very generalized terms and bears some resemblance to how I describe the movement of action in sequences. For example, the action for Gen 12:10–20 is stated in five steps: problem, plan, execution, complication, and outcome (42). As Niditch moves down the scale through the other three levels of her model, these five steps are given ever increasing specification and become increasingly explicit. By working on different levels, one becomes aware of very general patterns that may exist in more than one culture, of more specific elements that are peculiar to the culture of ancient Israel, and of features that are unique to a given story. Niditch seeks to describe the style of stories in terms like "popular-economical" or "baroque rhetorical," thus attempting to relate the patterns of text to patterns of human behavior.

Examples of Action Sequences

In this section a number of action sequences will be delineated, and examples will be provided for each type. Nine different sequences will be identified and grouped under six main headings and nine subheadings.

A. Punishment Sequences
    1. *Wrong/punished*
    2. *Injury/avenged*

B. Rescue Sequences
    3. *Difficulty/rescued*
    4. *Difficulty/escaped*

C. Achievement Sequences
    5. *Desire/achieved*
    6. *Task/accomplished*

D. Reward Sequences
    7. *Good deed/rewarded*

E. Announcement Sequences
    8. *Announcement/happened*

F. Prohibition Sequences
    9. *Prohibition/transgressed*

Each of the six main categories will be described and then illustrated with examples from biblical narrative. Since very few stories contain only one sequence, all sequences in a given story will be noted during the description. The six categories of sequences are simply those that have come to my attention. What follows is not a complete inventory of all possible sequences, nor are all examples from biblical narrative cited. While the list includes those sequences that seem to turn up most frequently, it is not implied that all biblical stories can be reduced to one or more of the sequences listed here. Let me reiterate what was said in the previous section. This mode of description has been developed largely for convenience. It has been tailored to the job at hand, a limited study of some repeated yet varied patterns in biblical narrative. There may be room for debate on a number of issues and there may be other ways of arranging the description than the way chosen here. Nevertheless, I believe that the following selection and description is sufficiently systematic and accurate to be useful.

In my previous work I collected a small group of stories on the basis of an apparent similarity: they all dealt with a miracle, a deception, or the like. These were then examined to see whether a common pattern of action could be discerned—a wrong which was punished or a person in difficulty who was rescued. Collecting stories by group not only brings to light the presence of a sequence but also defines the level of abstraction at which the sequence is stated.

At this stage, I seek to identify different kinds of action sequences. While a number of biblical stories will be employed to illustrate the various action sequences presented, the biblical examples will be described with a minimum of detail. Comments will be made only to the degree necessary for illustration even though there may be other features in the stories worthy of interest and deserving of fuller discussion. In the next chapter, some attempt will be made to go beyond the simple stage of identifying action sequences and to take other important features of the text into account in order to assess the particular way patterns have been varied.

A. Punishment Sequences

Two types of punishment sequences will be introduced and illustrated: *wrong/punished* and *wrong/avenged*. The distinction between the two is related to how the divine and human are involved. In the first type, the deity constitutes the party wronged and administers the punishment. The second type operates on the human plane in that a person who is wronged avenges the wrong done.

1. *Wrong/punished.* There are a number of stories in the Bible that tell about a person or a group doing something which is viewed as wrong by the deity so that divine punishment follows. The main action sequence in such stories is likely to be a punishment sequence, which can be given the descriptive label *wrong/punished.* Stories in which this sequence is central can be conveniently called punishment stories. Some examples have been discussed in Culley (1980a).

It is rare to find a story so short and simple that it contains the action sequence *wrong/punished* without any elaboration at all. Still it is best to begin with a very short example containing little elaboration so that the movement in the story and the shape of the action sequence will be relatively clear.

(a) In 2 Kgs 2:23–25 Elisha curses some boys (Culley, 1980a:169). While this narrative is part of a series of stories about Elisha in which Yahweh frequently intervenes, it records a self-contained incident with a beginning and an ending. As Elisha is on his way to Bethel, some little boys make fun of him. He curses them in the name of Yahweh. Immediately two bears come out of the woods and attack the boys. The main movement in the action in this story goes from wrong to punishment. Making fun of the prophet is defined as a wrong because it brought on a punishment and not because of the action itself, which may or may not appear deserving of punishment to us. From one point of view the boys were being boys. Perhaps they unknowingly crossed the line between acceptable and unacceptable behavior in dealing with a special agent of Yahweh who was capable of invoking divine power in the sphere of human affairs.

The second element of the sequence, the punishment, is not a single action but itself consists of two elements: a curse is uttered, and it is immediately realized. This may be defined as an action sequence embedded in the larger punishment sequence. The pronouncement of a curse followed by its realization can be identified as an action sequence of the type to be discussed below, an announcement sequence in which the action may be defined as *announcement/happened*. It is not uncommon that one or the other, or even both, of the paired elements making up an action sequence may consist of an embedded action sequence.

The action sequences of 2 Kgs 2:23–25 can be displayed in a diagram as follows:

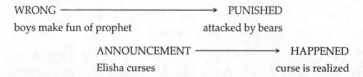

WRONG ————————————→ PUNISHED
boys make fun of prophet   attacked by bears

                ANNOUNCEMENT ————————→ HAPPENED
                Elisha curses   curse is realized

(b) The fate of Lot's wife provides another short example of a punishment sequence. This sequence is included in a longer and rather complex story found in Genesis 18–19 (see Culley, 1978:37; for more detailed discussion, see below) and consists of only two verses separated from one another in the text, Gen 19:17 and 26. When the divine messengers bring Lot out of Sodom along with his wife and daughters, Lot is warned not to look back (v. 17). A discussion then ensues concerning the goal of the flight. When this is settled, Yahweh destroys Sodom. At this point (v. 26), Lot's wife looks back and becomes a pillar of salt. A wrong is committed and then punished. In this case, the first element depicting the wrong consists of an embedded action sequence of the type *prohibition/transgressed* (see below). A warning is given not to look back. Lot's wife does. Thus, a specific action is expressly forbidden and subsequently disregarded; in other words, there is a movement from prohibition to transgression of the prohibition. Once the divine prohibition has been transgressed, a wrong has been committed, and a supernatural response in the form of a punishment may be expected. The action sequences regarding Lot's wife may be displayed as follows:

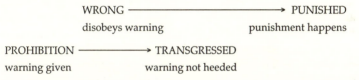

WRONG ⟶ PUNISHED
disobeys warning   punishment happens

PROHIBITION ⟶ TRANSGRESSED
warning given   warning not heeded

(c) A third example of a punishment sequence appears in 1 Kgs 20:35,36 (Culley, 1980b:173); again it is part of a larger story. A member of the prophetic order instructs a companion through a divine word to strike him. The companion refuses to do so. The original speaker then announces that, because his companion did not obey Yahweh, he will be attacked by a lion. This happens. A wrong is committed and punished. Here, however, both elements of the sequence, the wrong and the punishment, are represented by embedded sequences. In the first element, an instruction is given and refused. It functions in the story in virtually the same way as a prohibition that is violated. The second element, the wrong punished, consists of an announcement followed by the occurrence of what was announced.

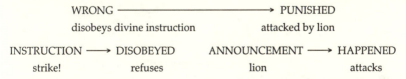

WRONG ⟶ PUNISHED
disobeys divine instruction   attacked by lion

INSTRUCTION ⟶ DISOBEYED   ANNOUNCEMENT ⟶ HAPPENED
strike!   refuses   lion   attacks

(d) Another example is the story in Num 21:4–9 about the serpents that Yahweh set on the people (Culley, 1976b:102–4). The punishment is recounted in three verses (4–6). The people journeying in the wilderness speak against the deity and Moses with complaints about the lack of food and water. They preface this complaint with a comment about being brought up from Egypt to die in the wilderness. This is a version of the so-called "murmuring motif" (Coats, 1968). The force of the complaint is that it challenges the whole enterprise of the exodus from Egypt so that the wrong committed here is not just a complaint about food and water but a charge that the deity has made a grave mistake. In response to the words of the people, Yahweh sends serpents that bite them and cause a good number to die. The punishment sequence is complete at this point. There is a movement from wrong to punishment that can be easily identified: the people complain and are punished immediately through supernatural intervention.

The story is not finished, however, and it may be worth indicating here what happens in the next stage. With the punishment in progress, the people approach Moses, admit that they have sinned in speaking against Moses and Yahweh, and ask him to pray so that the serpents might be removed. Moses does. Yahweh instructs him to make a serpent and place it on a standard so that everyone bitten could see it and live. Moses does so, and people are cured. The continuation of this story takes the form of another kind of action, which will be discussed below under the heading "rescue sequence." It is often linked to punishment sequences in order to mitigate the punishment. The punishment produces a dangerous situation from which may arise an appeal for rescue: the serpents are biting the people, and the people are dying in substantial numbers. In response to this dangerous situation the people admit their wrong and appeal to Moses to intervene. Moses prays and receives instructions that he follows with the result that the danger is averted. The sequences in this story may be displayed in the following way.

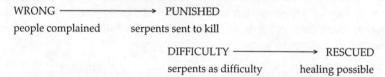

It is of interest that the punishment in the first sequence becomes the difficulty from which rescue is needed in the other sequence. In other words, the attack of the serpents is an event with a double function. It is both the second element in the punishment sequence and at the same time the first element in the rescue sequence.

These four examples should be sufficient to illustrate the punishment sequence of the type *wrong/punished*. Further examples of this kind of sequence will be met in the biblical material to follow, and a few of these will be discussed more fully in subsequent sections of this work (see also Culley, 1980b, 1976b:100–8). A few well-known instances may simply be noted. Gehazi is punished for performing a deception in order to gain some goods he wanted (2 Kgs 5:20–27). In 1 Kgs 20:33–43 the king of Israel treats the king of Aram with generosity instead of putting him to the ban; but, after an elaborate section in which the king of Israel declares himself guilty, punishment is announced for him. The story of Cain and Abel (Gen 4:1–16) has a punishment sequence with a mitigation. The Garden story (Genesis 2–3) has a punishment sequence as a major, if not the major, sequence, in which the wrong consists of a prohibition followed by a transgression. The story of Achan (Joshua 7) involves a punishment sequence as a major feature. Finally, there is the strange story of the lying prophet in 1 Kings 13, where a prohibition is transgressed and results in punishment.

2. *Injury/avenged*. In all the above stories, the wrong is apparently understood to be against Yahweh, and so the punishment comes about through or by means of divine action, whether directly or indirectly. There are, however, stories in which a wrong takes the form of an action carried out by one person against another so that an act of vengeance is instigated by the injured party. Of course, from a broad perspective, it may be said that any such injury may be viewed as a wrong against the deity. Nevertheless, in defining sequences, the action is labelled as "wrong" or "injury" depending upon the nature of the reaction, divine punishment or human vengeance. In these stories everything seems to happen on the human plane, even though it is possible in an ultimate sense to attribute all such actions of revenge to divine action governing human affairs. Sometimes the larger context of the narrative implies that one should interpret it this way. Sequences that express vengeance will be taken as a variation on the punishment sequence and will be distinguished from the others by being labelled *injury/avenged*. Two examples will be given. These are both longer and more complex than the examples given so far and as such deserve a much fuller discussion than they will receive. At this stage, however, I am only concerned to identify the basic action sequences that govern the movement of the narrative.

(a) First, there is the story of Amnon and Absalom in 2 Samuel 13. A wrong, Amnon's rape of Absalom's sister Tamar, is avenged by Absalom. The action constituting the wrong is itself a sequence of a type to be listed below and identified as an *achievement sequence*. In this embedded sequence, Amnon desires to have Tamar and, following the advice of a friend, succeeds by means of a deception. The treatment of

Tamar contains two injuries. One is the rape in which Amnon forces himself on the woman, an action that she describes as an act of folly that should not be done in Israel (v. 12). The second is the rejection of Tamar by Amnon immediately afterwards, which is described by Tamar as a worse wrong than the first (v. 16). Nevertheless, it appears to be the first injury that motivates Absalom's vengeance (v. 22). The results of the second injury serve to draw his attention to what Amnon did. In spite of the magnitude of the crime, as Tamar describes it, their father David grows angry but does nothing. From the point of view of narrative action, David's inaction leaves open the possibility for Absalom to act.

Since Absalom needs to create a situation in which he can execute his revenge, he must prepare the way by a careful deception. Absalom's vengeance may be viewed as an embedded action sequence of the sort described below as an achievement sequence. Like Amnon's taking of Tamar, this action involves a desire that is achieved by means of a trick. Since, however, Absalom's action is driven not by a desire to murder but by a desire to avenge, the sequence will be defined as having the form *task/achieved*. This kind of sequence will be described and illustrated below. Although my label of the last action sequence is open to argument and therefore tentative, the following diagram appears to me to be a sufficiently accurate sketch of the movement within the story.

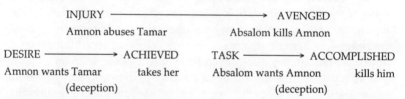

(b) The second example is the story about Dinah in Genesis 34. Shechem saw her, took her, and forced himself on her. In contrast to the reaction of Amnon, Shechem fell in love with the woman and wanted her for a wife. Jacob hears that Dinah has been defiled but holds his peace while his sons are away. When his sons learn of the incident, they are both upset and angry because, as the narrator points out, such a flagrant act has been committed in Israel. Hamor's attempt to arrange a marriage presents an opportunity to the sons of Jacob, and they proceed with an act of vengeance against the perpetrator and his family. This action can be construed as an embedded sequence in which a desire is achieved by means of a deception. The wrongdoers are tricked into thinking that a marriage will take place if they undergo circumcision. After they allow themselves to be circumcised and while they are recovering, they are murdered by Dinah's brothers Simeon and Levi, and their city is plundered. Jacob, who has not participated in the revenge, rebukes his sons for the action because of the dangerous situation it might create, but the sons retort that it had to be done.

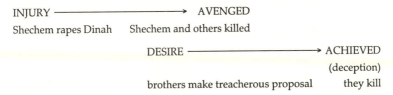

INJURY ⟶ AVENGED
Shechem rapes Dinah   Shechem and others killed

DESIRE ⟶ ACHIEVED
(deception)
brothers make treacherous proposal   they kill

B. Rescue Sequences

Two types of rescue sequence will be identified: *difficulty/rescued* and *difficulty/escaped*. Again, the distinction between the two has to do with the involvement of the divine, or supernatural. In the first type, the deity intervenes either directly or indirectly. In the second, the action seems to remain on the human plane.

3. *Difficulty/rescued*. There are numerous stories in the Bible in which a person or a group find themselves facing some sort of problem but are rescued from it by the deity (Culley, 1976b:71–100). One such sequence has already been encountered above in the discussion of punishment sequences. It was suggested that the story about punishment by serpents (Num 21:4–9) also includes a rescue sequence in which a means of healing is offered to some of those afflicted by the serpents.

Rescue sequences, at least those that have been brought together here, exhibit considerable variety, especially with regard to the difficult situation from which rescue is accomplished. One could make a number of distinctions within the group. For example, there are stories in which there is a real threat to life, anything from a hostile power such as an enemy to the lack of a necessity of life such as food. There are also stories that deal with lesser problems, unpleasant but not life-threatening ones. However, the term "rescue" will be understood here in a very broad sense, and no subgroups will be identified. This decision is largely a matter of convenience, and I do not believe that it is misleading to include a number of different possibilities under the label *difficulty/rescued*. The act of rescue usually involves a miracle, either through direct intervention of the deity or through an agent of the deity who speaks the proper words or performs the correct actions.

(a) A short account containing a rescue sequence may be found in 2 Kgs 2:19–22 (Culley, 1976b:72–75). Men from a city come to Elisha with a problem. They point out that the water and land are both bad. The reference to the bad land may result from a faulty text since it is not mentioned further. In any case, the problem dealt with in the rest of the story is bad water. The prophet asks for a new dish and some salt; he throws the salt into the water and pronounces a word of Yahweh to the effect that the water has now been restored and will no longer present a problem. The story concludes with the comment that this indeed happened just as Elisha had said. The basic sequence is *difficulty/rescued*, and it is little elaborated. The difficult situation is described very briefly in a comment to the prophet. Once the prophet is aware of the difficulty, he gives instructions and takes action. The rescue involves not only direct action but an announcement in a Yahweh word that immediately takes effect. This could be described as an embedded *announcement/happened* sequence.

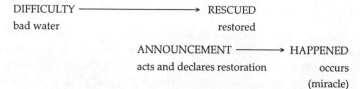

DIFFICULTY ———————————→ RESCUED
bad water   restored

ANNOUNCEMENT ———→ HAPPENED
acts and declares restoration   occurs
(miracle)

(b) A second example of a rescue sequence may be found in the story about a lost axe-head, 2 Kgs 6:1–7 (Culley, 1976b:81–83). While clearing space for a new settlement, the axe-head of one of the workers, and a borrowed one at that, falls into the Jordan. This is the difficulty. It is not a matter of life and death by any means but a problem. The prophet throws a stick in the river at the place where the axe-head fell in, and it floats to the surface. This story appears to have just the one sequence, although it is elaborated by dialogue and details.

DIFFICULTY ———————————————→ RESCUED
the axe-head falls in river   prophet recovers it
(miracle)

(c) A third example of a rescue sequence is the story of the boy healed by Elijah in 1 Kgs 17:17–24 (Culley, 1976b:87–91), which is similar to a story about Elisha in 2 Kgs 4:18–32. This Elijah story is a more complex example of a rescue sequence than those already mentioned.

The complication lies in the fact that the difficult situation in the story can be viewed from two angles. Elijah is a guest in the house of a woman whose boy becomes ill. The sick boy represents the kind of difficulty that a divine agent like Elijah might be expected to do something about, and he does. However, the mother of the boy does not ask for help, as one might expect; rather she charges the prophet with being responsible for the misfortune by bringing her sins to light.

There is a double aspect. First of all, the challenge to the prophet and his subsequent vindication can viewed as a rescue sequence. The prophet finds himself in difficulty because he is charged with causing the mortal sickness of the boy. In response to this he takes the boy, performs actions on him, and prays to Yahweh twice. The first prayer does not ask that the boy be healed but, in effect, appears to remind Yahweh of the important fact that he, Yahweh, has brought misfortune upon the widow in whose household the prophet is residing. When the boy is healed and taken back to the mother, she responds by saying that now she knows that Elijah is a true man of God and that the word of Yahweh is truly in his mouth. Thus the widow's initial charge and the prophet's first prayer stress the fact that the prophet is himself in difficulty, one that can only be resolved, and indeed will be resolved, by healing the boy. This is confirmed by the final comment of the widow, which indicates that the sickness of the boy has indeed brought into question, at least in her eyes, the validity of Elijah's office. The prophet is cast in a difficult situation; and in bringing about the healing of the boy through Yahweh he, too, is rescued by divine action.

Second, within this sequence regarding the prophet there is the loss of the son and his restoration to the widow. This can be identified simply as another way of looking at the same sequence, or, for purposes of discussion, could be called another sequence parallel to the first. Here, the woman finds herself in a difficult situation, to which the prophet responds with help. The second prayer of Elijah specifically asks that the boy be restored, although this action is also essential for the first sequence just discussed. The actions and prayer of Elijah are effective, and Yahweh restores the boy to the mother. The sequence about the restoration of the boy appears to be subordinate to and framed by the one about the challenge to the prophet, although the two are closely interconnected. One diagram serves for both.

DIFFICULTY			RESCUED
prophet charged	acts and prays	boy healed	vindicated
mother has sick boy		boy healed (miracle)	restored to her

(d) A fourth story with a rescue sequence comes from Exod 15:22–27 (Culley, 1976b:78–81). Searching for water the people come to Marah, but the water is bitter and they cannot drink it. They complain to Moses, and he cries out to Yahweh who shows him a tree. When Moses throws this into the water, it turns sweet. This is a very brief story in which the rescue sequence is clear.

DIFFICULTY ——————————————→ RESCUED

water is bitter   appeals, shown   tree makes sweet

Some other stories containing rescue sequences and involving divine intervention or miracle may be noted as further examples. There is the prophet story about the poison stew in 2 Kgs 4:38–41. Similarly, help is given to a widow by Elisha in 2 Kgs 4:1–7. In Exod 17:1–7 Moses produces water from a rock to quench the people's thirst.

4. *Difficulty/escape*. There are also stories in which persons solve a difficulty without direct divine intervention. Sometimes they rescue themselves; sometimes they are helped by others. They may do this by means of their wits, as by deception, or by means of their strength, as in combat. Some of these were treated in an earlier article as deception stories. There I was stressing the mode of rescue or escape, and that this action developed on the human level (Culley, 1974:174–78).

(a) The short account of the midwives in Exod 1:15–21 contains this kind of sequence. The king of Egypt, in the context of his actions against the Israelites, instructs two midwives to kill the male children at birth. Since the midwives fear God, they do not do what they are asked, explaining to the king that the Hebrew women give birth too quickly. The account is very brief and does not give many details. In response to their predicament the two midwives use the only weapon at their disposal, their wits. They save the people by ignoring the king's instruction and covering up with a story, which also saves themselves. That they succeed, at least temporarily, is clear from the report in v. 20 that the people grow in numbers.

DIFFICULTY ——————————————→ ESCAPED

abhorrent instruction   disobeyed and lied   escaped
                                                    (deception)

(b) A second story containing a rescue sequence of this type also involves a deception. In 1 Sam 19:11–17 we find Saul sending messengers to David's house to kill him. The difficulty is clear. Here, however, it is not David who responds to the crisis but Michal who takes the initiative.

She lets David down through the window so that he may escape. She then fixes his bed so that it looks as though he is in it and tells the messengers that he is sick. This buys some time, but when Saul sends the messengers again, they discover the fraud. Saul complains to his daughter that she has been treacherous, but she manages to cover up her own participation in the escape.

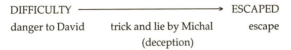

DIFFICULTY ⟶ ESCAPED

danger to David   trick and lie by Michal   escape

(deception)

(c) A third example is the story of the Gibeonites, Josh 9:3–15 (Culley, 1974:176). Apart from some signs of unevenness, the section follows the outline of a rescue sequence in which the potential victims use their wits to escape from a dangerous situation. The Gibeonites have heard of what happened to Jericho and Ai before the advancing Israelites. They seize the initiative and perform a deception involving a masquerade and a false story. They ask to make a treaty on the grounds that they are not of the land but have come from afar. Taken in, Joshua accedes to their request and makes a treaty, and the Gibeonites save their skins. It may be noted in passing that the rest of the chapter (whatever its origin) takes vv. 3–15 as an embedded story that delineates a wrong which, once discovered by the Israelites, is avenged by making the Gibeonites woodcutters and water carriers. At least they are not killed.

DIFFICULTY ⟶ ESCAPED

danger to Gibeonites   trick and lie   escape

(deception)

A few other examples can be noted (Culley, 1974:174–78). In Genesis 14, when Lot is captured and carried off by foreign kings, Abram pursues, attacks, and rescues Lot. The story of Tamar (Genesis 38) also moves from a difficult situation to an escape, at least in a general way. Tamar has not received something owed to her, an obligation that has been set aside. She can only gain it by using her wits to perform a clever deception. Finally, in 1 Sam 21:11–16 David flees to Gath only to be recognized. Fearing what King Achish would do, David feigns madness and is let alone so that he is able to escape.

C. Achievement Sequences

This section will deal with two kinds of sequences: *desire/achieved* and *task/accomplished*. The common factor is that a goal has been set either as something desired, which a person then sets out to gain, or as task laid on someone, which he or she must accomplish. Actions motivated by desire function on the human plane. Tasks may be set by other humans or by the deity.

5. *Desire/achieved.* In identifying here examples of this kind of sequence, the notion of desire will be kept fairly specific since many actions in stories likely involve to some extent the desire of a person to perform some feat or gain some object. The notion of desire will be limited here to cases where the desire to possess an object or perform a feat is the only, or at least the major, motivation for an action and where the desired object or action is not easily obtainable or achievable but can only be gained or accomplished with a certain degree of effort, skill, or ingenuity in the face of difficulty.

Two examples of this type of sequence have already been mentioned because they have been found embedded in other sequences: in 2 Samuel 13, Amnon wants Tamar and deceives to get her, noted above in 2(a); in Genesis 34, the sons of Jacob want to take revenge on Shechem and his family, noted above in 2(b). Two other examples will be mentioned here, but only briefly because they will be dealt with more fully in the following chapter. First, in 1 Kings 21, Ahab wants Naboth's plot, but the latter's refusal to sell stands in the way. Ahab's wife takes action and employs a trick to eliminate Naboth. Ahab then proceeds to possess his heart's desire. Second, in 2 Kings 5, when Naaman offers valuable gifts to Elisha and they are refused, Gehazi wants to have some for himself and obtains them through a deception. In both stories, the deception sequences are embedded, functioning as the wrong that is subsequently punished. With four examples already noted and two more to come it will be sufficient to discuss just one further example at this point.

In Genesis 27 Isaac is tricked into bestowing his blessing on Jacob. There is no mention at the beginning of the story of any particular longing or desire of Jacob's to gain his brother's blessing. The possibility for gain arises when Rebekah overhears Isaac's instructions to Esau, and she takes the initiative by approaching Jacob with a plan to deceive Isaac. The role of the one who desires, plans, and gains is divided between two characters both of whom stand to profit. In fact, Jacob appears to be reluctant (v. 11), at least to the extent of realizing what is at stake in the dangerous game. After being reassured, Jacob carries out the preparations for the deception and succeeds in fooling the father. The blessing is given to Jacob. Here the sequence *desire/achieved* does not serve as a wrong that leads to a punishment. By most standards lying and cheating a father and a brother for no other reason than personal gain is reprehensible, but in this narrative neither Jacob nor Rebekah are charged with any wrongdoing by the father, nor is there any explicit mention by him or by the deity of any kind of punishment. Esau, of course, is enraged and bent on revenge, but he does not get any farther with this than chasing Jacob away. This is one version of why Jacob left home, vv. 42–45. Behind all this another force is at work, because Jacob is moving into the position already announced for him by Yahweh (Gen 25:23). Read in this larger context, this story is embedded in an announcement sequence and indicates how the announcement came true.

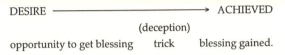

DESIRE ⟶ ACHIEVED

(deception)

opportunity to get blessing   trick   blessing gained.

6. *Task/accomplished.* In this kind of sequence, as with the sequences about a desire, a goal is established that entails gaining or doing something, which may present at least a measure of difficulty. The establishment of the goal does not derive principally from a desire to have or do but is a response to some external factor or situation. The distinction here between *desire/achieved* and *task/accomplished* may be too fine in the end to be worth maintaining, but for the present it seems useful to make it. One example of this sequence has been noted above in the discussion of the story of the rape of Tamar in 2(a). When Absalom discovers what Amnon has done, he appears prepared to avenge it. He has a goal and his task is set; to achieve it requires a deception, which he performs successfully.

One further example can be noted. Genesis 24 tells the story of how a wife was procured for Isaac. Here a person is given a task to be carried out. Abraham charges a servant with the duty of going to the old homeland and bringing back a wife for Isaac. This charge involves a journey, leading far from home and back again. This long trip affords the narrator ample scope to include any number of adventures that may happen along the way. Between the departure and return, there is the meeting at the well, the meeting with the family, and the problem of getting away again to return home. The task may not appear to be unusually difficult but there is at least the problem of heading off into the unknown and selecting just the right woman, all of which is aided by Yahweh (vv. 12–27).

TASK ⟶ ACCOMPLISHED

bring back wife   brings back wife

A story dealing with a test, administered and achieved, may be a variation of the *task/achieved* sequence. Stories dealing with a test do not appear to be very common in biblical narrative, but one famous example can be cited. When God decides to test Abraham (Genesis 22), a task in the form of an instruction is given to Abraham. Of course this test is complicated by the fact the Abraham is kept completely in the dark about it. He is given a task and seems to take it at face value, since he does not appear to know that a test is involved. However, the narrator has warned the audience at the very beginning that a test is in progress. Thus, the real task assigned to Abraham (although he does not know it) is the test, and passing the test does not require the completion of the apparent task he has been given. This story has fascinated countless commentators and could lead to a lengthy discussion. It will be sufficient here simply to note that in this story the test is something like a task assigned and achieved.

D. Reward Sequences

7. *Good deed/rewarded.* This sequence is opposite to the punishment sequence. A good deed is performed and a reward is given. While punishment sequences are common in the biblical tradition, reward sequences are relatively rare and for that reason can be identified with less confidence. Some possible examples follow.

(a) In 2 Kgs 4:8–17 a woman of Shunem and her husband become regular hosts to the prophet Elisha on his travels; they even set aside a room for him. In gratitude for their kindness, the prophet wants to grant the woman a favor. When his servant Gehazi suggests a son, Elisha calls the woman and announces to her that she will bear a son. She does.

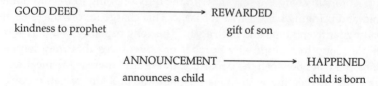

GOOD DEED ⟶ REWARDED
kindness to prophet   gift of son

ANNOUNCEMENT ⟶ HAPPENED
announces a child   child is born

(b) Another example comes from the story about the midwives in the first chapter of Exodus; it has already been discussed in 4(a) above since it also contains a rescue sequence. The description of the action of the midwives is given in vv. 15–19. It is clear that this whole action—the refusal to do what the king of Egypt has instructed—may be taken as a good deed because in the next two verses, 20 and 21, it is explained that

God is good to the midwives. He provides them with families, seeing that they fear him.

GOOD DEED ⟶ REWARDED

midwives do not kill   given a reward

(c) In the story of Exod 2:15–22, in which Moses meets his wife, there may be a *good deed/rewarded* sequence. Moses comes to the aid of the daughters of the priest of Midian at the well. When the priest hears of this action, he has Moses brought home for something to eat. Moses stays with him and is given the priest's daughter as a wife. This story is so condensed that the links between the actions are not made explicit. It may or may not be that the giving of the daughter functions as a reward for the rescue.

E. Announcement Sequences

8. *Announcement/happened*. This is intended to be a rather general label to cover a wide range of possibilities. It may in the end be too broad a category, but it will serve for the present. In a broad sense, the term "announcement sequence" will be applied to a movement in narrative that opens with an indication that something is going to happen and closes with the occurrence of the anticipated event. The most obvious example of this, at least in biblical narrative, would be an oracle or pronouncement from the deity indicating that this or that will occur followed by the report that it did indeed occur. This kind of supernatural announcement may issue directly from the deity or be transmitted through a human agent, usually a prophet, speaking explicitly or implicitly with divine authority. However, I will include among announcement sequences other kinds of story movements that begin with an indication that something is going to happen and then proceed to recount its occurrence. The tension in such a sequence consists in seeing how and when the announced event comes about. The lapse of time between an announcement and the occurrence may be very brief or stretch out for a long period of time so that the span may be contained within a brief story or extend through large sections of narrative collections.

Frequently, announcement sequences in which a pronouncement is made by the deity or an agent function as embedded sequences. Announcement sequences have already been noted above as components of punishment sequences (*wrong/punished*). The second phase, in which the punishment occurs, takes the form of an announcement of retribution, which then comes to pass. This may occur immediately or at some time in the future. In the brief account of Elisha and the boys (2 Kgs 2:23–25), the punishment comes about by having the prophet pronounce a curse in the name of Yahweh that is immediately realized by the appearance of the animals, which attack the boys. Something similar happens in the story about a confrontation between two members of the prophetic order. By a word of Yahweh one orders the other to strike him, but this is refused (1 Kgs 20:35–36). The one who issued the instruction then announces a punishment for the other because he did not obey Yahweh. It is announced that a lion will attack the culprit, which happens as soon as he takes his leave. In the reward sequence about Elisha and the Shunammite, the prophet announces the birth of a son. The woman becomes pregnant and bears a son.

The above are examples of embedded announcement sequences, but are there examples where an announcement sequence governs the main action of a story? I am going to suggest that this may be so. There are stories that simply relate what happened at a certain point of time, how something happened on a certain occasion, or how a given state of affairs came to be. When readers learn at the beginning of the story what the story will be about, they know in general what kind of event will take place, and the tension in the story exists in following through the details of the announced event until it is complete. It is clear that this may be stretching the notion of an *announcement/happens* sequence. Nevertheless, it may be worthwhile to present a few possible examples for consideration.

(a) In 2 Kings 2, a story is told about how Elijah is carried off to the heavens, bringing his stay on this earth to an end. I would maintain that the story is governed by a narrative sequence of the form *announcement/happened*. The narrator introduces his story by informing us that this narrative will tell what happens when Yahweh takes Elijah up to the heavens in a whirlwind. This statement right at the beginning of the story tells us what to expect and what we can look forward to. The subject matter of the account is found again in v. 3 when the members of the prophetic community ask Elisha if he knew that Yahweh was going to take Elijah. As the story unfolds, Elijah is indeed taken up in the whirlwind. When this happens, we know that the action sequence has come to an end. What was "announced" has happened. But the story continues, describing a search for Elijah that is subordinated to the main story. The search confirms that he has really disappeared from the earth. The tension in the story consists in knowing what is going to happen in general but having to wait to see how it will happen in particular.

ANNOUNCEMENT ——————————→ HAPPENED
indication that   story tells
Elijah will be taken   how this occurs

(b) Similarly, one may understand the creation story of Genesis 1 to be governed by an announcement sequence as I have broadly defined it. The first verse indicates the topic of the account: the story will be about the creation of the heavens and the earth. We also know that we are at the beginning of that process. Barring any other complications introduced into the narrative, one then anticipates an account of how the world came to be, and this is what we get. When creation is completed, the story is over. The *announcement/happened* sequence governs the whole story. It could also be argued that Genesis 2–3 also begins with a sequence of this sort, indicating that we will learn about how the world was created, and so we do. However, other sequences are introduced that take over and become more dominant than the announcement sequence of the creation. The movement in Genesis 1 may be indicated as follows.

ANNOUNCEMENT ——————————→ HAPPENED
creation of   events of creation
heavens and earth   narrated to completion

(c) Another possible example may be found in 2 Kgs 4:42–44. The action begins with an instruction, although a very unusual one: a man is asked to distribute a small amount of food to a hundred men so that they may eat. In other words the man is instructed to perform a task which on the face of it is impossible. The man realizes this full well and immediately objects, pointing out the problem. Even though the story is cryptic, one may assume that the prophet knew exactly what kind of instruction he was issuing. Thus the objection the man raises is not meant to inform the prophet of a difficulty about which he was unaware but rather to stress the impossibility of the instruction. It might be argued that the impossible instruction functions as an announcement of a miracle that is about to take place. The objection is a common enough elaboration of announcement sequences, as will be seen.

ANNOUNCEMENT ——————————→ HAPPENED
impossible instruction   (objection)   obeyed and is effective

Announcements sometimes extend beyond individual stories. One of the most famous of these is Gen 12:1–9, where an announcement is made to Abraham about land and people, an expectation that appears to remain important for the larger narrative as it continues in the books following Genesis. Indeed, the promise is repeated a number of times. There is, however, no clear marking of the exact point in the later narrative when the announced situation is deemed to have been realized. Another example is the oracle given by Yahweh to Isaac (Gen 25:23), which was mentioned above. The oracle concerns the two sons in his wife's womb and indicates that priority will be given to the younger one. In a sense, the Jacob narratives that follow work out the movement of Jacob from second to first position. On a smaller scale, an announcement of a son for Abraham is related in Gen 18:10. This announcement is, of course, met with some measure of skepticism by Sarah, who cannot help laughing to herself. After a rebuke for this expression of doubt, the announcement is restated in 18:14. The anticipated event occurs a few chapters later, following the present form of the text, in Gen 21:1.

There are some interesting features associated with announcement sequences that may be noted here. Since announcements often point to unusual events or events that one would not normally expect to occur, such announcements may evoke an expression of doubt. Sarah's reaction to the news of a son has just been mentioned. Since her laughter is not taken as an affront to the deity, only a mild response is forthcoming along with a reassertion of the announcement.

Sometimes, however, persons respond to an announcement by attempting to avoid the realization of the announced event. The story in 2 Kings 1 would seem to be an example of such a response to an announcement of punishment. Injured in an accident, King Ahaziah sends messengers to the god of Ekron to inquire about his health. This appears to function as the wrong in a *wrong/punished* sequence. Prompted by Yahweh, Elijah meets Ahaziah's messenger and announces, apparently as a punishment, that the king will not arise from his sickbed (v. 4). This is what happens (v. 17). The king's response to Elijah's announcement is to send the military after him, but of course to no avail. It is not clear from the text what the soldiers were supposed to do, kill him or arrest him. Nor is it clear what motivated the king to send them, whether because Elijah had the audacity to pronounce an oracle against the king or because he hoped by killing the prophet he might avoid the announced punishment.

Another instance of this kind of response to an announced punishment is 1 Kings 22, the famous story of the prophet Micaiah. When the prophet announces that he saw Israel scattered before the enemy like a flock without a shepherd, indicating the defeat of the people and the death of the king, three responses ensue. First, the king puts the prophet in jail until he returns. Second, the prophet proposes a test of whether or not his announcement is a true word from Yahweh as opposed to that of the other prophets: if the king returns safely, then Yahweh has not spoken through him. Third, the king of Israel disguises himself when going into battle. Although the reason he does this is not explicit, one may assume that he hopes to avoid the fate announced for him. Of course, he does not succeed.

F. Prohibition Sequences

9. *Prohibition/transgressed*. Punishment sequences in which a wrong is committed imply that some sort of prohibition has been transgressed. Most often no specific prohibition appears. In these cases, the transgression stands in opposition to what is generally known of the divine will, or it may be that the transgressor performs some action that is generally accepted as something that ought not to be done. As was noted above, wrongs or transgressions in stories are not identified primarily in terms of the action itself but rather according to whether or not the action is punished. It follows that sequences involving a prohibition and a transgression are to be found embedded in *wrong/punished* sequences and stand in the position of the wrong.

A clear example may be found in the story of the punishment of Lot's wife, one of the punishment sequences enumerated above. The wrong consists of a prohibition sequence. The prohibition not to look back is given in Gen 19:17; the violation is reported in v. 26 and followed immediately by the punishment.

Two further examples may be cited from stories that will be discussed in the following chapter. One is the Garden of Eden story in Genesis 2–3. If the problem of one or two trees in the middle of the garden is set aside, there is a clear prohibition not to eat the fruit of the tree of the knowledge of good and evil. When this prohibition is disobeyed, punishment results. Another example of a prohibition can be found in the story of the lying prophet in 1 Kings 13. The narrator does not present us with a scene at the beginning of the narrative in which a prohibition is actually given to the prophet, but we learn of it later after the experience at the altar. When the king invites the prophet to come and dine with him, the prophet refuses, saying that he has been forbidden to eat or drink in this place; he even quotes the word of Yahweh containing the prohibition (vv. 8–9). Subsequently, after being tricked into transgressing this prohibition, he is condemned and punished for rebelling against Yahweh by disobeying the instruction he had been given.

CHAPTER THREE

The Variations

If the foregoing chapter looked at the "themes," this chapter will concentrate on the "variations." The emphasis in the previous chapter was on how similarities among stories could be described in terms of action sequences. It was possible to identify a number of action sequences (rescue, punishment, and the like) that could be found repeated in many stories. In this chapter, attention will be directed more to individual stories and how sequences are expressed, linked, and elaborated in specific instances in order to see how individual examples of a given sequence (punishment, rescue, and the like) vary from each other.

One might also say that the variations are realizations of sequences. Clearly sequences only exist as abstractions, as formulas that state a common pattern shared by a number of stories. They simply represent a way of stating similarities among groups of stories. It is less clear what status these patterns have and whether they can be said to produce variations. I am making no particular claims in this direction beyond the fact that I have been able to identify sequences and have found it helpful to discuss them as repeated and varied patterns in biblical narrative. Accordingly, I will continue to speak of sequences being realized in variations. The following stories will be treated individually, but always in the light of their relationship with other stories with similar action sequences.

In the previous chapter, the shortest possible stories were selected in order to simplify identification and comparison of action sequences. Most of the examples were less than a chapter in size. Here the stories under discussion will be longer, usually a chapter or more in length. As a consequence, they will yield more complex arrangements of sequences within individual stories.

Before proceeding to the examples, I would say a word about combinations of sequences. Several of the examples presented in the previous chapter contained more than one sequence since a story usually has more than one. It was also seen that sequences may be linked together in different ways. Some of the common kinds of linkage identified in examples given in the foregoing chapter can be listed.

(a) *Embedding*. This occurs when one phase of a sequence is itself a sequence, as in the case of Lot's wife (Gen 19:17–26). This is a punishment sequence with two phases, the first having to do with the *wrong* and the other having to do with the *punishment*. The phase containing the wrong consists of a prohibition followed by a transgression of that prohibition, in other words, a prohibition sequence. Then again, in the punishment sequence about the two prophets (1 Kgs 20:35, 36), the *wrong* phase involves an instruction that was not obeyed (an embedded *prohibition/transgressed* sequence) and the *punished* phase is an embedded announcement sequence in which the punishment is announced and then happens.

(b) *Adding*. One sequence can be followed by another so that a story in which a sequence has come to a conclusion may continue by moving into another sequence. This was seen in the story about the serpents in Num 21:4–9, where the people do wrong and are punished. Since the punishment takes the form of serpents with a deadly bite, a danger remains for the people who are still alive. It was suggested that this could be seen as the beginning of a *difficulty/rescued* sequence in which the deity rescues the remaining people from the danger. The serpents, then, have a double function. In the first sequence they are the punishment for the wrong but in the second they are the difficulty from which rescue is needed.

(c) *Concurrence*. Sequences may run side-by-side in a story. It was noted that the healing of a sick boy by Elijah in 1 Kgs 17:17–24 appears to have two sequences related in this way. The sickness of the boy is both a difficulty from which the mother needs to be rescued and a difficulty (a challenge) from which the prophet must be rescued (vindicated). It is possible that the difficulty of the woman is subordinated to the difficulty of the prophet, but the two sequences still run side-by-side.

Apart from noting how sequences vary and how they combine, some other matters will be kept in mind and brought into the discussion when appropriate. I am referring to the features of text discussed in Chapter One. There is the question of the traditional and composite nature of biblical narrative and what happens when the arrangement of sequences is examined in a text composed of different traditions and different sources. Another issue is the relationship between divine and human action in biblical narrative, which I place under the religious aspect of the text. It was pointed out that the participation of the divine and the human in narrative can be examined apart from analyzing sequences. However, since identifying sequences is one way of tracing the movement of action in stories, it may prove interesting to consider the question of the divine and the human from the perspective of sequences and combinations of sequences.

While the biblical stories to follow have all elicited substantial scholarly comment, little of this has been devoted directly to the kinds of action movements I wish to examine. I will not therefore enter into a discussion of all the problems posed by individual stories but limit myself to sequences and related matters. As a result only selected references will be made to the available scholarly literature.

The examination of biblical material in this chapter has been divided into five sections. Section A deals with eight stories of punishment and rescue where kings and/or prophets play significant roles. Section B turns to the book of Judges, where a pattern of punishment and rescue is stated in the framework of the book and then displayed concretely in the stories about the judges. Section C treats some of the stories about the conquest in the book of Joshua. Section D examines longer and more complex stories by considering four of the most famous punishment stories in the Hebrew Bible: the garden, Sodom, the flood, and the spies. Finally, Section E deals with two long stories of rescue, the Exodus narrative and the Joseph story.

A. Eight Stories of Punishment and Rescue.

The first group of eight stories form a somewhat miscellaneous collection, although each does contain a punishment sequence. In the first five stories, the punishment sequence appears to be the most important sequence, while in the last three the punishment sequences play a rather minor role, as they are subordinated to rescue sequences. All the stories involve either kings or prophets, and frequently both.

The first four stories make up an interesting group. It consists of two stories about the punishment of Saul in which Samuel plays a role and two stories about the punishment of Ahab in which Elijah plays a role. There are, of course, many issues that might be discussed relating to how the two accounts about Saul or the two accounts about Ahab are related to each other within the text of Samuel or Kings (on the Saul accounts, e.g., cf. Van Seters, 1983:259–63, and Polzin, 1989:126–31). Here I am limiting myself largely to a consideration of all four as expressions of punishment sequences.

1. *1 Samuel 13:1–14.* This is the first of two stories about punishment for Saul. The chapter begins with an incident involving Jonathan and the Philistines. Jonathan attacks a Philistine outpost. This leads to the mustering of a vast Philistine army at Michmash. At Gilgal Saul leads a very nervous group waiting for Samuel to come. Earlier (10:8), Samuel had told Saul to go to Gilgal and wait seven days. At this time, Samuel would come, offer sacrifices, and tell Saul what he should do. When Samuel does not arrive after seven days, the people begin to scatter. Instead of waiting any longer, Saul then takes the initiative and offers up the burnt offering. Just as he finishes, Samuel arrives and immediately rebukes him. Even though Saul offers reasons for his action (v. 11, the people were dispersing, Samuel was late, and the Philistines were gathered at Michmash), Samuel rejects his justification and holds to the simple charge that Saul has not observed the instruction of Yahweh, presumably the instruction of 10:8. The penalty is that Saul's kingdom will not stand.

This account involves a punishment sequence. Saul does wrong and is punished—or at least his punishment is announced. The *wrong* consists of an embedded prohibition sequence in which an instruction is given but not followed. The punishment consists of an announcement that does not take effect until the end of the book.

WRONG ————————————————→ PUNISHED

INSTRUCTION ———→ DISOBEYED   ANNOUNCEMENT ————————→
to wait   does not   kingdom will not stand

It seems to be simple. Saul was told to do something and he did not. Still, the story makes clear that Saul did wait the seven days required. Saul also presents plausible reasons for his action. Should this not change the situation? The story suggests not. The presence of Saul's justifications may be a means of stressing the point that nothing, not even good common sense (from a human point of view) can excuse disobedience to a prophetic instruction. Saul deserves no sympathy. On the other hand, the very reasonableness of the justification can work the other way and create sympathy for Saul. He did not deliberately flaunt the instructions, yet he is finished. From this point of view, his crime is at most an error in judgment.

2. *1 Samuel 15*. Again, Saul does wrong and is punished. So much is clear. But this chapter contains some remarkable features. First of all, the story is linked by action sequences both to an event in the past and to an event in the future. When Saul is instructed to attack the Amalekites, this is portrayed as an act of punishment for what the Amalekites did to Israel shortly after the exodus from Egypt (Exod 17:8–16). In other words, this is the second phase of a *wrong/punished* sequence begun in Exodus.

The punishment of Saul here has more than one aspect. If the punishment is seen as the divine rejection of Saul as king (v. 26), this rejection has already happened, or happens with Samuel's declaration to Saul. The punishment is instantaneous. However, if the rejection is linked with the actual removal and replacement of Saul (v. 28), then the punishment of Saul's wrongdoing is not completed in this story. I have chosen to treat this as an announcement sequence in which Yahweh announces the rejection and replacement that will only find its realization much later. From this point of view, then, the punishment comes in the form of an embedded announcement sequence (*announcement/ happened*). If so, the announcement of the rejection and replacement of Saul (coupled with that of 13:13–14) remains a major tension in the larger narrative of 1 Samuel in that the reader looks forward to the time when Saul will be set aside.

The main movement in the story consists of the punishment sequence, in which Saul does wrong and is punished, or his punishment is announced. However, the significant feature of this sequence is that almost three-quarters of the story is devoted to one stage of the action, the meeting of Samuel and Saul in which the guilt of Saul is declared and eventually accepted by him.

To sum up briefly, this chapter is the second phase of a sequence about the punishment of Amalek. Within it, is a punishment sequence concerning Saul. The *wrong* phase is itself a prohibition sequence and the *punished* phase, as I have understood it, is an announcement sequence that does not reach completion until much later.

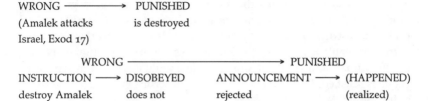

WRONG ─────────→ PUNISHED
(Amalek attacks   is destroyed
Israel, Exod 17)

          WRONG ─────────────────→ PUNISHED
INSTRUCTION ──→ DISOBEYED   ANNOUNCEMENT ──→ (HAPPENED)
destroy Amalek   does not   rejected   (realized)

As this summary shows, the punishment sequence concerning Saul expounds the *wrong* in terms of a prohibition sequence which in this case consists of an instruction disobeyed. Samuel gives Saul a word of Yahweh that he should attack Amalek and put it to the ban, showing no mercy but killing all living things, human and animal. Saul immediately embarks on this venture, and the events connected with this mission are recounted very briefly. By v. 7 a successful attack has been made that should bring the mission to a successful completion. However, in the very next verse it is reported that Saul has taken Agag, the king of Amalek, alive, thus disobeying the instruction of Yahweh. In fact, Saul and the people spared not only the king but also best of the spoils. A wrong has now been done, and we anticipate hearing of a punishment.

What follows is an elaborate account of Samuel's confrontation with Saul, the guilty party. If we may judge by the amount of space devoted to this encounter, it would seem that the narrator wishes to draw special attention to this part of the sequence. As we have seen in the previous chapter, in some punishment sequences the action can move very quickly from wrong to punishment. However, elaboration is possible in a variety of ways. The action here has been elaborated by using embedded sequences for both the *wrong* and the *punishment*. Further elaboration can be achieved, especially when an intermediary of Yahweh is involved, by portraying a confrontation with the guilty party in which the guilt of that person is demonstrated, displayed, or declared. This kind of elaboration will be found in other punishment stories. In 1 Samuel 15, not only is such a confrontation present; it takes up most of the story.

The confrontation follows several steps: It begins with a word of Yahweh to Samuel disclosing that the deity now regrets having made Saul king because he has not carried out the instructions given him by Yahweh. When Samuel meets Saul, a curious dialogue ensues. The king immediately proclaims a successful completion of the task assigned to him, although the story has made clear that he has not. When challenged about the presence of animals, Saul indicates that the people spared the animals in order to sacrifice to Yahweh—although this was not mentioned as a motive when it was first reported that the animals were taken. At this point Samuel declares plainly that Saul has done wrong. Once again Saul insists that he has obeyed his commission. Only Agag has been spared, and the people have kept the best of the animals for sacrifice. In reply to this, Samuel insists that obedience is better than sacrifice and announces that, because Saul rejected Yahweh, Yahweh has rejected Saul. Saul finally admits that he has indeed transgressed Yahweh's instruction ("I have sinned," v. 24), and asks for his sin to be forgiven, adding by way of excuse that he feared the people. It is again pointed out to Saul that the kingdom has been taken from him, with the additional comment that it will be given to a colleague better than he. The decision is firm and unchangeable (v. 29). Again Saul confesses, "I have sinned" (v. 30), but this time he does not ask for forgiveness. The discussion has come to an end.

This conversation is remarkable. Either Saul is incredibly naive or he is devious, and if he is devious, his attempts to cover himself seem heavy-handed. How can he deny the obvious? Perhaps Sternberg is on the right track when he suggests that the narrator has developed this section in order to discredit Saul and show that he does not merit sympathy (482–515). Certainly by the end of the conversation, the reader may well be prepared to doubt even the sincerity of Saul's confession, although Saul's ineptness in handling the situation might still evoke sympathy for him as victim.

The story affirms clearly that to do wrong, to disobey, means punishment, and that this decision once taken is firm and irreversible. However, it is possible that the lengthy discussion may betray some unease about the severity of the judgment and the implacability of Yahweh once the decision has been made. Yahweh is not a human that he should change his mind, but the point about the rejection of Saul is that he did just that.

The next two stories concern Ahab.

3. *1 Kings 20*. The story in this chapter includes a sequence about the punishment of a king who did not obey, although this is preceded by two rescue sequences. Thus, three major sequences have been linked together, two rescue and a punishment.

The first sequence (*difficulty/rescued*) governs the action for about half of the chapter. The *difficulty* is created by the invasion of Ben-hadad, King of Aram, and thirty-two kings who then besiege Samaria with King Ahab inside. Negotiations with the besiegers break down, and the Arameans prepare to attack in earnest. Then comes the *rescue*. An unnamed prophet approaches Ahab and through a word of Yahweh announces that the enemy will be delivered into the king's hands, even indicating who will start the attack. Israel gains a great victory. In sum, rescue is announced and effected. There is no divine intervention other than through the prophetic word.

The prophet again appears, this time with a warning that the king of Aram will return. Indeed, the Arameans are planning an attack, only they intend this time to fight on the plain, believing that the divine power supporting Israel is only effective in the hills. A man of God approaches Ahab with a word rejecting this theory and announces that the enemy will fall into his hands. This quickly happens and thus represents another rescue sequence in which the difficulty consists of danger posed by an enemy. The rescue transpires without divine intervention, apart from the announcement of the victory that immediately comes to pass.

After these two rescue sequences comes the punishment sequence. The *wrong* takes place in connection with the flight of the Aramean army. Following the advice of his officials, who point out that the kings of Israel are generous, Ben-hadad appeals for his life. In response the king of Israel concludes a favorable treaty and spares his opponent. The narrative so far gives no hint that this is an improper act, although battles in which Yahweh participates frequently involve the requirement to kill the conquered enemies. In any event, it is soon made plain that the king's action in sparing Ben-hadad is an error.

As in the previous story about Saul, a prophet acts on Yahweh's behalf to declare guilt and to announce punishment. As in the previous story, the confrontation is elaborated. From the meeting between the king of Israel and Ben-hadad, the scene shifts abruptly and introduces a brief but rather peculiar punishment sequence. An unnamed prophet instructs a companion through a word of Yahweh to strike him. The companion refuses. This unfortunate creature is immediately charged with disobeying Yahweh and a punishment is announced. A lion will attack him as soon as he leaves. This happens. Given the same instruction, another complies with the request. The prophet is wounded and wraps his head with a bandage. This is performed to provide a disguise so that the king whom he wishes to confront will not recognize him. Thus disguised, the prophet presents the king with a story about a captive given into his charge who has run away, and the king is called upon to judge whether or not the wounded man must forfeit his life. The king declares him guilty. Thereupon the deception is over; the prophet tears off his disguise and pronounces a word of Yahweh that turns the judgment back on the king. Because Ben-hadad, the man of Yahweh's ban, was let go, the king must forfeit his life; and this judgment is extended to his people as well.

The very brief punishment sequence involving the colleague of the prophet who refused to obey the command to strike him appears at first glance to be of little consequence for the story. However, it indicates clearly that an instruction through a word of Yahweh must be followed no matter how bizarre it appears to be. The command to kill the enemy king is not explicit, as it was in 1 Samuel 15, although the announcement of punishment implies that the king of Israel should have known that he was in a holy war situation (v. 42). Thus, even though the declaration of wrong indicates that he had no excuse and deserves to forfeit his life, the act itself does not seem to be a flagrant and willful act of disobedience; it could be read as a shrewd settlement of political differences. Since the sparing of Ben-hadad may be less obviously a wrong, perhaps the incident with the prophet is meant to strengthen the point that disobedience means punishment (see Polzin, 1989: 139–47 for a view of Samuel's role.)

This incident is similar to 1 Samuel 13 in that the motif of being punished for wrongly sparing a captured king is the same. That these two examples represent two instances of a widespread motif used in traditional narrative one cannot say, but it is possible (but see Van Seters, 1983: 258–64).

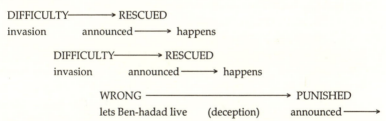

4. *1 Kings 21*. In the story of Naboth, the outline of a punishment sequence is clearly evident. A wrong is committed when Naboth is murdered and, as Ahab takes possession of the vineyard of Naboth after the murder, Elijah appears to pronounce him guilty and announce the punishment.

The depiction of the *wrong* could be a story in itself and may be construed as an action sequence embedded in the larger punishment sequence. This embedded sequence can be described as an achievement sequence, *desire/achieved*. Ahab wants something and gains it, although the action is more complex than this. While Ahab wants Naboth's vineyard, he does not seem to have the same measure of initiative and determination as does his wife Jezebel. Having learned of Ahab's frustrated desire, she takes over and arranges to have Naboth murdered in order to clear the way for her husband's seizure of the land. Jezebel's plan to get the vineyard for her husband involves the murder of Naboth by means of a deception, or "dirty trick," which allows the murder to take place without the usual consequences for the murderers.

As the text now stands, the punishment element consists of a pronouncement of guilt and an announcement of punishment, both initiated by Yahweh and carried out through the prophet Elijah. The announcement involves two things, the death of Ahab (v. 19) and a disaster for the people (v. 21). This latter expands the wrong and the punishment from a personal error that must be atoned for to the more important issue, the broader concern in the books of Kings with the rise and fall of kings and dynasties. A punishment is also announced for Jezebel (v. 23). At this point the narrative is brought to a satisfactory conclusion in the sense that the problem of the wrong has been met by the announcement of a punishment, even though the punishment has not yet actually happened. But the narrative continues. Another comment, vv. 24–26, returns to the broad picture by relating Ahab's punishment to the theme of doing wrong in the sight of Yahweh and by committing abominations in going after idols. This links up with what was said about Ahab in 16:29–34 about dealings with other gods, as though the punishment really has to do with this issue and as though the vineyard incident is simply the occasion to settle it by removing Ahab from the scene.

The final stage in the story is a mitigation of the punishment, vv. 27–29. Because Ahab displays his remorse through acts of penitence, Yahweh modifies the punishment to Ahab by indicating that the promised disaster to the people will not happen in Ahab's days but in the days of his son.

In this last section on the punishment (vv. 17–29) there is some unevenness in the text as well as the presence of Deuteronomistic language, problems long recognized by scholars (for discussion, see Rofé, 1988a,b; Oeming; and Zakovitch, 1984). The story of Naboth may well have been secondarily expanded. One of the effects of the unevenness has just been mentioned: the crime of a murder over a vineyard has been linked to Ahab's association with idols; thus gaining for it the dimensions of *the* crime against Yahweh. Another problem has to do with the roles of Ahab and Jezebel in the affair of vineyard. One might expect that

Jezebel's clear participation in the murder would mean that she would be the major, guilty party so that any punishment would concern her, at least primarily. It is not clear from the present narrative to what extent Ahab even knows about what his wife is doing. Her punishment is announced as part of this last section.

On the one hand, the story steadily flows through a punishment sequence from wrong to punishment. The continuation into a mitigation is not unusual in punishment stories (Culley, 1980b and 1976c:100–8).

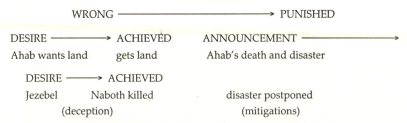

On the other hand, this simple movement is complicated by the issues just mentioned: the placing of the main punishment on Ahab rather than Jezebel, and the linking of this to the Deuteronomistic reading of Ahab as one who did wrong by dealing with other gods.

As with Saul, there are two stories about Ahab that elevate a wrong into the broader question of the fitness to rule. Ahab's first wrong may have left open some questions about the weight of the punishment when measured against the crime. Here the punishment of death fits the crime of murder, except that Ahab is less directly in line for the punishment than Jezebel. Taken together, the four stories involving Saul and Ahab produce a curious effect. They all repeat the outline of the punishment sequence stressing and confirming the fact that disobedience to the deity will be punished. Yet at the same time the individual variations each contain features that conspire to render the notion of punishment somewhat problematic. While the concept of wrong and punishment is not challenged as such, the puzzling features of the variations call for a much more nuanced and intricate assessment of the theme. The following story about the lying prophet adds even further complexity.

5. *1 Kings 13.* This is the famous story about the lying prophet (for recent views including discussion of scholarship, see Walsh and Van Winkle). The main action in the story is a punishment sequence involving a man of God, although this is set within a larger framework. The man of God was sent to make an announcement to King Jeroboam, one

that does not come true until the time of Josiah, according to the larger text of the books of Kings.

At the beginning of chapter 13, the man of God arrives from Judah with a word of Yahweh while Jeroboam is standing at the altar. The word of God is addressed to the altar and announces that Josiah will sacrifice the priests of the high places on that very altar. In the report about King Josiah in 2 Kgs 23:15–16, it is related that he burned human bones on the altar, and explicit reference is made to the announcement about the altar uttered by the man of God. This then is an announcement sequence that stretches over a long section of text and therefore takes a very broad perspective in view.

Once this announcement has been made, the story moves into the punishment sequence concerning the man of God. The transition occurs through some further interaction between the king and the man of God. In response to the announcement the king stretches out his hand and orders that the prophet be taken into custody. His hand withers and is only restored upon a petition to Yahweh by the prophet, offered at the king's request. These events seem to have restored a measure of civility to the relations between king and man of God, at least to the extent that the king extends an invitation to dinner. This is significant because through it we learn that a prohibition has been laid on the prophet by the deity: he is not to eat food, drink water, or return by the same way. The *wrong* in the punishment sequence is an embedded *prohibition/transgressed* sequence.

In refusing the king, the man of God demonstrates his firm intention to hold to the prohibition. And so he would have except for an unusual intervention by a local prophet. This prophet is a rather mysterious figure in the narrative for a number of reasons. Readers are not told why the prophet intervenes. He invites the man of God to eat with him, assuring him that a word of God, spoken through a divine messenger, has ordered him to bring the man of God home to eat and drink water. The narrator indicates quite clearly, however, that the man was lying when he said this (v. 18). The man of God complies. Through a deception the local prophet tricks the man of God into transgressing the prohibition, and he is immediately denounced for rebelling against Yahweh and disobeying his instruction. The wrong has been done, and the punishment follows. It is announced that his corpse will not reach the grave of his fathers.

Upon leaving the home of the prophet, a lion kills the transgressor. This punishment takes the form of an embedded *announcement/happened* sequence. The story is brought to a close with the prophet burying the man of God and affirming that the word he addressed to the altar will indeed come to pass.

The punishment sequence is clear. Disobey Yahweh, it implies, and the consequences will be disastrous. If one experiences some uneasiness in reading the previous stories about the punishment of Saul, Ahab, and the unfortunate prophet who was killed by a lion for not striking his comrade, this story gives grounds for serious misgivings (but see Van Winkle). The man of God is not deceived into transgressing the prohibition by an enemy who wishes him ill but by a prophet, one who establishes his authenticity by pronouncing the punishment. Behind the prophet then lies Yahweh, who was apparently testing the man of God by standards neither made clear nor justified by the story (but see Van Winkle, 40, who argues the prophet should have known). One gains the impression that the divine decision to punish may remain inscrutable on the human plane (see also Greenstein, 1989a:61–64). This reinforces the sense of puzzlement with the judgment in the previous stories. To be sure, the punishments are based on acts of disobedience, and this message comes through in each story. Yet, signs of discord in the stories suggest that divine punishment is much less clear than first appears. The ability of humans to understand divine judgment may well have severe limitations.

There follow three stories in which punishment sequences may be found but in which a rescue sequence has at least equal weight.

6. *2 Kings 6:24–33 and 7.* This is a story about the remarkable deliverance of a besieged and starving city, except for one unfortunate officer who does not survive to enjoy the happy occasion. The main action appears to be a rescue sequence. The people of Samaria find themselves in a difficult situation because the Arameans have laid siege to the city and the people are starving. Yahweh intervenes, drives off the enemy, and rescues the people from their difficult situation.

This simple outline of a rescue sequence has been elaborated in a number of ways. The first may be seen in the depiction of the difficult situation, which is described in 6:24–30. These verses contain some activity but nothing that appears to be an action sequence. While walking on the city wall, the king meets a woman who makes an appeal to him. She has a grievance of an especially grisly sort. Following an agreement made with another woman, the two of them have eaten the first woman's child. But on the following day, the other woman will not allow her baby to be eaten in accordance with the agreement. So severe is the famine, so desperate the population, the king can only tear his garments in despair.

This opening situation leads into another movement in the action, one which does not appear to lead to any conclusion. The affair is sketched so tersely that it is difficult to make out clearly what is transpiring. The case raised by the woman seems to be the last straw for the king. He swears that he will have the prophet Elisha's head, invoking God's intervention if he fails to do so. The next few verses (31–33) appear to move in the direction of carrying out this threat, as though the king, holding Elisha responsible for the situation in the city, seeks to take his revenge on him, although there is nothing in the story to indicate why Elisha should be blamed. Is he held responsible for having had a hand in causing the situation, perhaps by announcing it as a punishment? Or is he is deemed culpable for having done nothing to rescue the people? At any rate, this incident begins like a sequence in which an injury has been done and revenge is going to be carried out.

However, once the intention of the king is declared, the scene shifts (v. 32) to Elisha, where we begin to see things from his point of view. The obscurity in the narrative continues. Although the king's messenger has not yet arrived, Elisha already knows, presumably through his prophetic powers, that a messenger has been sent by the king and what the messenger's task is. He orders that the door be shut and held closed. This is something like a rescue sequence in the sense that the prophet's life is in danger and he takes steps to avert this threat. This action, however, does not seem to be brought to its conclusion. In any case, the threat of the king is not carried out, and it is implied that the prophet somehow prevented it.

At the very least, this section has the function of bringing the king and Elisha together so that Elisha can announce to him that the famine will soon end, that deliverance is near. But is there more? Perhaps the anger of the king against Elisha introduces into the narrative an element of challenge. The prophet is put on the spot. He is responsible for a nasty situation either by having a hand in causing it or by doing nothing about it. This kind of challenge was discussed in the previous chapter with regard to the story of Elijah and the dead child (1 Kgs 17:17–24). That is to say, in order to vindicate himself the prophet must act to remove the famine. At the same time, the incident shows the king's hostility toward the prophet and may be a way of casting the king in a bad light.

Once the prophet and the king are face to face, Elisha responds to the crisis of the city by making an announcement (7:1). The *rescue* element of the sequence takes the form of an embedded announcement sequence. Elisha declares in a word of Yahweh what the food prices will be the next morning at the city gate. One may deduce from this that something very unusual will have to occur to bring this about. The narration of this announcement sequence is filled with interesting material, and some of these elaborations may be noted.

A dramatic miracle takes place. The narrator describes it to the reader, but because none of the participants—neither the king nor any other person in the story—witness the event, none of them knows what really happened apart from the evident result. The event comes to the reader in a flashback introduced at a later point in the story. Yahweh frightened the enemy off so that they fled leaving all their goods and supplies behind (vv. 6–7). Food prices become those announced by Elisha (v. 16). The focus of attention through most of the announcement sequence is a group of four lepers. They are important to the rescue sequence in that they are the ones who discover the empty camp and bring this news back to the city. When faced with death from starvation, they decide it would be better for them to risk going to the enemy (either quick death or food). It is at this point that the narrator by means of a flashback (v. 6) brings us up to date on what has happened at the enemy camp. There is a further elaboration. At first the lepers look out only for themselves, but upon second thought decide they had better tell the king. The city is rescued.

Even though the king is rescued, and therefore the beneficiary of divine favor, he does not appear in a particularly good light. He is not directly criticized in the story, but his hostility to the prophet raises some questions. Furthermore, it is not the king who first discovers that rescue has occurred but a group of outcasts, lepers. In spite of their initial opportunism, they later display great generosity of spirit and a sense of responsibility in deciding to report back to the king despite the great temptation to take care of themselves alone. Even when the lepers bring back the good news, the story is delayed further by having the king suspect a trap. He goes out to the camp only after a party has been sent first to investigate. This may be a natural reaction, even a prudent one, but in light of the announcement of Elisha perhaps too prudent.

The fact that someone very close to the king is punished, may reflect on the king indirectly. This event forms a short punishment sequence (*wrong/punished*). When Elisha announces the food prices (7:2), an officer beside the king calls in question the word delivered by the prophet (a *wrong*). In response, the prophet immediately declares that the officer will not be able to participate in the good fortune of the city (*punished*).

The punishment is expressed by means of an embedded announcement sequence. The announcement of punishment comes in v. 2, and the announced event happens in v. 17 when the officer is trampled and killed by the people at the gate.

7. 2 *Kings 5.* Two sequences, a rescue sequence about the healing of Naaman and a punishment sequence about Gehazi, are linked together here. The action flows from one into the other and Naaman, Elisha, and Gehazi play a role in both.

The first story (2 Kgs 5:1–19) has the pattern of a rescue sequence (*difficulty/rescued*). The action seems straightforward. Naaman, the officer of the Aramean King, has leprosy. When he hears that Elisha has power to cure, he goes to visit him and is cured. Nevertheless, some of the elaborations of this simple pattern provoke interest. It is a humble servant girl who tells the high officer about Elisha. The importance of the officer is further stressed by several factors: the official letter from the king of Aram to the king of Israel, the escort, the valuable gifts, and the evident fear of the king of Israel. This image of importance and power that the ailing foreigner projects stands in contrast to the way Elisha deals with him—not directly but by sending instructions through a messenger. After an initial fit of anger at this treatment, the stricken man finally does obey the instructions and is cured. The change in his attitude is striking. Not only does he try to get Elisha to accept the gifts he had brought from home but he confesses faith in Yahweh, asserting that he will henceforth sacrifice only to him. He even expresses concern that he will have to become involved in the worship of another deity because of his official duties.

Naaman is no ordinary victim. He is a foreigner, holds a powerful position, and has great influence with the king of Aram. As a foreigner he is pictured in a good light. He is easily persuaded to swallow his pride and become an enthusiastic convert. From this perspective, the story is about an intelligent and pious foreigner who is perceptive and sensitive enough to recognize Yahweh when rescued from a difficulty.

Then there is the prophet. He is neither frightened, in contrast to the king, nor even impressed by the important foreign visitor. Elisha dismisses Naaman with a brief instruction which nevertheless effects the cure. He will accept no gifts. From this perspective, the story draws attention to the extraordinary power that Elisha has at his disposal and the supreme confidence that he can deal with all eventualities. The power derives, of course, from Yahweh, as Naaman recognizes. In the end, attention seems less directed to the notion of rescue from difficulty than to the divine power at the disposal of the prophet.

The punishment of Gehazi that follows the story about the rescue is relatively brief. A wrong is done. It is punished. However, the wrong is expressed in terms of an embedded achievement sequence. Gehazi desires some of the gifts that Elisha refused to accept and finds a way of getting his hands on a portion of them. To achieve this desire he must perform a deception, and this he does by telling Naaman a lie. The crime is discovered because of Elisha's special gift to observe events at a distance, for Elisha knows about what Gehazi has done. Elisha declares Gehazi guilty and announces a punishment, which takes effect immediately. In this story the interest appears to lie with Elisha and his remarkable power to discern wrongs and punish them.

8. *1 Samuel 25*. The story of David and Abigail. Two actions are especially important in this account and they need to be identified before any judgment can be made as to how they are related to each other.

The opening of the story suggests that the action is going to be developed along the lines of a punishment sequence of the type *injury/avenged*. It all begins when David sends messengers to Nabal at sheep shearing time with a request for a little something in return for protecting him over the past while. Nabal dismisses the messengers with a disparaging remark about David. Upon learning of this response, David orders his men to put on their swords and sets out at the head of an armed band four hundred strong. It is clear what David intends to do, and comments later in the story make his intention explicit (vv. 22 and 34). He has been insulted and intends to retaliate, although he never completes what he sets out to do.

At this point in the action, the scene changes, and there is a corresponding shift from David's perspective to that of Nabal's people (vv. 14–17). We find one of Nabal's workers reporting the whole affair to Abigail. The worker has understood clearly the implications of his master's rudeness. Explaining that David's men have rendered great service to Nabal, he urges Abigail to take steps to avert the impending disaster, which in narrative terms amounts to commissioning her for a task. In other words, when viewed from the perspective of Nabal's people, David's act of revenge represents a difficult situation from which the people need to be rescued or escape. Abigail accepts the task and sets out to meet David. Indeed, she succeeds in this delicate and dangerous undertaking, persuading David not to take action against Nabal. This action can be identified as a rescue sequence in which Abigail is able to avert a disaster for herself and her people.

The means used by Abigail to effect the rescue add further complication to the action of the story. She is not in a strong position. Nabal appears to be in the wrong; his action cannot be justified. She has only her wits and her words. Abigail makes a long speech to David (vv. 24–31). While there are some difficulties in these verses because the syntax is not always clear, the main thought seems sufficiently evident. Abigail uses two strategies. First, she asks that the guilt be shifted to her. Nabal does not really count because he is a fool, just as his name indicates. On her part, she did not see the men David sent. This attempt to shift attention seems a clever move. If Abigail can remove Nabal from the discussion, then David must deal with her. The next step is ask forgiveness for herself (v. 28).

In case this does not work, a second argument is developed that leads in another direction. It seems to be alluded to as early as v. 26 but becomes more explicit in v. 31. Abigail points out that David, in intending to take up arms against Nabal, is acting rashly and stands in danger of compromising his anticipated role as Yahweh's leader. In drawing this to David's attention, Abigail brings forward an important argument against David's carrying out his attack on Nabal. As already noted, the argument works, the attack does not take place, and the rescue sequence is complete.

This argument adds a new dimension to the narrative. Abigail is not only seen as a rescuer of her own people but is also cast in the role of the rescuer of David. David himself seems to recognize this, going so far as to attribute her action to the intervention of Yahweh. From this point of view, another rescue sequence becomes apparent (*difficulty/rescued*). Here it is David who is in danger by reason of his intended attack on Nabal because his actions will not be appropriate to his future role in Israel. From this precarious position Abigail rescues David by persuading him of the danger he faces. Thus, by the same action Abigail is at the same time performing two rescues, saving her own people and David as well. Abigail's second argument saves David from himself and is the clinching argument that rescues Nabal's people. Two concerns are at work. Or is it only one? Is this to be seen primarily as a very clever act of persuasion on the part of Abigail, almost a deception? Although the story as a whole is more concerned with David than with Abigail, perhaps it is. Even though it does not appear to start out as a rescue of David by Abigail, the story ends up emphasizing this feature. Since David clearly attributes

Abigail's action to Yahweh (v. 32, also vv. 26, 33, and 39), Yahweh is the real rescuer.

While the two rescue sequences, the one concerning David and the other concerning Nabal's people, draw to a conclusion when David accepts Abigail's appeal, the story does not end there. There is still one loose end. Nabal's insult to David precipitated the crisis; that is to say, the difficult situations for both David and Nabal's people, which led to the two rescue sequences, remains unresolved. It could have been left at that. However, Nabal did insult David. While this was viewed initially as an injury to David that called for revenge, it is now in the last part of the story reread as a wrong by Nabal against Yahweh, who then carries out a punishment. Thus the story continues. Abigail returns home. When Nabal has sobered up after a heavy bout of drinking, she recounts what happened. It is reported that in response to this news his heart dies and turns to stone. Whatever this means, Nabal's reaction, apparently one of paralyzing terror, does not kill him. But after ten days Yahweh strikes him and he dies (v. 38). When David hears of Nabal's death, he interprets it as an act of Yahweh, who has taken up his case and dealt with the insult done to him. This event casts the opening scene in a slightly different light. At first, it appeared to be an injury against David. Now it may be seen as a wrong against Yahweh and functions as the first phase in a punishment sequence of the type *wrong/punished*. Thus, the opening action of Nabal retains a double aspect. It represents a wrong done by Nabal against Yahweh, who then punishes him; nevertheless, the sense of personal injury against David of is still retained (v. 39).

It is possible to identify one more sequence, albeit one that is not especially clear. At the end of the story (vv. 39–43) David takes Abigail as a wife. This could be construed as a reward sequence. That is to say, Abigail performs a good deed by preventing David from doing something he will regret. After the death of Nabal, David rewards her by making her his wife. This is not particularly evident since there are any number of reasons, signaled in the narrative, that David might see it to his advantage to take this action. Abigail is attractive. She has shown herself to be intelligent, perceptive, and courageous. There is one small point that may support the assumption that this is a reward. In her speech, Abigail speaks of David's future role as leader in Israel, and she adds that, when Yahweh makes David prosper, he, David, will remember her (v. 31). In other words, David owes her something.

It is rather difficult to chart the sequences because they overlap. The nature of some of the sequences only becomes apparent after they have begun so that one must reassess what is going on in the course of reading. What follows will give some approximation of how they are related.

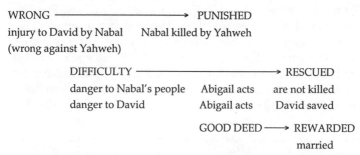

WRONG ⟶ PUNISHED
injury to David by Nabal   Nabal killed by Yahweh
(wrong against Yahweh)

DIFFICULTY ⟶ RESCUED
danger to Nabal's people   Abigail acts   are not killed
danger to David   Abigail acts   David saved

GOOD DEED ⟶ REWARDED
married

There is both divine action and human action in the story. Up to the speech of Abigail (vv. 24–31) the story proceeds on the human plane with no intervention of Yahweh either directly or indirectly. It appears that Abigail, using whatever powers of persuasion she has at her disposal, will try to rescue her people from the wrath of David. But, as we have seen, part way through her speech to David her words begin to suggest that we must understand what has happened in a different light. Yahweh has been intervening after all, but only indirectly through the actions of Abigail. This is a hidden role for the deity, who works behind and through human actions. The punishment of Nabal is more direct—at least the narrator describes it this way.

Concluding Comment on the Eight Examples. Simply on the basis of this small group of stories, a number of features have come to light. The last example, the story about David and Abigail, showed that combinations of sequences can become both rich and complex. Elaborations of basic rescue and punishment sequences were also found, for example, the use of an agent in punishment stories who acts on the deity's behalf by declaring guilt and by announcing punishment. Variations within sequences were seen, as when a parable was used as a means of declaring guilt (1 Kings 20). Or in rescue accounts it was noted that rescue can vary from a major event like the deliverance of a city from famine to an individual matter like the healing of a leper (the foreigner Naaman). The relationship between the divine and the human displayed a range of possibilities. Divine action could be direct, as in the punishment of Gehazi, or indirect through apparently ordinary events hidden in the complexities of life, as in the David and Abigail story. The punishment stories were of particular interest because of the way in which they at the same time affirmed and obscured divine punishment.

B. Stories of the Judges

The book of Judges claims special attention because separate stories about different judges have been placed within a framework that comments on them as a group (for a literary-historical approach, see Brettler). This framework of commentary is usually identified as Deuteronomistic, although some scholars distinguish layers in the material that stem from different periods (e.g., Boling:29–38; Soggin:42). It will be sufficient in the following discussion simply to distinguish between framework and story. The framework has a broad perspective. The Deuteronomistic view, whatever precise role it plays in the framework, treats the people of Israel as a whole, and this is true also in matters of rescue or punishment. The people as a whole is deemed to possess a historical tradition that goes back to the time in Egypt. On the other hand, within the individual stories, the perspective is usually restricted to a specific geographical area and a particular tribe or group of tribes oppressed by external enemies. Yet, even within the stories, the language and perspective of the framework emerges from time to time in particular blocks of material, and some of these will be noted.

Within the framework material in Judges 2, the narrator delineates a pattern that is said to repeat itself in the events associated with each of the judges. Of course, the narrator does not describe patterns of events he observed but rather patterns in the traditions about the judges he received. In other words, he is really talking about story patterns. The narrator appears to be quite conscious of his function as a commentator on the traditions he is passing on. He wants readers to be aware of the pattern in the traditions because he considers the former important for understanding the latter.

Five stories will be considered here: Ehud, Deborah and Barak, Gideon, Jephthah, and Samson. Before discussing them individually, it will be important first to see them within the context of the framework given to them in the book of Judges.

The pattern in question is set out by the narrator in Judg 2:11–17. Israel does wrong by abandoning Yahweh to follow other gods. Yahweh becomes angry and hands the people over to their enemies (v. 14). This in turn creates a difficult situation for the people. Yahweh then raises up judges who save them from their enemies. But when a judge dies, the people resume their attention to other gods. The first appearance of the full pattern identified in Judges 2 comes in Judg 3:7–11. This is a short account about a certain Othniel. The story does little more than add names to the basic outline of the pattern with the result that the language used to describe the pattern in 2:11–19 is largely repeated.

If we look at this pattern more closely, it is possible to distinguish three patterns rather than one, and two of these resemble sequences discussed above. First, there is the pattern of a punishment sequence: the people do a wrong and are punished. Second, there is the pattern of a rescue sequence: the people find themselves in difficulty and are rescued. Third, there is the pattern of the story of someone's life. By this I mean very little, only that one can identify a movement in the text from the birth (even birth announcement) or early life of a judge to the death of that person. This is something like a sequence, in that each judge functions from the time of his participation in a rescue (or call/birth announcement) until death. This amounts to a kind of movement from a beginning to an end, but its structure is sufficiently vague that I have decided not to treat it as a sequence, at least as I have defined it. The life story pattern is not an uncommon feature of biblical narrative in that a number of characters appear in the narration at birth or call and remain until death and burial. While it certainly merits consideration, I will only note its presence. The significant patterns in Judges for the purposes of this study appear to be the first two just mentioned, the punishment and rescue sequences, which are linked together in such a way that the difficult situation created by the punishment becomes the opening situation for the rescue.

A further observation can be made. In Judges the punishment sequence is always found at the beginning of each story and is stated very briefly in the language of the framework. That is to say, there are no stories about punishment, only brief statements that summarize this pattern of action. At the end of each story are brief closing statements in language like that of the framework. Thus, the punishment sequence seems to belong to the framework or commentary that encloses the stories about the judges. In contrast, the rescue sequence appears to form the main action in the stories of the judges. Some of these stories are quite lengthy and seldom reflect the style or language of the framework. As a pattern common to these stories, the rescue sequence, reduced to its simplest form, amounts to this: the people are in difficulty and Yahweh responds by producing a leader who rescues them. However, the individual stories are quite distinct from each other and elaborate this pattern in different ways.

What has been said so far is not new. But, as I have already indicated, what strikes me as worthy of interest is that the commentary on the stories provided by the framework comes from an ancient commentator (or commentators) who not only saw a pattern in a set of stories but suggested that seeing this pattern was important for understanding what these stories are about. Even with all the differences and marks of individuality displayed by the stories, one must also pay attention to the pattern they share. At least this seems to be the claim of the commentator. The task of the rest of this section will be to examine this claim in more detail in order to see to what extent and in what way it can be said that stories very different from each other (Ehud, Deborah and Barak, Gideon, Jephthah, and Samson) reflect a common rescue sequence.

1. *Judges 3:12–30*. In the story of Ehud, the punishment sequence is brief and couched in the language of the framework. The Israelites do wrong and Yahweh sends Eglon, king of Moab, whom they serve for eighteen years. As already noted, the language of the framework works with a perspective of Israel as a whole so that all events related to the judges are viewed in this light, even though the stories appear to deal with local situations. Here, apparently in the introductory comments of the framework (v. 13), it is said that Eglon attacks Israel (the broad perspective), but he is reported to have captured only Jericho (the narrower perspective of the story). The rescue sequence begins with the language of the framework, which indicates that the Israelites cried out to Yahweh and he raised up a rescuer (v. 15). At this point, Ehud is introduced and his act of rescue begins. The punishment and rescue sequences are linked in that the punishment leads to a difficult situation from which the people need to be rescued.

In this story, the narration of the rescue does not begin with a message or visitation from Yahweh and a formal selection of the rescuer. Divine intervention at the beginning is entirely absent. No task is proposed, no instructions are given about how to proceed, nor is there a promise of victory. We know Ehud is the rescuer because the first part of v. 15 identifies him as such. When Ehud is introduced, he has been appointed to convey tribute to Eglon. The fact that he conceals a weapon on his body implies that a specific action against Eglon is contemplated. In other words, he has set a task for himself, and this can be construed as an achievement sequence (*task/accomplished*).

The assassination of the foreign king will open the way for the rescue of Israel by the expulsion of Moab. As the weaker party, Israel cannot move openly against the more powerful invaders; Ehud must resort to a trick or deception. Once he has carried out the mission he set for himself and has made good his escape, Ehud mobilizes the Israelites and leads them against the enemy. The Moabites are soundly defeated because the Israelites have seized the ford of the Jordan so that the Moabites cannot escape to their homeland. Neither in the assassination nor in the battle is there any mention of a miracle or direct, divine intervention. Still, Yahweh is referred to at two critical points in the narrative, which relates him to what is happening. First of all, as Ehud prepares to stab Eglon, he announces that he has a word of God for the foreign king (v. 20). Then, as Ehud calls Israel out against Moab, he announces that Yahweh has given Moab into their hands (v. 28). Thus, it is made clear that, while these events are carried out entirely on the human plane, they are nevertheless related to Yahweh (but see Klein:46).

The sequences may be set out in the following way. The punishment sequence is linked to the rescue sequence. The achievement sequence is embedded in the rescue sequence.

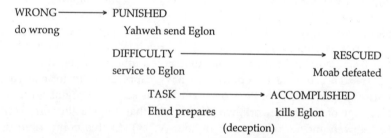

2. *Judges 4*. The story of Deborah and Barak. This narrative follows the general pattern discussed above: a punishment sequence followed by a rescue sequence. The punishment sequence comes in the familiar language of the framework and is brief. The first three verses explain that the Israelites have done wrong and that Yahweh has turned them over to a foreign king, Jabin, who ruled at Hazor with his general, Sisera.

The rest of the story is a rescue sequence (*difficulty/rescued*). The difficulty is stated in v. 3 and the rescue occurs in defeat of the enemy in vv. 15 and 16 together with the death of Sisera (vv. 17–22). The first phase of this sequence, the *difficulty*, finds its beginning in the brief statement of the punishment sequence since the punishment creates a difficult situation from which the people have to be rescued. Thus, with the comment that the people cried out to Yahweh (v. 3), the shift from punishment to rescue is clearly marked, although this comment is still couched in language close to that of the pattern story about Othniel (Judg 3:7–11). The second part of the rescue sequence, the rescue itself, starts in v. 4 and continues to the end of the chapter. The rescue is reiterated in a summary statement in v. 23. Language similar to that of v. 23 comes at the end of the stories of Ehud (3:30) and Gideon (8:28), which indicates that there is framework language at the end of some stories as well as at the beginning, although this particular phrase was not part of the language of the pattern introduced in Judg 2:11–19 and 3:7–11.

If we look more closely at the rescue phase, vv. 17–22, further elaborations can be identified. First, an agent is selected to carry out the rescue. While this is not essential to rescue sequences, it is part of the stories in Judges where a rescuer is usually depicted as acting on Yahweh's behalf. Further, and this is where the rescue phase begins (v. 4), a messenger is sent to select the rescuer and assign him his task. Deborah the prophetess here plays the role of the intermediary who presents Barak with his divine commission.

The wording of the commission introduces three smaller sequences that function in the rest of the story: an achievement sequence (*task /accomplished*) and two announcement sequences (*announcement/happened*). First, there is the achievement sequence in which Deborah gives Barak an instruction in the name of Yahweh to move against the enemy (v. 6), and this instruction is obeyed in v. 10.

Second, in addition to this instruction to mobilize against the enemy, Deborah makes two announcements. The first states that Yahweh will draw the enemy out to meet Barak once he has followed the instruction to gather men together and go out against the enemy (v. 7). This happens in v. 12–13. The second announcement states that the enemy will by delivered into Barak's hands. In this announcement sequence a promise is enunciated in v. 9, reiterated in v. 14, and fulfilled in vv. 15–22. In this case, the occurrence of what was announced comes about through the direct intervention of Yahweh who panics Sisera and his army (v. 15). The Israelite army is then able to move against the enemy. Thus, the rescue sequence has three main elaborations. The rescuer receives a commission to go to war, which he does. There is an announcement that the enemy will come out, which they do. Finally, a promise that the war will be successful, which it is.

There is further elaboration. A subordinate line of action is created and moves along parallel to the main action of the rescue. The commissioning of Barak does not run smoothly. While Barak does not reject the task laid on him, he sets out a condition: he will go if Deborah comes along, a suggestion that is not well received by Deborah. In fact, Barak's proposal is treated like an act of wrongdoing so that what emerges here is very much like a punishment sequence. Barak does wrong by suggesting that he will not go unless Deborah comes with him. For this impropriety a punishment is announced. Barak will not gain glory in his campaign because Sisera will be turned over to a woman. In other words, the punishment is an embedded announcement sequence: the punishment is announced in v. 9 and this announced event happens in vv. 17–23.

The occurrence of this announced event (vv. 17–23) is itself elaborated. Verses 17 and 18 depict Sisera fleeing to the tent of Jael, expecting to find safety there because of the peace between the king of Hazor and the Kenites. But readers know something Sisera does not. It has already been announced that Sisera's doom has been sealed by Yahweh and further that he will fall into the hands of a woman. It was also pointed out in v. 11 that Heber, the Kenite, had pitched his tent in the neighborhood. By vv. 17 and 18, readers know what is going to happen and that Yahweh is behind it. However, as readers, we do not know why the woman decides to kill Sisera. No motivation is given, although this may not matter to the narrator as long as the action is seen as the completion of Yahweh's announcement. A more important problem emerges. How will an unarmed woman dispatch a warrior? In other words, this section presents an achievement sequence in which a difficult task is accomplished. Here, Jael accomplishes her task by means of a deception. She gives no hint of hostile intentions until Sisera is safely asleep. Then she dispatches him. The story closes (v. 22) when Barak confronts this situation and sees for himself that the word announced has indeed happened.

The sequences can be outlined in a diagram.

WRONG ⟶ PUNISHED
people do evil and Jabin comes

      DIFFICULTY ⟶ RESCUED
      under power of Jabin   freed by Yahweh and Barak

        TASK ⟶ ACCOMPLISHED
      Barak to call the men to war   he does

        WRONG ⟶ PUNISHED
    Barak sets a condition   glory goes to a woman

          ANNOUNCEMENT ⟶ HAPPENED
          glory to a woman   comes true

          ANNOUNCEMENT ⟶ HAPPENED

will draw Sisera	does
will give into hands	does so

TASK ———→ ACCOMPLISHED

Jael to kill Sisera   she kills him

(deception)

A number of things are worth noting. Most of these sequences have to do with the elaboration of the rescue sequence. The assignment of a task to the hero and the promise of victory are both logical expansions of the rescue. Barak's punishment for his hesitation introduces a new line of development in the story, although it functions within and remains compatible with the rescue. The punishment given to Barak is no problem for Yahweh who accomplishes his ends through the woman Jael so that the death of Sisera remains part of the rescue. In fact, Jael functions as a rescuer and provides a certain contrast to Barak.

This contrast may be part of a larger contrast in the story regarding divine and human action. Yahweh plays a significant role in the story. While we are told nothing about the commissioning of Deborah, she confronts Barak with an instruction from Yahweh, part of which is phrased as Yahweh's direct speech. Furthermore, when the two armies confront each other, Yahweh intervenes directly by creating panic among the enemy forces. Other things happen at the level of normal human events, but it is made explicit that Yahweh is ultimately responsible for them. For example, it is announced that Yahweh will draw the enemy out, and indeed Sisera does bring out his troops. The most important example may be found in the murder of Sisera by Jael. It is announced beforehand that Sisera will be handed over to a woman, and so it is to be understood that Yahweh is acting indirectly here. Yet the story proceeds without any hint of this. Jael is not spoken to by Yahweh, nor is she given any instructions. In fact, we are not told what motivated Jael to kill Sisera, especially in the light of Sisera's supposition that there is peace. Unknown to herself, she becomes Yahweh's agent, carrying out the punishment announced for Barak and completing the rescue promised by Yahweh. Neither called nor commissioned, she acts on her own and fulfills Yahweh's intention. Barak was openly selected and commissioned as a rescuer, and he was given an assurance of victory—but he hesitated.

The story gives the impression that Yahweh is in control of the action from start to finish. This is made especially clear by the announcement sequences that predict what will happen. Even so, there is a shifting back and forth between obvious intervention by Yahweh and absence of any overt action, although Yahweh is assumed to be directing the course of events. Of course, there is one point where things do not go according to Yahweh's plans, when Barak hesitates. Still, this hesitation becomes a problem for Barak, not Yahweh, and it is handled immediately.

3. *Judges 6–8.* The story of Gideon is longer than the others discussed so far and might well have been included among the longer stories discussed in a section below. It seems to me better to consider Gideon in the framework of the book of Judges (but see Auld on this question). However, to examine every element in the narrative action would lead to a lengthy and complicated discussion. What is needed for the present review is simply a general outline of the rescue sequence in the Gideon story along with some of the main ways in which it is elaborated. As in the other stories, the Gideon account contains both punishment and rescue. The punishment sequence is outlined in only one verse, 6:1, and appears in the stereotyped language of the framework. The people did wrong and Yahweh turned them over to the Midianites. The following verses (2–6) describe the ravages of this punishment; but in doing so they depict at the same time a difficult situation that, after an appeal for help (v. 6), leads to rescue by Yahweh. The rest of the story, 6:8 to the end of chapter 8, completes the rescue sequence (*difficulty/rescued*) by providing its second phase, the rescue, which consists of Yahweh's response to the difficult situation.

The first step in the rescue is the selection of a leader (6:8–24). Yahweh sends a divine messenger to Gideon. During this encounter, two things happen that establish the structure of the rescue: the messenger issues an instruction and makes an announcement. The instruction issued to Gideon tells him to go save Israel from Midian, which he does. This can be construed as an achievement sequence, described above as *task/accomplished.* The accompanying announcement simply declares that the mission will be a success (v. 16), which it is. This may be construed as an announcement sequence (*announcement/happened*). Thus, there are parallel sequences embedded in the second half of the rescue sequence and they govern the action of the rescue.

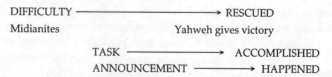

DIFFICULTY ⟶ RESCUED
Midianites   Yahweh gives victory

TASK ⟶ ACCOMPLISHED
ANNOUNCEMENT ⟶ HAPPENED

Gideon, then, is given a task and assured of success. The fact that success is assured by the divine announcement suggests that the tension in the story does not reside in whether or not Gideon will succeed but rather in *how* he will succeed. Indeed, the announcement is restated at later points in the story (7:7, 9, and indirectly 14). The certainty of victory is emphasized further in Yahweh's reduction of the fighting force to a mere three hundred persons (6:4–6) in contrast to the size of the Midianite and Amalekite armies in which the soldiers are as numerous as locusts and the camels as abundant as the sand on the seashore (7:12).

Since the outcome seems certain—it would appear so from the point of view of the reader—it is remarkable that Gideon requires two special confirmations of the announcement: a sign from the messenger (6:17) and a double execution of the sign of the wool (6:36–40). Yahweh even adds further confirmation by instructing Gideon to visit the enemy camp where he hears the account of a dream signifying victory (7:14)

The extended coverage of the rescue (6:33–8:21), deals with how Gideon obeys his instruction by going to battle against Midian and Amalek. In all this, the actual clash of the armies receives relatively little space. Most of the attention is focussed on elaborations, including a substantial account of the preparations before battle and an extended narration of the pursuit and execution of the leaders after the battle. The preparation, or the steps leading up to the battle, includes the announcements of victory, the signs and confirmations, and the reduction of the army.

The actual confrontation and victory (7:16–22) involves two elements. The first is a trick or deception. Gideon's force is divided into three groups and supplied with horns and torches hidden in pots. Blowing the horns and smashing the pots to reveal the torches cause the enemy to flee, although the text may not be entirely clear. At this point in the story, the second element is introduced: Yahweh intervenes to set the enemy soldiers against one another with their swords. Thus, the rescue is accomplished by a victory in battle in which the enemy is routed at the human level by a trick and at the divine level by an intervention, as though action at both levels is needed to effect the desired result.

While the story might have ended with this action, the narration continues to describe the pursuit and execution of the enemy leaders. Only after this final episode does the language of the framework (8:28) declare that Midian was humiliated and did not interfere any further. As a result, the land was quiet for forty years during the days of Gideon, a fact that formally signifies that the rescue is complete. It is worth noting, however, that other material pertaining to Gideon—the kingship and the ephod—surrounds this verse. What is said goes beyond the rescue pattern. There is also information about the number of sons born, as well as the death and burial of Gideon. In other words, the rescue sequence seems to be set into something like a life story. In fact, the following story of Abimelech in chapter 9 is a continuation of the story about Gideon's family.

4. *Judges 10:6–12:7*. The story of Jephthah tells of his victory over the Ammonites, an action attributed to Yahweh. There are several unusual features in this account. Even the opening provided by the framework is remarkable. It begins in the usual way with a statement of wrong and punishment, but this is expanded far beyond the framework comment in the other stories (10:6–9). The wrong is not only stated but spelled out: the Israelites had worshipped the Baals and the Ashtaroth, the deities of neighboring peoples; they had abandoned Yahweh; and they did not serve him. This brings the standard response: Yahweh became angry and handed them over to the Philistines and the Ammonites, and the resultant difficult situation leads, as usual, to an appeal. However, a curious section follows. The people not only cry out but confess their wrongdoing, their abandonment of Yahweh and their worship of other gods. In response Yahweh points out that this has happened several times before and that he has rescued them when they cried out. But not this time. The people are referred to the other gods. Although Israel confesses wrongdoing again and appeals for help, going so far as to remove the foreign gods and worship Yahweh alone, Yahweh does not appear to relent (v. 16).

Within this broad perspective of the framework, the story itself provides a narrower focus, Gilead confronted in battle by the Ammonites. The rulers of Gilead have no leader who can take up the task of fighting the Ammonites. They select Jephthah, formerly driven out of the city, and lure him with the promise of leadership. This selection occurs without any action of Yahweh either in word or deed, although it is said that the agreement between the elders of Gilead and Jephthah involved Yahweh (vv. 10, 11) and was conditional upon Yahweh giving Ammon into the hand of Jephthah (v. 9). While the introductory comments of the framework appear to leave Yahweh refusing to help, these comments have implicated him in the arrangements with Jephthah. We have here an achievement sequence (*task/accomplished*): Jephthah has been charged with a task that he proceeds to carry out.

Once this agreement is struck, the confrontation can begin. But, and this is another unusual feature of this story, Jephthah tries to settle matters peaceably through diplomacy. Another remarkable feature immediately follows. The hostile action of the Ammonites has been precipitated by a dispute over land that is traced back to the time of the wilderness wanderings of Israel, all of which broadens the perspective of the story again to that of the framework, all of Israel and its history.

With the failure of negotiations, a combat becomes inevitable. The narrative shows little interest in the battle itself, which is described in only two verses (32–33). Still, Yahweh is active here, at least to the extent of having his spirit fall upon Jephthah, which seems to confirm divine participation in the selection of a rescuer. It is also noted that Yahweh gave the Ammonites into the hand of Jephthah.

The real interest surrounding the battle appears to focus on the fateful vow, which provides yet another striking element in the story. The vow functions like an announcement sequence: an intention to do something is announced, and later the announced action is carried out. But the vow is remarkable for two reasons. In the first place, the vow involves a human sacrifice (if that is what v. 31 implies, an unusual practice in Israel). Secondly, it is the daughter of Jephthah who turns out to be the designated victim, and neither the father nor the daughter appear to think that the vow can be changed or broken. Nor does the narrative offer any hints in this direction. The remarkable irony of a father having to kill his own daughter draws considerable attention to the vow sequence and thus colors the rescue sequence.

With the victory over the Ammonites, the rescue is accomplished, although the account continues with one further incident stemming from the battle. This consists of the complaint made by the Ephraimites that they had not been called to participate, a dispute that is only settled by a battle. As in the story of Gideon, the narrative ends with the death of the hero. The sequences governing the rescue aspect of the story are limited to two, apart from the implied punishment sequence in the introduction. There is a rescue sequence and within it an achievement sequence carried out by Jephthah. The complications have been noted. The announcement sequence of the vow can, because of the unusual features just mentioned, draw much of the attention in the story, even though the vow is not integral to the rescue.

WRONG ⟶ PUNISHMENT

DIFFICULTY ——————— refusal to help

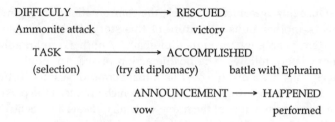

DIFFICULY ――――――→ RESCUED

Ammonite attack   victory

TASK ――――――→ ACCOMPLISHED

(selection)   (try at diplomacy)   battle with Ephraim

ANNOUNCEMENT ――→ HAPPENED

vow   performed

5. Judges 13–16. The story of Samson is another long story I am including here because of its setting in Judges. The story reflects a rescue pattern and so bears a relationship to the other stories of the judges, although the rescue does not stand out to the extent that it does in the other narratives. Many things are going on in the Samson story, and it differs significantly from the other stories just considered. Consequently, the account of Samson will only be treated briefly and in summary, without a detailed analysis of sequences. The birth story is a selection narrative but does not come in direct response to a specific threat as in the previous stories. There are also tensions between what one might expect Samson to be and his actual life style. The struggle between Samson and the Philistines is more like a vendetta marked by retaliation and revenge than a battle to escape their domination. Samson eludes all attempts to capture him except for the last, but even there he turns the tables, although it is at the cost of his life. The last scene amounts to a victory of sorts over the Philistines, but it is not decisive. To be sure, the birth announcement had only promised a beginning. There are some hints in the story that invite the reader to assume that Yahweh is acting behind all that happens and to take the Samson story as a kind of rescue story. One of these hints consists of the curious comment in 14:4, where it is said that the business of wanting a Philistine wife was Yahweh's way of establishing grounds for a quarrel. Another comes when the spirit breaks out on Samson, implying Yahweh's intervention. In sum, the story offers a curious tension: part of the text suggests a kind of rescue, and yet part resists any simple reading of this sort.

Comments on the Stories of the Judges. I have already discussed the relationship between the frame and the stories, but one or two further observations can be made. In these stories two important elements were noted that can occur as elaborations within the rescue sequence: the selection of the leader and the confrontation with the enemy. Selection played an important role in the stories of Gideon, Deborah and Barak, Jephthah, and even Samson, although it happened differently in each case. With

Gideon the selection involved rather direct divine intervention, yet with Jephthah things developed on a human level. Confrontation in battle and victory occurred in all but the Samson story. The actual battle was not elaborated in any of the stories, although events preceding or following this crucial point were. Here again, the role of the divine and human varied in that sometimes direct divine intervention was involved and other times not.

C. Stories of the Conquest

In this section I will examine the action sequences in four stories in the book of Joshua: the spies and Rahab (chap. 2), the capture of Jericho (chap. 6), the sin of Achan (chap. 7), and the capture of Ai (chap. 8). The stories to be considered here tell of the conquest of the two cities Jericho and Ai. The main action governing these stories deals with capturing and taking possession, although rescue and punishment sequences are present. These four chapters are closely linked and, as we will see, action sequences function between stories as well as within each story individually. Significant examples of tension may be found within some of these narratives, and this, too, will be examined. I will also continue the discussion already begun in connection with the stories about the judges and give some further consideration to the relationship between divine and human action.

Before we turn to the four stories, a few general comments on Joshua 1–12 are necessary. In the present form of the text, the book of Joshua opens with a speech of Yahweh announcing that the land will be given to the Israelites and ordering that Joshua cross the Jordan. This announcement is realized in Josh 11:23, where it is reported that Joshua has taken all the land. In other words, the general announcement about the acquisition of the land at the beginning of the book introduces an expectation that establishes the general direction of the action of the narrative in these chapters. When the expectation is fulfilled at the end of Joshua 11, the story of the conquest is at an end. This movement from announcement to realization is an announcement sequence that seems to govern the story of the conquest as a whole. The use of the announcement sequence here leaves open the precise stages the action may follow as the story proceeds. In fact, the narrative moves by means of several subordinate stories largely complete in themselves but usually marking a step on the way toward the conquest. Among these are stories of the crossing of the Jordan, the capture of cities, and dealings with the people of the land.

Even though the story of the conquest gives the impression of a coherent movement from announcement to realization, most scholars have assumed that the narrative has probably attained its present form only after a long period of growth and development, perhaps reaching back to oral tradition (but see Van Seters, 1983:324–31). It has also been noted that the number of stories is rather select since what we have relates only part of the conquest and records only a small number of the battles that would have been required to complete the conquest of the land by means of a single campaign under Joshua. Much of the conquest is given in a summary form (Josh 10:28–43).

1. *Joshua 2*. This chapter tells of the spies and their encounter with Rahab (for an earlier version of what follows, see Culley, 1985b). The narrative action can be described by identifying three narrative sequences. The first sequence presents a task assigned and carried to completion (an achievement sequence). Joshua sends out two men as spies, and they eventually return with a report, thus completing the task assigned them. As it happens, the task is difficult and the men are fortunate to return alive. A similar pattern is found in Josh 7:2–3 where Joshua sends spies to Ai, although in this case the instruction to spy is followed immediately by the report, and no incident intervenes. What in Joshua 7 is a small part of a larger story appears in Joshua 2 as a framework for the story as a whole. The report the spies bring back from Jericho is what they heard from Rahab.

The second action sequence entails a rescue and takes place in Jericho: the men, having landed in a dangerous situation, are rescued by Rahab. When they arrive in Jericho and enter the house of Rahab, the men are threatened by the king, who has heard of their presence and has sent messengers to take them into custody. The rescue by Rahab takes place in two stages. First, the men are hidden, while their pursuers are sent off on a wild goose chase. Then the spies are lowered out of a window, placing them outside the city. After hiding in the hills for a brief period to elude their pursuers, they return safely to Joshua.

A third action sequence begins in this chapter but does not conclude until Joshua 6. While this movement is more difficult to describe and does not seem to fit easily into any of the categories of sequences mentioned in Chapter Two above, it is still worth mentioning. The woman succeeds in persuading the men to promise that she and her family will be spared when the city is taken. In other words, she makes an appeal to which the men respond positively. The response has two elements: a promise to save Rahab, given immediately, and the future fulfillment of the promise at the capture of Jericho. One could think of this negotiation in terms of a sequence in which a good deed is rewarded: the woman has rescued the men and then makes an appeal for a reward, which she gets. But the idea of reward, while implicit, is not obvious. Perhaps the woman's request constitutes a veiled threat, seeing that the spies are still very much in her power. If they do not accept Rahab's terms, she has no reason to let them go. Possibly neither sense can be ruled out, although reward seems to be more likely. In any event, a request is made and granted.

The structure of the narrative action in Joshua 2, then, may be summarized in terms of an achievement sequence and a rescue sequence along with another movement that can be described as a request made and granted. There is no necessary connection between the task of spying and the act of rescue. One simply happens within the framework of the other. The request granted is closely linked to the rescue and depends on it. The request also links the story of the spies to the fall of Jericho in chapter 7 because it is then that the request is acted on. Similarly, the task of spying is located within a larger story context, in that the mission of the spies is a first step in the conquest of Jericho and the land.

While the arrangement of the action sequences gives the impression of a coherent narrative structure, a careful, clause-by-clause reading of the text of Joshua 2 turns up signs of unevenness, consisting of significant gaps and tensions. This text may, therefore, provide a useful opportunity to discuss the matter of disturbances in the text.

A recent attempt to deal with this aspect of the text may be found in Floss. Working largely within the approach developed by Wolfgang Richter, Floss works through problems raised by textual criticism and literary criticism (traditions and sources), seeking to determine whether or not the text is an original unity and to what extent the work can be attributed to authors and editors. Floss' study is extremely thorough and detailed, so that it will provide a useful basis for a brief discussion.

At the level of textual criticism, Floss compares the Massoretic text with the Septuagint. There are a number of different readings, mostly words and phrases present in the MT but not in the LXX. Following scholars like Orlinsky and Auld, Floss gives substantial weight to the LXX and considers it a better witness to a Hebrew *Vorlage* than the MT. Thus, Floss frequently reads with the LXX. For example, he reads "youths" with the LXX rather than the MT "men" in Josh 2:1.

At the level of literary analysis (traditions and sources), Floss employs the presence of doublets along with the existence of tensions and contradictions as criteria for determining lack of unity. Using these criteria, he identifies places in the text where unevenness should be taken as a sign of different authorship. On the basis of his analysis, Floss proposes (79) that the earliest unit of the text consists of vv. 1–3, 4c–6, 15, 22, and 23. The rest of the chapter he regards as material added at later stages. His proposed analysis is bolstered by an extensive examination of the form of this unit, using methods based on and developed from the work of Richter. Within the earliest unit, Floss distinguishes a preliterary stage that tells of a prostitute who finds that two of her customers have been charged with spying (217). She takes their side, sends their pursuers on a false trail, and later helps them to safety. According to Floss, this oral story has been picked up by a later author and provided with a framework that turns it into a story about the sending of spies to prepare the way for Joshua's conquest.

Floss' proposal represents an interesting possibility, and his argument possesses a measure of plausibility. Tensions and gaps can be identified in the text (see more recently, Zakovitch, 1990). Yet in spite of Floss' extraordinary effort, I remain less confident than he about our ability to delineate the stages of development in the text with any likelihood of probability rather than plausibility. Explaining why tensions appear in texts is a very complicated business for any number of reasons. We know so little about what has really happened to texts, and when it may have happened. For example, many stories in the Bible are rather short, surprisingly short in fact, when one considers that many may go back to a living narrative tradition. It is as though a process of condensation has occurred in which the stories, for one reason or another, have been reduced to a summary form. If this were so, then the task of explaining the reasons for gaps and tensions would become even more complex than already imagined.

A possible instance of condensation might be the first several verses of Joshua 2. They read like a summary, an account reduced from a much longer story. The present text lacks a great deal of information that readers would like to know. For example, the spies arrive in Jericho and are immediately located in a prostitute's house. We are not told how or why they did this, business or pleasure, carrying out their mission or straying from it. Nor do we know how their identity and mission was discovered so that it could be reported to the king of Jericho. When the king sends to Rahab, demanding that the men be handed over, it is not indicated by whom the instruction is sent, nor is the arrival of messengers at the house recounted. However, the woman is already in the act of hiding the men without our knowing what prompted her action. She speaks immediately to the emissaries of the king as though their presence had precipitated the hiding. We are not told how Rahab could have dealt with the messengers and hidden the men all at the same time. This condensed section of narrative manifests the difficulty of distinguishing clearly which tensions and repetitions are due to different authors and which reflect condensation and summarization.

One would think that with all the gaps I have just mentioned, the narrative would fall apart, but, even with so much information missing, the general outline of the rescue sequence remains clear: the spies are in danger, and the woman rescues them by misleading the messengers of the king. It would appear that the story line manages to hold the narrative together in spite of gaps and distortions in the text. Even though these difficulties may be noticed by a reader, they do not need to disturb one unduly because the main movement of the action is clear.

This discussion of condensation leads to the question of perspective or scope, which was raised earlier in connection with the story of Naboth. By perspective or scope I mean the extent to which the focus in a story rests on the immediate story being told or the larger context in which the story is found, in this case on the rescue sequence or the achievement sequence. While the rescue story seems surprisingly short, the speech of the woman to the men hidden on the roof is remarkably full. Here the words flow. Moreover, they flow in a style and vocabulary reminiscent of the tradition of Deuteronomy. In its content and style, this speech shifts to the perspective of the conquest of the land. In other words, the speech has less to do with the rescue of the men than with their task as spies. The report that the spies take back has to do with what Rahab has said about the condition of the people of the land in the face of the invading Israelites. The mission of the spies, viewed as preparation not only for the capture of Jericho but also for the conquest of the land, governs the story of Joshua 2. The present version of the story subordinates the rescue sequence to the framework sequence of the spy mission through the prominence of the speech of Rahab that forms the substance of the report taken back by the spies.

It may be worth noting briefly how the various characters are distributed among the action sequences in Joshua 2. This touches on the relationship between the divine and human. Yahweh's power is an important element in the chapter because it is his reputation that has debilitated the people of the land, and this is what the spies report to Joshua. But Yahweh is not a participant. He does not send the spies. In fact, he is not even consulted in the matter. Nor does he intervene to rescue the spies. He has nothing to do with the promise made to Rahab and her family. In short, he is remarkably absent from the action. Other characters play important roles. Joshua sends the spies and receives their report. Rahab supplies the report to the spies, rescues them, and gains their favor, if not a reward. The spies complete the task assigned to them, are rescued from danger, and make a promise to Rahab and her family. Both Rahab and the spies take surprisingly bold initiatives. They improvise responses to the situations they meet, surviving by their wits. It is true that the power of Yahweh may be at the bottom of it all but only indirectly and in the larger perspective.

As far as tensions are concerned, it is not being argued that tensions do not exist, or do not matter, or that they disappear in reading (see Greenstein, 1982). It is only being suggested that, as long as a reader grasps the direction of a narrative at the level of action sequences, difficulties like gaps, tensions, and other marks of unevenness appear as disturbances of greater or lesser degree within a story rather than as disruptions that pull a story apart and make it impossible to read. They would be like static, or to change the metaphor, blurring at certain points in the text where things remain uncertain. On the other hand, disturbances may be a more positive factor in texts, more like conflicting signals than static. Indications of more than one message are present, thickening the text, so to speak. In these cases, one might speak of a shimmering rather than blurring, since a reader may be shifted back and forth between one perspective and another very rapidly.

A possible example of this can be cited in Josh 2:1. Here the word "Jericho" follows the word "land" directly in such a way that there appears to be a disturbance in the text. Even though the city name "Ai" and the word "land" appear in the same context in Josh 7:2, the juxtaposition in Josh 2:1 looks odd. However, it was noted above that the story itself appeared to have a double function, being preparation for the capture of Jericho as well as for the conquest of the land. The juxtaposition of the words "land" and "Jericho" matches this double function and produces a shifting back and forth, a shimmering, between two perspectives.

2. *The capture of Jericho (Joshua 6).* This chapter consists of a single action sequence. An opening speech of Yahweh (vv. 2–5) contains two things. First, an announcement is made assuring Joshua that Jericho has been delivered into his hands. Second, instructions are issued pertaining to what the warriors and priests should do. The warriors are to go

around the city once a day for six days. Seven priests are to carry seven horns before the ark. On the seventh day, the march around the city is to be performed seven times and the priests are to blow their horns. At the sound of the horn, the people are to raise a shout. The walls of the city will fall. These instructions are followed. It is reported in v. 20 that the walls fall. The people go up and capture the city. The movement of the action runs from the announcement that the city will be delivered, more specifically that the walls will fall, to the occurrence of what is announced when the walls fall and the city is taken. The tension in this announcement sequence is that between knowing something is going to happen and then watching it happen. This is the same sort of movement mentioned above that controls the whole conquest story from Joshua 1–11.

The narrative proceeds from announcement to occurrence by means of small movements much like action sequences: an instruction is given, and then it is reported that the instruction has been obeyed. For example, the instructions about going around the city (vv. 3–4) are repeated to the people in an abbreviated and slightly modified form in v. 7. The performance of these instructions is reported in vv. 8–9 with even further modifications. In v. 10 Joshua gives another instruction, warning the people not to shout until he instructs them. Following this, vv. 11–16 describe the march around the city on the seventh day, at which point (v. 16) Joshua intervenes with a command to shout followed by an instruction to put the city to the ban save for Rahab and her family. After the city is taken (v. 20), the instruction regarding the ban and Rahab are carried out.

While there are no other action sequences in Joshua 6, there are parts of action sequences present that link this chapter with two other stories. We have already seen how the sequence involving the promise to Rahab made in Joshua 2 remained incomplete and could only be fulfilled at the capture of Jericho. And it is indeed fulfilled in the form of an instruction. Just before the capture, Joshua instructs the two spies to bring the woman and her family out of the city, which they do.

The other link looks ahead to the story of Achan. In Josh 6:17–19 Joshua announces the ban of the city and warns against taking anything of it lest the camp of Israel be put under the ban, thereby causing it trouble (the same verb as in 7:25). It is not just that this alludes to the Achan story. The warning is in fact a prohibition, which, as we are told at the beginning of Joshua 8, Achan transgresses. As we have seen, a prohibition can function as part of an embedded sequence in a punishment story—in other words, the *wrong* is realized by the sequence *prohibition/transgressed*.

While in Joshua 2 Yahweh took no active part in the story, here he is a major participant. He initiates the action, declares what will happen, and presumably sees that it does happen. How the miracle occurs is not explained, nor is the exact relationship between the action of the people and the falling of the walls. Joshua and the people do what they are told. Joshua passes on the instructions. The people carry them out. The central role of Yahweh creates a sense of inevitability. The enemies pose no real threat or difficulty. They remain passive and play no active role, almost as though they were an obstacle to be removed rather than an enemy to be defeated in battle.

Even though the general movement of the narrative is clear, the details are not. The tensions are obvious and may well be due to a history of development in the text, although no consensus has been reached among the commentators as to the stages of growth (Van Seters, 1983:327, for example, blames the confusion on P). The most evident tensions may be seen in the details of the procession. The first description of the procession (vv. 3–5, a speech of Yahweh to Joshua) mentions warriors, seven priests with seven horns, and the ark. In v. 7, the people are to march around the city with an armed contingent going before the ark. In vv. 8 and 9, a rear guard is added. Blowing the horns is also viewed differently. From vv. 4 and 16, the impression is left that the horns are to be blown on the last day only. However, vv. 8, 9, and 13 have priests blowing the horns on each daily round. Nevertheless, since the general action of narrative is fairly coherent, the confusion in details only amounts to some blurring in the story.

The tension in Joshua 6, as I have already suggested, consists of a fairly smooth movement from the announcement to fulfillment. There is no struggle. Rather, this movement is characterized by a rhythm produced by a whole series of short narrative movements involving an instruction given followed by a report that the instruction has been carried out. This rhythm creates the impression, at least in my view, of a sense of order and inevitability. This is further heightened by the content of the instructions themselves, in that they entail a ritual-like procession around Jericho repeated for six days followed by a sevenfold circuit on the seventh day. Even though the details vary through the story, the impression of an orderly ritual remains. It has already been suggested that the central role of Yahweh contributes to this impression. Whether or not this narrative stems from an actual ritual is not an issue here (for a discussion of this possibility, see Wilcoxen). Rather, the point is the effect produced by the ritual-like quality of the instructions and their contents.

3. *The Sin of Achan (Joshua 7)*. Even though Joshua 7 tells of the beginning of the conquest of Ai described in chapter 8, it can be discussed separately because the sin of Achan provides the main interest. The striking feature of this story, at least as far as action sequences are concerned, is the way in which two major action sequences are intertwined throughout the narrative. The first tells about a punishment: Achan does something wrong and is punished for it. The other focuses on Israel: a difficulty has arisen that must be resolved. According to the description of sequences presented in chapter two, this would fall under the general heading of rescue sequence. The crime of Achan has its effect on the people in that it has led to the failure to capture Ai, although initially the people do not know about what Achan has done and how it is affecting them. From the point of view of the people, the failure along with the loss of men poses a problem that needs to be solved before the conquest can continue. The people need to be rescued or delivered from this difficult situation.

The first sequence involving Achan is a punishment sequence. The first phase, the *wrong*, consists of an embedded prohibition sequence, as was noted above in the discussion of Jericho story. The prohibition is declared in Josh 6:17–19 and the transgression of this prohibition is reported in 7:1, which, by the way, is a comment made by the narrator to the reader. In other words, the narrator and the reader know what the other participants, apart from Achan, do not know. Thus, in order to move from wrong to punishment, the hidden crime and its unknown perpetrator must be exposed and recognized. The disclosure of this wrong takes place in three stages. First, an appeal to the deity by Joshua following the defeat at Ai evokes a response from Yahweh (v. 11) in which he points out only that Israel has sinned and transgressed the covenant. The next stage consists of a selection process, ordered by Yahweh, which leads to the identification of Achan as the culprit (v. 18). The punishment is also specified: the guilty party must be burned. The last stage comes when Joshua confronts Achan demanding that he tell the truth. Achan confesses that he has sinned (v. 20). The secret crime is now public knowledge. Punishment quickly follows. After being taken to the vale of Achor, Achan is executed by stoning, burning, and then stoning again.

The second sequence begins in the very first verse of the chapter with the indication that Israel has acted faithlessly. While this might sound like a declaration of a wrong deserving of punishment, the statement points in another direction, a rescue sequence (*difficulty/rescued*). It parallels the statement about Achan's crime and, like it, forms a comment made by the narrator to the listener or reader. The Israelites do not yet know that something has gone awry. The same steps followed in the Achan situation to expose the crime here reveal the cause of the people's difficulty and effect its removal. The defeat at Ai and Joshua's appeal lead to Yahweh's speech in which he reveals the problem: material taken from the ban rests in the camp. Yahweh then gives instructions about how the guilty person may be found and decrees what must be done. The person who took the material as well as all that he has must be burned so that no trace of contamination remains. Once the guilty party has been brought to light, the people know what they did not know before and are able to deal effectively with the situation in accordance with Yahweh's instructions. The difficulty has been removed and the conquest of Ai may now continue.

Chapter 7 is a single story, revolving around what Achan did. But the two intertwined sequences give two views of the series of events in the chapter. On the one hand, Achan does wrong, is discovered, and then punished. On the other hand, Israel faces a problem revealed by the failure to take Ai so that they must take steps to discover the cause. This involves uncovering a perpetrator. When this is done, Achan and the banned material he took must be removed from the camp. The main events of the story have double functions in that they work in both sequences in different ways to move each sequence to its conclusion.

Some other features of Joshua 7 can be briefly noted. First is the selection process by which the identity of the sinner is discovered. This ritual-like movement, working down in stages from the unit of the tribe to the individual, evokes something of the same sense of inevitability and orderliness that was noted above in the story of the capture of Jericho. There is no struggle or difficulty involved in gaining the information. It is revealed in a straightforward way as the people go through the steps of the selection process as it gradually works its way down to the culprit. Then, there is the role of Joshua in the story. Joshua sends the spies and presumably accepts their advice to send only a small party to attack the city—but all this without any advice from Yahweh. It is only after the disaster has occurred that Joshua turns to Yahweh. After suitable acts of mourning, Joshua utters a reproach that recalls the murmuring tradition. Further, he appeals to Yahweh, pointing out what the loss of the people would mean for the deity's great reputation. While this has all the appearances of an appeal in the face of a real crisis—a genuine attempt to move the deity to rescue Israel from a difficult situation—the plea must be taken ironically in the present form of the story, since the readers already know what the problem is and that it concerns Israel rather than Yahweh.

4. *The Capture of Ai (Joshua 8)*. As in Joshua 7, the capture of Ai (Josh 8:1–29) is governed by an announcement sequence. Yahweh announces that the city has been given into the hands of Israel and this happens. The announcement creates the expectation that the rest of the narrative will recount the events that move toward the point at which the announcement becomes a reality. Along with the announcement in the opening speech of Yahweh come two instructions. First, Yahweh orders that booty and cattle be exempted from the ban, and this is carried out after the capture of the city. Second, Yahweh demands in a single terse statement that an ambush be set behind the city, but he provides no further information as to how this should be done.

The instruction about the ambush is obeyed. The ambush functions as a deception or trick. A trap is laid for the enemy, and they fall into it so that the city is captured by means of a ruse. Although Yahweh gives the basic instruction to set an ambush, it is Joshua who elaborates the more detailed plan to capture the city by this means (vv. 4–8). He selects a group who are to station themselves behind the city. The main army will advance toward the city but retreat as soon as the enemy forces come out from the city to meet them. When the enemy pursues the retreating Israelites, the ambush will make its move, seize the city, and set it on fire. The trick works and the enemy forces are caught out in the open (vv. 14–26). Actions like an instruction given and obeyed or a trap set which then works are much like action sequences. However, as I explained in the previous chapter, I have decided to exclude several of these smaller movements.

Divine and human action work together here. The announcement sequence represents the action of Yahweh. He makes the key decisions and controls events. On the other hand, the ambush is action on the human level. Joshua does the planning. The army, including the party in ambush, accomplishes the victory. But the two modes of action, divine and human, are intertwined even further. Yahweh not only gives the order for the ambush, but he also intervenes at one point in the story by instructing Joshua (v. 18) to stretch out his weapon. From what follows, it appears that this is a signal to the ambush; but it may also have something to do with affecting the tide of battle. This instruction to Joshua comes as a surprise; there is no mention of this earlier in the story when Yahweh gives his initial order about the ambush.

Even though divine and human action are intertwined, the basic tension created by placing the two together is not removed. The juxtaposition of divine and human activity is curious here because of the fact that a trick is needed to gain a victory. Usually a trick or deception is required only when an enemy is fairly strong and is likely to win. Thus, at one level the story proceeds as if Israel is faced with a powerful enemy that can only be overcome if it is caught in a trap. On the other hand, the announcement at the beginning of the story makes clear that Yahweh has everything under control. The only indication of this in the story is the unexplained instruction to Joshua to raise his weapon. These two different perspectives may reflect stages in the growth of the story, but they remain side by side in its present form. Nevertheless, the tension created does not pull the story apart. The result is a shimmering effect, which moves the reader back and forth between two perspectives.

Commentators have noted other tensions in the story. These may be further evidence of different stages in the growth of the text. For example, the references to an ambush of one size in v. 3 and one of another size in v. 12 remain confusing. Still, since the main lines of the narrative action are fairly clear, smaller tensions like the one just mentioned only produce a blurring of the sort discussed above.

Concluding Remarks on the Stories in Joshua. In this examination of four stories of the conquest narrative of Joshua 1–11, it was seen that each has a reasonably clear structure, at least at the level of action sequences. At the same time, instances of unevenness, tension, and gaps are evident. When one reads these texts concentrating on the fairly clear story lines, many of these discontinuities simply appear to be points in the story where details remain fuzzy. I have described this as a blurring. Minor disturbances of this sort can be virtually ignored or discounted, or even reinterpreted to fit into the story. On the other hand, if one chooses to give some discontinuities weight as features of the text that need to be accounted for, then one may need to read again, paying more attention to the existence of unevenness, tensions, and gaps. Some may be signs or traces of other perspectives which, once brought to attention, can put a different slant on the story being told and yield a richer text.

But I have also spoken of a shimmering. It was noted in Joshua 8 that there appeared to be a juxtaposition of two different perspectives, one focusing on divine action and the other on human action. This was described as a shimmering rather than a blurring effect because the tension seemed to invite the reader to move back and forth between two possible ways of looking at what was happening in the story. The presence of more than one perspective invites readers to engage in the interaction created by the presence of two different perspectives in the one story.

It is also possible to see a shimmering effect at work among the four stories in terms of the way that divine action and human action are set side by side. With regard to divine action, the fall of Jericho and the sin of Achan involve a ritual-like activity implying order, control, and inevitability. This is especially true of the Jericho story, where the fall of the city is announced at the beginning and the capture proceeds in an orderly fashion. In the Achan story, there is some sense of disorder in the abortive attempt on Ai and the sin of Achan itself, but the uncovering of the crime and its remedy move smoothly to a conclusion. With regard to human action, Joshua sends the spies to Jericho without consulting Yahweh. The spies work things out completely on their own, even to the point of promising safety for Rahab and her family. The intermingling of these two may result from combining different traditions, but the result is a textual richness reflecting more than one perspective.

It was also seen that these four stories are linked together by action sequences which begin in one story and finish in another. The rescue of Rahab promised in the story of the spies is effected in Joshua 6. The prohibition regarding banned material pronounced in the Jericho story is transgressed at the beginning of Joshua 7. There is no such link between Joshua 7 and 8, although the first attempt to capture Ai is found in chapter 7.

D. Four Stories of Punishment: Longer and More Complex Examples.

Apart from a few examples like the stories of Gideon and Samson, most of the texts considered so far have been relatively short. In this next section, attention will be more consistently focussed on longer and more complex texts. In these examples, there will be less of an attempt to identify all the sequences; only the most important ones will be noted. I will examine the Garden story (Genesis 2–3), the destruction of Sodom (Genesis 18–19), the flood story (Genesis 6–9), and the story of the spies (Numbers 13–14). The investigation of sequences in each of these texts raises in one way or another the issues of traditional and composite texts discussed in Chapter One. The relationship of the divine and the human in these stories will require less comment, not because there is nothing to be said but because the divine presence is on the whole very strong.

Once again, and especially with these well-known stories, only very selective reference will be made to secondary literature.

1. *The Garden Story (Gen 2:4b–3:24).* As a creation story, this account has generated an immense amount of commentary (for an earlier version of what follows, see Culley, 1980b). Quite apart from the general subject matter, many features of the text have elicited discussion. For one thing, there are a number of tensions in the text, and it is entirely possible that diverse traditions have come together, leaving traces of different perspectives. While there are no clear indications of different sources, some scholars have posited the existence of sources and stages of redaction (e.g., Weimar). From the point of view of sequences, the most striking feature of the Garden story consists in the fact that two sequences, pointing in different directions, run alongside each other: a punishment sequence, in which the couple and the snake do wrong and are punished; and an achievement sequence, in which the woman and the man see an opportunity to gain something, the ability to know good and evil, and seize the opportunity to better themselves. In addition to these sequences, two others can be distinguished: a rescue sequence *(difficulty /escaped)* in 3:22–24, where Yahweh God delivers himself from an awkward situation, and an announcement sequence in 2:4b–24, in which acts of creation are recounted. These four sequences will be discussed in the order just given. Further sequences will be noted, but they are embeddings within or elaborations of these four (for a quite different reading, see Rosenberg).

We may begin, then, with the punishment sequence, since it stands out clearly. Westermann has worked out the structure of the garden narrative in terms of a punishment story (1984:263–64). He identifies two main sections, one having to do with a prohibition that is transgressed and the other concerning the punishment of the transgression. These elements were mentioned in my earlier attempt to identify the action sequences in this story (1980b). In what follows, I will identify the same sequences but modify my description of them somewhat and expand on some issues not fully developed in my earlier study.

In the punishment sequence, the first phase (the *wrong*) is an embedded prohibition sequence. The prohibition is stated in 2:17, warning that fruit from the tree of the knowing of good and evil may not be eaten, although fruit from all the other trees in the garden may. Two trees were mentioned in v. 9, the tree of life in the middle of the garden and the tree of the knowing of good and evil, but the prohibition relates only to the one. Yahweh declares that, if the fruit is eaten, the eater will die. The prohibition is mentioned again in the conversation between the snake and the woman, although with some curious variations. The snake asks the woman whether it is so that Yahweh forbade all the trees of the garden (3:1). The woman replies that the prohibition concerns the tree in the middle of the garden and that they may not eat its fruit or even touch it. If they do, they will die (3:3). With the transgression of the prohibition in 3:6, the wrong is committed. They eat the fruit that was forbidden. Since the woman took fruit from the tree, ate it, and gave some to her husband, both are implicated in the wrong.

The second phase of the punishment sequence (the *punishment*) is elaborated in two ways. First, there is a description of how the wrong comes to light. Yahweh encounters the pair, who admit what they have done. All this is played out in a little scene. Yahweh looks for the man in the garden, and the man becomes aware that he is naked. The conclusion is drawn that the man has eaten from the forbidden tree. He confesses his act and explains that the woman had given it to him. For her part, the woman explains that the serpent deceived her, and so she ate.

The second elaboration involves the declaration of punishment. The punishment for each is pronounced separately, for the woman because she ate (v. 16), and for the man because he listened to his wife (v. 17). The punishment for the woman seems to come into effect immediately, although the particular consequences regarding childbirth will only be felt in the future. The punishment for the man, which will also effect the woman, is that the ground will be cursed. It is not said whether this ground is inside the garden or outside the garden or both. One assumes outside, but the expulsion only comes later in another sequence and is carried out for different reasons. The punishments meted out to the man and the woman do not coincide, however, with the penalty Yahweh had predicted when he announced the prohibition, if instant death was meant. The two did not die when they ate the fruit. Indeed, the snake had assured them that this would not happen, and he was right.

Closely intertwined with this punishment sequence is another punishment sequence concerning the snake. The snake does wrong by persuading the woman to eat the prohibited fruit. No explanation is given for why he approaches the woman with his suggestion (3:1–4). The woman's interpretation of the snake's action, at least as she explains it for Yahweh's benefit, is that the snake deceived her (v. 13). In a way, the snake's action seems to have been a general act of mischief of the sort that villains usually perform in stories, for that is the role that the snake is playing here; and as with most villains, he is punished for his efforts

(vv. 14–15). The snake's role in the larger punishment story is important because he makes possible the breach of the prohibition.

Alongside the main punishment sequence another line of action can be discerned that works in tension with the punishment. Why did the woman decide to eat the fruit? The only insight into the motives of the woman comes in v. 6. The narrator tells us that the woman was attracted to the fruit because it looked good to eat, was attractive to the eyes, and could give insight (or whatever this means precisely). The snake had told her, claiming that God knew this as well, that they would become like God, or gods, in the sense that they would know good and evil (3:5). Indeed, when they eat, their eyes are opened, and they realize that they are naked. One assumes, although it is not made explicit, that this has something to do with knowing good and evil. At the end of the story, the deity notes that the man has become like "one of us" to the extent that he knows good and evil (3:22).

On the basis of the snake's description of the fruit, the woman sees something to be gained, and so she takes a risk that she and the man may obtain it. And so they do. Even though they are punished, they do not lose the remarkable quality they have gained, the kind of knowing only God or the gods possess. I would suggest that this action is akin to an achievement sequence in which something is desired and then acquired. Objects of desire can be obtained by means of deception or simply by heroic effort. Neither is very clearly involved here, although a real risk was entailed in accepting the snake's opinion of what would result rather than the warning uttered by Yahweh God. As it turned out, the snake was right about eating the fruit, but Yahweh God still administered a punishment, as he had warned.

The last section of the garden story (3:22–24) is closely associated with this achievement sequence. The expulsion from the garden has more to do with the successful attempt to achieve the prize of knowing good and evil than the punishment pronounced. Because the man has gained this prize of being like God, or the gods, in that he knows good and evil, he becomes a problem to Yahweh God. That he should now also eat from the tree of life and be able to live forever appears to be unacceptable to Yahweh, who expels the man from the garden to till the soil from which he was taken. This last phrase makes a connection with the punishment announced for the man (v. 19). The episode follows the pattern of a rescue sequence in the sense that a difficulty is perceived by Yahweh from which he escapes or which he manages to avoid.

There remains to discuss only the first part of the story, vv. 2:4b–24. This small section appears to be a creation story. It tells about how the first man, the animals, and the first women came into existence. The earth and sky are simply there at the start. In my *Semeia* article (1980b), I suggested that the movement of this story might be tentatively described in terms of an achievement sequence: Yahweh God set himself a task and then completed it. Now, I would be inclined to construe it, as I did with Genesis 1 above, as an announcement sequence. This may not be the most satisfactory description of the action in this kind of story, but I favor it for the time being. As I argued that Genesis 1 very soon reveals itself as an account of how something came to be, so in Genesis 2 I would suggest that the opening of the story may imply the same thing, although only in an indirect and general way, through what is said in vv. 4b and 5. V. 4b indicates the time of the account: when God made the heavens and the earth. V. 5 indicates the conditions at the beginning of the story: no vegetation, no rain, and no human. All this is enough to suggest what kind of story is being recounted, a story of creation. The specific direction of the action is not made clear, but the creation of a human being will likely be involved.

If we may tentatively take 2:4b–24 as an announcement sequence, then two further sequences can be detected. First, a human is formed and put in a garden, another announcement sequence. The creation of a human being is signaled and then happens, with the human being set in a garden. Here the action takes a different direction. Yahweh God perceives that it is not good for this human to be alone and proposes to fashion a counterpart. This statement includes two issues that invite action. There is a difficulty that needs to be solved (a form of the rescue sequence): the human is alone, and this is not good. There is also a task to be accomplished (an achievement sequence): to make a counterpart. It is not absolutely vital here to make a final decision about all the sequences in Gen 2:4b–24 as long as an adequate account of the action can be given.

What effect do the sequences have on each other in this Genesis account? In the present arrangement in the garden story, the punishment sequence appears to have a dominant role. This is highlighted even more in the context of Genesis 1–11, in which further punishment sequences are present (Cain, the flood story). However, other sequences in the garden story produce significant tensions with the punishment sequence and in doing so may modify its impact. For example, the more the punishment sequence is seen as central to the garden story, the more the creation section (2:4b–24) can be seen as simply a background to or a setting for the punishment sequence, since it sets the stage for the prohibition and subsequent transgression. Nevertheless, because of its subject matter alone the creation story claims attention and retains impact beyond any subordinate role assigned to it in the arrangement of sequences.

The major tension has already been noted. Alongside the punishment sequence, which appears to hold the central position, runs an achievement sequence. Eating the fruit leads to loss of the garden home through the expulsion, but over against this there is the gain of the divine characteristic of knowing good and evil. Which is better, to be in the garden without the knowledge or outside the garden with the knowledge? Part of the problem lies in the fact that the advantage of the knowledge of good and evil is not fully explained. The only immediate effect on the couple is that they can see that they are naked, which troubles them.

The tensions produced by the sequences are heightened by a number of other tensions, or at least lack of clarity, with regard to certain details in the story. These have been widely recognized. There is, for example, the question of the trees. At the beginning of the story two trees are mentioned specifically (2:9) out of all the trees growing in the garden. One of these is prohibited and all others are permitted, leaving it unclear as to whether or not the tree of life is permitted. At the end of the story (3:22) it appears as though the tree of life had not been available up to this point. Through most of the story only one tree plays a role, the one referred to as the tree in the middle of the garden (3:3) or the tree that was prohibited (3:11). There is also a tension between what Yahweh said would happen when the fruit was eaten and what the snake said would happen. Death did not occur, unless the expulsion meant that they were now to be cut off from the tree of life they had been eating all along.

As we have seen before, the presence of tensions in the story, both those engendered by different sequences and those produced by different details, do not necessarily work negatively in the reading the text. One may, of course, seek to identify possible layers of tradition and redactors, as some have done. Or one may stress a certain pattern of coherence, like the punishment sequence, so that tensions fade into the background and are subdued by the focus on one perspective of the story. On the other hand, it may be more fruitful to allow the play of perspectives to reveal different angles and aspects of the text which reading produces.

2. *The Destruction of Sodom (Genesis 18–19)*. These two chapters narrate a series of closely related events: the visit to Abraham, the visit to Sodom,

the rescue of Lot followed by the destruction, and the incident involving Lot and his daughters (for an earlier version of what follows, see Culley, 1978). They are not only related to each other chronologically but also by the fact that some of the participants appear in more than one of these events. What precedes chapter 18 and follows chapter 19 is sufficiently different to set these two chapters apart from their surroundings. Within the chapters, neither the visit to Abraham nor the incident about Lot and his daughters is integral to the destruction of Sodom. Rather, they are related to it with respect to chronology and participants. The loose relationship of these episodes to the main event may be one indication that Genesis 18–19 may consist of material stemming originally from different backgrounds, material that has been brought together without being completely smoothed out. The primary aim here, of course, is not to sort out the different sources, traditions, and stages of development but rather to ask about their relationship in terms of action, specifically action sequences.

A major feature of these chapters is the destruction of Sodom and Gomorrah, and one can discern here the outlines of a punishment sequence, a wrong that calls for a response from Yahweh in the form of a punishment. This sequence, however, will need to be examined more closely. The first part of the sequence, the *wrong*, develops in an unusual way. The first indication of a punishment sequence comes in 18:16–22. The visitors leave Abraham's encampment and reach a place where they can look down on Sodom. They cannot have gone too far since Abraham is still with them in order to see them off. Yahweh has decided to tell Abraham what he is planning. The reason given is Abraham's special role as the forerunner of a great nation, that is, the perspective of the promise which governs the larger Genesis narrative (vv. 18–19). But Yahweh does not pronounce a judgment on Sodom and Gomorrah at that time. He only asserts that the outcry against these cities is great and their sin is grievous that he must investigate in order to establish whether or not things are as bad as they seem. Nothing has been decided at this point. The clear announcement of a punishment does not come until 19:13, when the divine messengers declare that they intend to destroy Sodom because the outcry is great. Thus, the second phase of the punishment sequence, the *punishment*, consists of an embedded announcement sequence: punishment is announced and the actual occurrence is vividly described at a later point (19:24–25).

It is clear that the necessary *wrong* and *punishment* elements of a punishment sequence are present, but there is need to sort out more clearly what is happening in the first phase of the sequence in which the wrong is stated. Unfortunately, no clear account of this can be given. In the first place, the wrong in this story is neither a single action nor the breaking of a specific prohibition but rather a condition in the city that has developed over some period of time. The story does not explain how this condition came about or why. The story simply begins by noting the possibility that such a situation might exist, and, after the investigation by the messengers, it concludes that it does indeed exist, making punishment inevitable.

A suggestion may be offered. The movement in the story works something like a test. If the men go, as the comment of Yahweh to Abraham suggests (18:21), to investigate whether or not Sodom is culpable, then one may assume that the reception they get from the men of Sodom decides the case. Consequently, their visit could be understood as a kind of test. Of course, beyond the general notion that the purpose of the visitation is to determine or confirm whether or not judgment should be passed, there is no explicit mention of a test. Nor is there a specific task or activity set up beforehand that the people of Sodom will be asked to perform or expected to accomplish so that the truth may be known. Nevertheless, the fact that the messengers will go to Sodom incognito may suggest that a test is involved. If so, one can distinguish something like an embedded sequence here: a question is posed about the state of Sodom and Gomorrah (18:21), and the conclusion is drawn that punishment is necessary (19:13). Thus, within this movement from question to answer, a test is posed (by the incognito visit) and failed (by the reception of the men of Sodom).

Another curious feature, with regard to the action of the punishment sequence, is the discussion Yahweh has with Abraham (18:22–33). The discussion amounts to an appeal by Abraham, set out in several stages, that Yahweh adjust the standard to be used in the investigation of Sodom. This lengthy interchange, which Abraham carries on at some apparent risk to himself, finally draws from Yahweh the assertion that he will not bring destruction for the sake of ten righteous men. But this standard is never explicitly applied in the subsequent narrative nor is it mentioned when the punishment is announced (19:13), where it is said only that the outcry was great. What is more, the messengers declare at this time that Yahweh has sent them to destroy the place, as though no test were involved. On the other hand, when the men of the city come to Lot's house to demand that his guests be brought out, it is pointed out that both young and old, the whole group without exception, came. Since all the men of the city appear to be implicated in the action, the conditions agreed to by Yahweh seem to have been met.

The attempt to mitigate the punishment by reducing to a very minimum the number of righteous men needed to save the city recalls appeals to reduce punishment found in other punishment sequences, where punishment is sometimes mitigated (Num 11:1–3, 21:4–9, 12:1–16, and Gen 4:1–16). However, mitigation occurs there when the punishment has taken effect, is in progress, or has already been announced. Thus, while Abraham is successful in his appeal, the discussion appears to be concerned more with the standards to be used in the judgment rather than a mitigation of the punishment.

The discussion between Yahweh and Abraham seems to be designed to comment on the action rather than to form a significant stage in it. Indeed, this suggests that it is a section that has been added to the story at a later stage, as many have suggested (see, e.g., Westermann, 1985: 283–93). Whatever its origin, the dialogue introduces a remarkable dimension into the larger account. On the surface Abraham appears more sensitive than Yahweh about the need to be fair to the righteous. It is Abraham who appeals to Yahweh to act in a civilized manner befitting his role as judge of all the earth. On the one hand, the passage can be taken as a signal to the reader—at least as it stands in the present form of the story—that when Yahweh brings about a terrible destruction, he does so with due respect to concerns of justice. On the other hand, the discussion confines itself to the number of righteous men required to stave off a punishment, and the larger question about the acceptability of destroying a population at all is not raised. It was noted above that some of the punishment stories appear to reflect some uneasiness or evoke questions about the fairness or appropriateness of divine punishments.

The second phase of the punishment sequence, the *punishment*, is relatively straightforward and takes the form of an announcement sequence. The messengers tell Lot that they are going to destroy the place (19:13). This happens (19:24–25).

Very closely related to this main punishment sequence and interwoven with it is a rescue sequence that traces Lot's deliverance from the conflagration. The first phase of the rescue sequence, the *difficulty*, is apparent from the situation. Since Lot is living in Sodom, the announcement of the destruction of Sodom is at the same time a threat to him. The *rescue* element is more complex and moves through a number of stages. First, even before they tell Lot of the impending destruction (19:13), the messengers instruct Lot to leave the city with those near and dear to him

(19:12). Next, at dawn, the messengers urge him on, finally taking Lot, his wife, and his daughters by the hand to get them outside the city (19:17). When Lot's family is warned to flee to the hills, Lot makes a counter-proposal, appealing for permission to go to a nearby city rather than to the hill country. This request is granted with the assurance that the city in question will not be destroyed (vv. 18–21). Finally, once this is settled, Lot is again urged to flee to the city so that the destruction can begin. Thus, the rescue is made possible by a whole series of interventions by the divine messengers through instructions and actions.

In addition to these two central sequences, the punishment of the cities and the rescue of Lot, other movements in the story may be mentioned. One of these is a small rescue sequence in the segment of the story dealing with the arrival of the messengers in Sodom (19:1–11). The two divine messengers arrive and accept Lot's invitation to stay with him. The men of the city make their demand and are rebuffed. They now threaten to treat Lot worse than the visitors, and they proceed to try to break into Lot's house. Lot and his two visitors are now faced with a difficult situation. The visitors, incognito divine messengers, have resources the other participants in the story do not know about. They rescue Lot by striking his adversaries blind. They also rescue themselves, although it is less evident how much they are personally in danger, given who they are and the miraculous powers they possess.

Also woven into the main rescue sequence of Lot is a very brief punishment sequence concerning Lot's wife, and this has already been noted in the preceding chapter. She commits a wrong and is punished. The *wrong* takes the form of a prohibition sequence. In one short clause (v. 17), a prohibition is given that no one should look back. Later, while the destruction is in progress, Lot's wife does. The wrong is done, and the punishment follows immediately. She becomes a pillar of salt (v. 26).

With the destruction of Sodom and the escape of Lot, the intertwined punishment and rescue sequences are at an end. However, almost any story can be continued simply by telling what happened next, and so a further incident follows reporting what happened to Lot and his daughters after their escape from Sodom. The action in this incident is governed by a rescue sequence of the type *difficulty/escaped.* The daughters find themselves in a difficult situation, or so they perceive it. The problem is that they are living in a cave in the hill country with no other men around apart from their father. In order to escape from the difficulty of having no children, they arrive at the novel idea of using their father to meet their needs. Since it does not seem likely that he will respond to a straightforward request, they employ a trick, or deception, and get the old man drunk first. This deception produces the desired results, so that the daughters become pregnant and bear sons, thereby escaping from their difficulty.

The visit to Abraham (18:1–15), too, is not an integral part of the intertwined punishment and rescue sequence concerning Lot and Sodom, although Abraham does play a significant role in the present form of the Lot and Sodom story. Abraham is told about the trouble with Sodom and, as we have seen, he pleads with Yahweh regarding the terms for the destruction. It is also noted, in a brief comment made after the rescue of Lot, that Yahweh arranged for the rescue of Lot because of Abraham. In other words, it is not inappropriate that the men should visit Abraham on their way to investigate Sodom. However, they have something more important to do, something that in the present context of the book of Genesis is far more significant than the destruction of Sodom. Yahweh announces to Abraham that within a short space of time, Sarah will have a son. This is the first part of an announcement sequence. What is announced here, however, does not happen until much later in the Abraham story (Genesis 21). This announcement sequence receives a slight elaboration when Sarah expresses doubt, very reasonable under the circumstances, by laughing to herself. This draws only a mild rebuke and the announcement is reasserted. In this broad picture, the announcement of a son does not stem from this visitation but goes back as far as the promise first given to Abraham in Gen 12:2–3 that implies that Abram will have male descendants. The lack of a son becomes a specific issue at other points in the tradition as well (Genesis 15, 16).

Two additional sequences may be mentioned. Two places suggest— but only suggest—the outlines of a reward sequence. The first is Gen 18:1–15. Three figures appear at Abraham's campsite. He welcomes them and prepares a meal. One of these figures then announces that Sarah will soon have a son. It is only after Sarah's expression of doubt that the narrator identifies the speaker as Yahweh, and then only to the readers. We are not told when Abraham recognizes the true nature of the visitors. Perhaps, recognition comes at the announcement of what amounts to a miracle, the birth of a son, but perhaps not. Because the announcement involves an unusual gift, one looks for some motivation for this. Strictly within the context of vv. 1–18, the act of hospitality to divine messengers travelling incognito can be taken as a good deed deserving of a reward. Commentators have recognized this possibility. With respect to reward sequences, I have already discussed the story of the prophet Elisha, who rewards a woman with the gift of a son because of her hospitality to him over a period of time (2 Kgs 4:8–17). In the case of Abraham and Sarah, however, it must be admitted that there is no explicit indication in the present text of Gen 18:1–15 that the hospitality was viewed as a good deed and the announcement of a son the reward for it. In the larger framework of Genesis, as we have seen, the announcement of a son has an obvious reason. But what function, then, does the act of hospitality have? Does it become background, a setting, for the long awaited announcement of a son? One might view the visit as a kind of test that Abraham passes by offering hospitality, thus clearing the way for the announcement.

A very similar situation appears in Gen 19:1–13. The divine visitors, only two this time, arrive in Sodom, and here Lot provides the hospitality. The similarity between Gen 18:1–8 and Gen 19:1–3 is rather close, extending even to the wording (Culley, 1976b:54–55). It could be argued that one may discern the outline of a reward sequence in 19:1–13. Lot displays hospitality to the divine messengers and, when the destruction of the city becomes certain, they rescue him, his wife, and daughters. However, there is no specific indication that the rescue should be taken as a reward for the hospitality. On the contrary, it is specifically pointed out in v. 29 that Lot was rescued because of Abraham.

Genesis 18 and 19 provide an interesting example of an arrangement of sequences in a text. On the one hand, when considered as a whole, the story flows fairly smoothly. The visitors pass by Abraham's campsite, and Yahweh reveals his intention to investigate the situation in Sodom. Following Abraham's successful appeal, the visitors (without Yahweh) arrive in Sodom. After the nasty incident at Lot's house, punishment is announced and the rescue of Lot is begun. Lot and his daughters are rescued, although his wife is lost, and the destruction comes. The story comes to an end when Lot is tricked into producing sons for his daughters.

On the other hand, when one reads with close attention to details, a number of tensions surface. These have been noted by commentators, and some have been alluded to in the above discussion. It is usually assumed that different traditions have come together in the stories about Lot and that the tensions evidence this diversity. This is not an unreasonable assumption, but whether or not all the tensions attest to different traditions need not be pursued any further here. What is of more interest to this study are the tensions produced in the present text as a result of its composite and traditional character.

A number of tensions within the text simply create a blurring of the story at certain points. That is to say, the disturbance they create is not strong enough to produce a serious disruption in the story. An example of this is the confusion over the identity of the visitors. Since three figures visit Abraham and only two go on to Sodom, it is assumed that the third one is Yahweh. Another small example consists in the fact that Sodom seems to be the only city involved for most of the story, but Gomorrah is introduced at certain points (18:16 and 20).

Set in its present context in the book of Genesis, the story of Genesis 18–19 offers two perspectives. First, the perspective of the wider Abraham tradition emerges in the promise of a son (18:1–15) and even more specifically in connection with Yahweh's disclosure of the Sodom mission to Abraham, where Abraham is described in terms of the promise (18:18–19). It is also noted in 19:29 that Lot is rescued because Yahweh remembered Abraham. This perspective stresses Abraham's role and encourages us to sense that the stories are told mainly because Abraham plays a part in them. But aside from these sections, the action of the main punishment and rescue sequences focuses on the destruction of the city and the rescue of Lot. Within this narrower framework one may discern hints of the reward of a son for hospitality. There is a slight shimmering between broader and narrower perspectives so that some of the incidents can be read in more than one way.

3. *The Flood Story (Genesis 6–9)*. The flood story, another familiar narrative from biblical tradition, has received ample comment. Genesis 6–9 is especially interesting because it is frequently cited as one of the best examples of a biblical narrative in which two distinct versions of a story have been woven together to form a single account. In what follows, the whole problem of the composite nature of this text will not be examined once again. The evidence for the two versions and the characteristics of each has been reviewed many times (e.g., Westermann, 1984; Emerton). I am prepared to accept this view of the text as a combination of two versions and to employ the usual "J" and "P" labels for them. The style and perspective of each version are sufficiently distinct that it is relatively easy to mark off the sections of text that belong to each account, and this can be done largely on the basis of differences in vocabulary and variations in descriptive details. By carefully dismantling the text it is possible to construct two separate versions (e.g., Coats, 1983). But does the existence of these two versions mean we must distinguish and read two texts instead of one? Perhaps the most striking feature of the flood account consists in the fact that a story so obviously composite runs as smoothly

as it does when read as one text. Indeed, there are those who prefer to begin with the text as it is, treating it as one text and concentrating on its coherence before going on at a later stage to identify discontinuities as indications of the prehistory of the text (e.g., Anderson:28–39).

I would attempt to read Genesis 6–9 as a composite text, noting features that suggest coherence and the possibility of reading it as one text, and features of discontinuity that reflect its composite character. My aim will be to look first at the combined text in order to identify action sequences and then from this point of view to note some tensions and differences.

As a story about a spectacular punishment, the flood narrative corresponds broadly to the story of the destruction of Sodom. A punishment for sin comes in the form of a massive destruction, and from this destruction one individual is rescued along with his family. We may anticipate a punishment sequence and a rescue sequence running side by side and interwoven with each other. In tracing these two sequences it will also be important to note how the two sources run parallel at key points in the sequences.

First the punishment sequence. As in the Sodom story, there is no specific wrong committed but rather a general condition of corruption that is completely unacceptable to the deity. A statement to this effect comes right at the beginning (Gen 6:5–13). Both versions seem to be present in this section, since the wrong is stated one way in vv. 5–6 and in another in vv. 11–12. Although the language differs these two statements amount to the same thing. The situation on earth is so that something must be done. Because the wrong that induces the punishment is described succinctly, interest appears to lie much more in the punishment and how it happens. The puzzling section at the beginning of the flood story (6:1–4) may, of course, represent an attempt to provide a reason for the sad state of affairs on the earth.

The second part of the punishment sequence, the *punishment*, comes in the form of an embedded announcement sequence: the punishment is announced and then happens. Announcements of a broad punishment occur twice. First, Yahweh declares that he will wipe humanity from the face of the earth (v. 7). Then, a few verses later, Elohim announces to Noah that an end of humankind has come and that he is going to destroy the earth (v. 13). Just as the two descriptions of the situation on the earth appear to derive from the two versions used, the same seems to be true of the announcements. Nevertheless, apart from differences in vocabulary, the two announcements amount to the same thing. Furthermore, because of their placement in the narrative, they do not stand out as simple duplications. The first announcement (v. 7, J) is spoken by the deity to himself, or to whatever audience may be presumed to be present where he resides. The second announcement (v. 13, P) is a statement made by the deity to Noah. Thus, if one simply follows the action in the present form of the story, the first announcement appears to be a decision taken by the deity, while the second is the communication of this decision to Noah. In fact, the communication of the decision to Noah seems to be presented as the ground or reason for the steps required to rescue Noah. This points in the direction of the rescue sequence, which will be discussed below.

Once the general announcement of destruction has been made, the occurrence of the announced event is then spelled out in specific terms, although, as we have seen, it is closely intertwined with the rescue of Noah. The nature of the destruction is specified in 6:17 (P), where it is indicated that a flood will serve as punishment. Since this is preceded directly by the instructions to build an ark, the coming of the flood appears to function as much as an explanation of why the ark needs to be built, pointing toward the notion of rescue, as a specification of punishment. The instructions about the animals to be taken into the ark follow, emphasizing once again the notion of rescue. In the next chapter, a J section (7:1–5) contains a specific announcement of punishment—rain for forty days and forty nights that will wipe out every living thing (v. 4). This, too, is set in the context of instructions regarding the rescue of Noah.

The embedded announcement sequence, as the second phase of the punishment sequence, reaches a conclusion with the statement that all life on earth has come to an end. This, of course, is preceded by material on the arrival of the flood (7:6, P) that is elaborated in subsequent verses, a mixture of both sources. Finally, the completion of the punishment is described in vv. 21–23, a mixture of P and J. The language of the P tradition notes that all flesh has perished (v. 21), while the language of J indicates that every existing thing has been blotted out (v. 23).

As I noted above, the rescue sequence runs alongside and is intertwined with the punishment sequence. In fact, the rescue sequence seems to capture most of the attention in the story so that the punishment sequence recedes more and more into the background. As early as the description of the bad situation on earth, Noah is introduced as someone who found favor in Yahweh's eyes (6:8, J) and as one who was righteous (v. 9, P). These statements imply that at least one person does not deserve to be destroyed along with the rest of humanity. Since Noah comes under the same threat as other human beings, he and his family need to be rescued. Given the scope of the contemplated punishment, the rescue will have to be rather unusual, to say the least. With Lot, it was just a matter of getting him, along with his family, out of the area of the conflagration. Here, the area of destruction covers the whole earth. Then too, if the world is to be restored to its present state after the destruction, some thought has to be given to the rescue of the animals as well. The scope of the punishment reaches its ultimate limits and creates the problem of ensuring that human and animal life will survive, since this appears to be what the deity wants.

The rescue sequence begins, then, with the indication that there is someone worth saving. Noah is introduced in v. 8 (J) as one who had found favor in the eyes of Yahweh and in v. 9 (P) as righteous and without fault. The first part of the rescue sequence, the *difficulty*, is identical with the announcement of punishment. The coming destruction endangers Noah. The second phase of the rescue sequence, the *rescue*, works itself out through a number of stages. The description of the rescue begins in 6:14 (P; there does not seem to be a parallel to this in J) with the command to build an ark and ends with the description of the drying up of the water (8:13, P and J?) and the emergence of Noah and his family from the ark (8:18, P but not in J).

As elsewhere in the flood story the intermingling of sources creates a text in which a careful reader can discern changes in expression and style with regard to details, for example, the number and kind of animals to be taken on the ark, the way the flood was produced, and the time scheme governing the duration of the flood.

Despite a certain amount of repetition, the stages in the rescue stand out with reasonable clarity. The ark is made. The animals are gathered. Noah, his family, and the animals enter the ark. The ark floats on the water. The water recedes gradually. The ark comes to rest. The earth dries up. Noah, his family, and the animals come out of the ark. The act of rescue is complete. Life can now begin again. Some of these actions are presented as instructions issued by the deity and then followed by Noah. For example, orders are given to construct an ark (6:14–16), to bring animals to the ark (6:18), and to take food (6:21). The completion of these instructions is apparently signaled with the general statement of v. 22, that Noah did everything he was told to do. While one encounters an instruction to enter the ark in 7:1, further instructions about the animals follow in 7:2–3. The action of rescue also ends with an instruction that is obeyed. The deity instructs Noah to leave the ark in 8:16, and it is reported that Noah does this in 8:18.

The story does not come to an end with the conclusion of the rescue sequence but is continued in two ways. First, it is made clear that such a catastrophe will not happen again. J depicts a sacrifice offered by Noah. When Yahweh inhales its odor, he says—apparently to himself rather than Noah—that he will not again disrupt nature and destroy all life. In P God promises to Noah by way of a covenant that life will never again be destroyed by flood, and the sign of the rainbow confirms that promise.

Second, a final episode is added to the flood story (9:18–29). Here we no longer have parallel accounts, only some P genealogical material at the beginning and end of this short section. Just as the story of Lot and Sodom closed with a remarkable incident involving Lot and his daughters, so the story of the flood concludes with an equally remarkable story involving Noah and his sons (9:20–27). This brief incident includes no less than three movements of action, even though they are given in the barest outline. One can distinguish a punishment sequence, a rescue sequence, and a reward sequence. In the punishment sequence, Ham does wrong when he sees his father uncovered in his tent in a drunken state. Upon waking, Noah becomes aware of what Ham has done and curses him with becoming the slave of his brothers. The rescue sequence appears in the form of an escape from a difficult situation. With the father lying in an uncovered state in his tent (a difficult situation), Shem and Japheth are able to find a way of placing a garment over Noah without looking at his uncovered condition (an escape). This good deed earns them a favorable mention, in contrast to the curse laid upon Ham.

The flood story stands, then, as a truly remarkable text. It has been produced by combining two distinct yet very similar versions, although we can only guess as to how and why this was done. On the one hand, the two versions can be identified to a remarkable degree and even reconstructed as separate texts. (Even so, the result does not yield complete versions, at least not for J, and the process of division is not without problems.) On the other hand, the combined narrative has been and can be read through as though it were a single story. This can hardly be achieved without some sense of disturbance in the text at the level of style and the details in the story. What helps hold the story together is the fact that the two versions follow each other so closely at the level of action sequences.

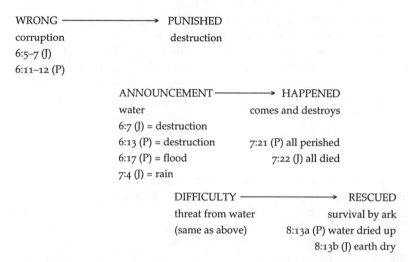

WRONG ─────────────────→ PUNISHED
corruption   destruction
6:5–7 (J)
6:11–12 (P)

    ANNOUNCEMENT ─────────→ HAPPENED
    water   comes and destroys
    6:7 (J) = destruction
    6:13 (P) = destruction   7:21 (P) all perished
    6:17 (P) = flood   7:22 (J) all died
    7:4 (J) = rain

        DIFFICULTY ─────────────→ RESCUED
        threat from water   survival by ark
        (same as above)   8:13a (P) water dried up
                    8:13b (J) earth dry

These sequences summarize the movement of the action in the story. As we have noted in the preceding paragraphs, the two versions provide comments at the critical points in the action, especially the beginnings and endings of sequences, as may be seen from the above chart. At these key points in the action, the same things are being said, although in different words, and so there do not appear to be significant disjunctions in the general movement of the narrative when the text is read straight through. In other words, the composite nature of the text is not especially signaled by tension between action sequences. In this respect the two versions are the same, having been carefully combined.

This kind of composite text leaves certain options open to readers. First, one may conclude that the impression of two versions is so strong that one cannot treat the text as a unity (Coats, 1983:75). Or one may simply wish to separate the two versions out and read them separately. This tactic certainly has its advantages. One may, for example, carry out a close reading on the Priestly version alone as in McEvenue. Of necessity, in this kind of stylistic study the difference between the sources is stressed in order to highlight the distinctive characteristics of each. In deciding to treat the versions separately, one may assume that reading the combined text does not produce much of significance: the whole is not greater than the parts. Thus, to read them separately and compare them may be deemed more productive than trying to read the combined text. This decision implies that the attempt to combine the versions did not work very well.

On the other hand, one might conclude that the sense of unity provided by the narrative action is sufficiently strong that one can read the text as a single story in spite of tensions created by the fact that two versions have been combined. In reading, concentration on the coherence of the text fosters an inclination to overlook tensions or play down their effect by ignoring or interpreting them in a way that integrates rather than contrasts. This may mean simply accepting a blurring in the text at several points, say, on the matter of the number of animals taken or the different time schemes. Or it could mean making connections that support the unity of the text rather than those that would pull it apart. For example, the story opens with two descriptions of the situation on earth, 6:5–8 from one tradition (J) and 6:9–12 from the other (P). Since repetition is a common feature in literature, an attempt to read the story as it stands would naturally lead one to read the two versions of the situation on earth as repetition functioning within the story to emphasize, reinforce, or add further dimensions to the depicted situation.

Now, is a third way of reading possible? It was suggested earlier in the discussion of the conquest stories that it might be fruitful to take account of a shimmering between different perspectives in texts. With regard to the flood account, this would mean following the story line, which gives substantial coherence to the text, while at the same time taking cognizance of the two distinct narrative voices alternating in the text, trying to give weight both to the perception of one story and one text as well as to the presence of two versions and trying to move back and forth between these two perceptions in the course of reading. The proposal seems simple, but many may find the procedure too unnatural to tolerate. The flood story represents something of a special case in that the combined versions match each other so closely. Yet I am not convinced that one is unable in the course of reading to keep track of both coherence and difference. A shimmering between two perspectives is, as we have seen, a feature of other stories in biblical narrative, and in the flood story two distinct voices do alternate and echo each other.

What is the effect of trying to read the text as a composite? It may create distance. In texts where a single narrative voice presents a fairly unified and coherent picture, readers are invited to accept this perspective and integrate all the material within the story. If two perspectives emerge and claim attention, then, one would accept each voice only tentatively and understand it always in the light of the other. In a sense one needs to stand at a certain distance from the text in order to observe what is happening. At the same time, however, this act of observing intensifies engagement with the text as one attempts to grasp its complexity.

4. *The Story of the Spies (Numbers 13–14).* This is another narrative that, like the flood story, contains striking evidence that different versions have been combined to form the present text. Long ago, S. R. Driver (62) argued that this story is made up of two accounts (J and P) both of which are almost complete. The identification of J and P has been fairly uniform from Driver's *Introduction* to Noth's *Pentateuchal Traditions.* Division into sources is usually based on the identification of doublets (e.g., 13:21 and 13:22–24, or 13:27,29 and 13:32,33). Differences in detail have also been noted. For example, one tradition (P) seems to have the spies sent to investigate the whole country (13:2). The other tradition (J) appears to have only Hebron in mind (13:22). There is no need to pursue the details of source analysis beyond this basic recognition of possible tensions in the text that may reflect the presence of different perspectives. In spite of the kinds of tensions pointed out by source analysis, the story seems to flow reasonably well from beginning to end. Accordingly, it should be possible to identify the action sequences that are functioning in this composite text.

Numbers 13–14 tells about a punishment and it is a punishment sequence that stands out as the principal movement in the action. The people do wrong when they refuse to proceed with the conquest of the land, and they are punished. Their punishment will be that the adults of the current generation will not be allowed to enter the promised land, so that the people must stay in the wilderness until the generation that refuses to invade the land dies off. The account of the spies and their subsequent report is built into the basic punishment sequence. The divided opinion of the spies places a choice before the people. When faced with two conflicting reports, they accept the view of the majority of the spies and reject the opinion of the minority. A wrong is committed. The mission of the spies is itself governed by an action sequence—an achievement sequence in which a task is assigned and accomplished. There is, however, little elaboration of this journey to spy the land. The emphasis lies not so much on the accomplishment of a difficult task as on the divided report given at the end, which, from the point of view of narrative action, presents an occasion to do wrong. When it comes to punishment, the spies who give a bad report are set apart and condemned to death by a plague.

The incident at the end of chapter 14, the subsequent attempt to take the land, forms a separate action that adds a further step to the punish-

ment sequence. The event is recounted briefly, and the action is not easily described in terms of sequences. The people belatedly conclude that
they were wrong to reject the proposal to take the land, and so they set
themselves the task of doing so. Moses declares that the project will not
succeed (*announcement*), and it does indeed fail (*happens*). This announcement sequence seems to be the most important one in the episode.
Failure is clearly what Yahweh wants and gets. Understood in this way,
the incident functions as a kind of affirmation of the punishment
sequence.

Thus, if the text is read straight through, the main movement of the
action from the opening situation about the spies to the failed invasion at
the end stands out clearly and runs fairly smoothly without significant
dislocations. This helps create the impression of a single story. Under the
influence of this sense of coherence, readers may be inclined to read
ambiguous or conflicting details in such a way that the ambiguity or
conflict is reduced as much as possible. For example, the section about
the mission of the spies (chap. 13) contains some repetitions that have
been taken as indications of different sources. The verb "they went up"
appears at the beginning of v. 21 and is repeated at the beginning of v.
22, and each of these occurrences of the verb is followed by a different
statement about what the spies did. The first (v. 21) says that they
explored the land from the wilderness of Sin to Rehov. The second (v. 22)
says that they entered the Negev as far as Hebron. The contrasting
details of these two statements may well suggest distinct sources, each
showing a different perception of the extent of the mission of the spies.
Yet, the relationship between these two statements can be understood in
a way that will be less disturbing: a general statement (the whole land as
a goal of the mission) followed by a more specific statement (Hebron as
the only place specifically discussed). Perhaps this is the way they were
understood when the composite text was produced.

Another example of repetition comes at the point in the text where the
return of the spies is described (13:27). They report that the land is
attractive but its inhabitants intimidating. Caleb exhorts the people to
proceed and assures them that they will be successful (v. 30). The rest of
the spies (Joshua is not mentioned here) declare that the Israelites will
not be able to succeed because the people of the land are too strong (v.
31). In the next verse, however, it is recounted that the men submit a bad
report about the land, claiming that it eats its inhabitants (whatever this
means precisely). Thus, this section (vv. 27–32) has been taken by source
critics to reflect two different reports from two different sources: one

expressing the fear of the inhabitants of the land and the other apparently expressing a negative attitude toward the land itself. However, the second is sufficiently ambiguous that it could be understood as a reiteration of the first, simply expressing in a more forceful way the fear of the inhabitants. Or, if the second is perceived as much stronger, it could be understood as an escalation in the argument of the spies revealing a much deeper objection than they first suggested.

For chapter 13, at any rate, a reader has three choices. One is to deliberately seek clues to sources. Significant tensions will be explained plausibly in terms of different sources or traditions, glosses, and so on. On the other hand, if one seeks to read the chapter as a coherent story and follow the movement of the action in the narrative, anticipating a reasonably harmonious account, then one will interpret the textual tensions in relation to one another, for example, as repetitions that add further information that in turn adds emphasis, reinforcement, or intensity. A third approach is to try to read the story as a composite text, as I have just done with the flood story. I will return to this approach below.

Chapter 14 begins with the response of the people. They complain bitterly in the familiar words of the so-called "murmuring tradition" (Coats, 1968) and propose a return to Egypt under a new leader, if that is what v. 4 means. When Joshua and Caleb speak against this negative attitude of the people and urge that they not be afraid, the people prepare to stone them. Once the refusal has been uttered, Yahweh speaks to Moses and begins to denounce it as an act of rejection and unbelief, making clear that the action is viewed as a wrong deserving of punishment. The people's refusal, then, constitutes the first part, or the *wrong*, of a punishment sequence, and we anticipate that a punishment will follow.

Indeed, a punishment is announced; but it is a punishment that will take place over a lengthy period of time. The announcement of punishment contains a significant elaboration (14:11–38), and so it merits closer attention. The first part of this lengthy section (vv. 11–25) consists of three related speeches (Yahweh, Moses, Yahweh). First, Yahweh announces a punishment. He will strike the people with pestilence, disinherit them, and then start over again with Moses by making him into a great people (v. 12). In his response, Moses makes an appeal against the punishment with a remarkable argument. Yahweh, he urges, will look bad in the eyes of other nations who will interpret his action to mean that he is unable to do what he says. Moses then issues a direct appeal to Yahweh to pardon the people. In reply, Yahweh agrees to pardon the people, but only to the extent that the punishment will be reduced.

Instead of destroying the entire people, only the present generation will be affected. They will not see the promised land (vv. 22–23). This element of mitigation is found as an elaboration in a number of punishment sequences. Even though some commentators have taken these verses (11–25) as a gloss on the J tradition (Coats, 1968), the elaboration of the announcement of the punishment by means of a mitigation fits very well into the movement of the narrative, at least at the level of action sequences. Only one exception is made to this punishment in this section of the narrative: Caleb will survive.

The second part of this section (vv. 26–38) consists, apart from the last two verses, of a long speech of Yahweh. The main theme here is the same as that in the foregoing section (vv. 11–25): announcement of the punishment. As in the previous section, these verses begin with a declaration of wrong by means of a question. Here the question concerns complaining (the so-called murmuring motif). The punishment announced is essentially the same as the one stated in vv. 11–25: the present generation will die in the wilderness. At the end of Yahweh's speech, a comment notes that the men who brought a bad report about the land die by a plague, as though their punishment is immediate, but that Joshua and Caleb do not suffer this fate.

As far as sources are concerned, both Noth and Coats take vv. 26–38 as P and vv. 11–25 as a gloss to J, or largely so (Noth, 1968:108–10; Coats, 1968:138–39), and there does seem to be evidence of two different narrators. However, as I indicated above, someone reading the story straight through would certainly notice that there are two pronouncements of punishment but would likely read the second as a reiteration of the first using different wording. The first section (vv. 11–25) is a discussion between Yahweh and Moses, almost a private discussion in which Yahweh can make proposals and speak more candidly, perhaps, than in a formal announcement. Moses is also free to raise objections, and indeed to do so with such persuasiveness that he makes his opinion count. The second section (vv. 26–38) shows Yahweh in a more formal role. He addresses Moses and Aaron, raises the problem of the complaints, and makes a formal announcement of punishment, which Moses (presumably, the verb is singular) is to announce to the people. The announcement comes in the form of an oath accompanied by the phrase "the speech or declaration of Yahweh" (v. 28), a phrase most frequently found in prophetic texts.

Even if one reads this section on the announcement of the punishment so that its two parts represent different stages, the sense of tension between them is not completely dispelled, not even sufficiently to be ignored. The fact that Caleb alone escapes punishment in the first section, while both Joshua and Caleb escape in the second may be a small discrepancy. But because it is the most visible indicator of textual tension, it invites the reader's attention to a number of less obvious yet more significant tensions between the two pronouncements of punishment. The fact that each of the two sections begins with a question that identifies or states the act of wrongdoing leads one to think along the lines of parallel rather than consecutive repetitions, especially since the wrong is identified in different terms in each case. In the first part, Yahweh declares that the people have rejected and do not believe in him, while in the second Yahweh states that complaining or murmuring is the problem. The latter explanation harks back to and resumes the language of complaint in the text at the beginning of chapter 14.

As I have already indicated, the tone of each of these two parts is quite different. On the one hand, the discussion with Moses leads to a kind of compromise punishment. On the other, the formal oath (like a prophetic oracle that announces punishment) elaborates the punishment very carefully. Here, it is not the result of compromise or debate. The punishment matches the crime: the children, whom the people in their complaining had argued would become booty, will be the ones to possess the land. The punishment will last forty years, just as the journey of the spies lasted forty days. I have already noted the two perceptions of Yahweh that emerge. There is the Yahweh who is apt to fly off the handle but can be brought around by a wise and perceptive Moses, who realizes what is at stake, advising against Yahweh's proposal even though he personally stands to gain by it. Then there is the Yahweh who solemnly announces punishments that are carefully worked out to fit the crime.

The more one allows oneself to become aware of two different perceptions juxtaposed at this point in the story when the punishment is declared, the more one may become more sensitive to differences elsewhere in the story. In the discussion above, a number of narrative tensions were noted, but in each case it was possible to view them in ways that lessened the tension. At this stage in the story, the rather sharp tension just described cannot be easily reduced. Therefore, we are encouraged to reconsider the earlier sections with a view to taking account of the tensions anew. We have noted, for example, the contrast between the broad scope of the whole land as the object of the spying expedition as opposed to the visit to Hebron and its environs only. Then too, there is the tension in the spies report between fear of the inhabitants and some deeper rejection of the land itself. Also, at the point where the wrong is committed, if fine distinctions are to be made, two perceptions may be present: a strenuous complaining that rejects the option of new land in favor of remaining in Egypt, set alongside a frank rebellion that rejects Yahweh and actually plans to return, under new management, to Egypt.

A rather unusual movement has been traced in my discussion of Numbers 13 and 14: the reader is pulled in different directions. I began by noting that source critics had fairly consistently agreed upon the presence of two sources in the text as though two stories had been woven into it. Then, I suggested that the movement of the narrative followed a punishment sequence (wrong/punished) that stands out clearly and consistently, moving from beginning to end with no serious dislocations, inviting the perception of a single story. Since, however, a doubling up at a critical point could not be suppressed, I have suggested that this beckons a reader to reconsider textual differences.

As a whole, then, the text of Numbers 13–14 may lead a reader in two directions: toward a recognition of the unity and integration of its diverse elements or toward the recognition of tension and diversity. Critics may lean in either direction, following the lines of force that pull the text apart. One may decide that the two traditions, J and P, be dealt with separately. McEvenue, for example, has read Numbers 13 and 14 in this way by isolating the P strand, just as he did with the Priestly version of the flood story. As I noted in connection with the flood story, this tactic makes sense for some kinds of literary readings, since working with only one source permits individual style to be given more weight. The disadvantage remains that the text that is produced by joining the two traditions and the new relationships that are created by intertwining them may rest unexplored. One may follow therefore the pull toward unity and treat Numbers 13–14 as a textual whole, seeking to bring all of its parts into a meaningful relationship as though it were the product of a single author (Robertson:6; cf. the notion of implied author invoked by Polzin, 1980:18). The advantage of this strategy is that it recognizes that the text can be read as one without major obstacles. The disadvantage is that such a reading may lessen some of the conflicting tensions in the text.

In connection with the flood story, I have already discussed how a composite text might be read. Such a reading would have to recognize the coherence that obtains in the composite text as well as the different perspectives that become apparent upon careful reading. The trouble is, as I have noted, that an attempt to read a composite text by giving weight to both lines of coherence and lines of tension may result in a rather unsettling mode of reading. In Numbers 13–14, at the point of the announcement of the punishment, the reader must be ready to shift gears, adjusting at one point to the dynamic of a debate between Yahweh and Moses about what kind of punishment should be assessed and at another point to the more static solemnity of style of the pronouncement that follows. As a character, Yahweh shifts from one who is ready to shoot from the hip and needs to be calmed on the one hand to a more controlled pronouncer of judgment in which the punishment fits the crime on the other. This sort of shift in perspective links up with other tensions in the story, such as the contrast between the journey of the spies to Hebron alone and the exploration of the whole land.

Numbers 13–14 tells one story but allows two versions to have their say. The presence of two perspectives does not reduce the coherence of the one story being told to the extent that the text breaks apart. Nor does one version dominate the other. Since, however, the two perceptions challenge one another, the reader cannot become fully drawn into either; one must stand back somewhat and try to observe what is happening within the tension. The distance does not mean less involvement in the text, but it is necessary in order to engage the complexity of the text more fully.

E. Sequences in Longer Texts: Joseph and the Exodus

This final section will examine sequences in two longer texts: the Exodus account (Exodus 1–14) and the Joseph story (Genesis 37–50). Both of these texts are well known and have been the subject of intense investigation and commentary. Once again, since my interest in these texts is limited to the question of sequences, I will not try to deal with all of the many important issues raised by these texts or discussed by the commentators. The primary aim of this section will be to examine narrative sequences in longer texts, although, as in previous sections, such matters as tensions in the texts and the role of divine and human action of these stories will be kept in mind. These two stories are particularly interesting because of the different ways divine and human action are portrayed in each. The explicit presence of the divine is quite limited in the action of the Joseph story but strikingly present in the Exodus account.

1. *The Exodus Account (Exodus 1–14)*. The story of the exodus is particularly complex because different sources and traditions have apparently been brought together in these chapters. As with previous

texts, I have no trouble accepting for purposes of discussion the traditional division into sources, especially where there seems to be a fair amount of agreement (Driver; Noth, 1972; Childs, 1974). In the following discussion, it will not be necessary to establish an exact source analysis. The text will be read as it stands, but as a text that is traditional and composite. Accordingly, tensions will be noted where relevant, usually when there is a blending of different perspectives. Identification of the sequences will provide the starting point. Since the story of the exodus recounts the rescue of the people of Israel from captivity in Egypt, the main sequence governing the story as a whole is a rescue sequence, as one would expect. Analysis will concentrate on this major sequence, although clearly a text as long as this will contain many smaller sequences that could be noted in a more detailed investigation.

The difficult situation that introduces the rescue sequence emerges in Exodus 1, although the matter is not as straightforward as would appear at first glance. The people of Israel have become numerous, which alarms a new pharaoh who did not know Joseph. An attitude of hostility and suspicion, heretofore not evident, arises on the part of the Egyptians so that the new pharaoh decides to gain control of the situation by submitting the Israelites to forced labor. While this measure might succeed in reducing the political danger of an unmanageable foreign population, it is not clear how forced labor would deal with the birth rate. Nor does it; and so, another measure is introduced. Pharaoh orders the Hebrew midwives to kill all male children at birth. This step does not succeed either because the midwives refuse to follow instructions. Finally, Pharaoh orders all his people to kill all males born to the Israelites by throwing them in the Nile. The extent to which this succeeds is not reported. The danger to newly born males is still present in Exodus 2, where the story of the birth of Moses assumes that the child faces certain death; a trick must be used so that he may escape this fate.

On the face of it, one might assume that the difficulty that the Israelites would feel most keenly and which would be at the center of their complaint must be the genocide. But, while this notion is a necessary assumption for the story of the birth of Moses, it is not mentioned again beyond Exodus 2. It is the hard labor that attracts Moses' attention when he grows up (v. 11), and it is the hard labor about which the Israelites complain in their cry to Yahweh (v. 23). Furthermore, it is the hard labor that Yahweh mentions when he appears to Moses (3:7). As a consequence, the hard labor must be identified as the difficult situation that preoccupies the narrator for the rest of the story. The genocide remains part of the story, but its early disappearance from the narrative is unexplained. Logically, a systematic massacre of all male children should become the central crisis in view of the implications of this policy for the future of the people. The presence of both hard labor and geno-cide seems to be one of the many tensions produced by the composite nature of the text.

There is another dimension to the difficult situation of the Israelites, although it lies in the background. Exod 1:8 notes that the new pharaoh did not know Joseph. This comment links the story about Moses and the escape from Egypt to the story of Joseph quite explicitly and indicates that the exodus story should be read in the context of the broad narrative about Israel that begins with the Patriarchs. From this perspective, the general issue of the promise to the patriarchs about the land stands, by implication at least, behind the specific difficulty of captive labor in Egypt. How can the promise be fulfilled if the people remain captive in Egypt? While this issue does not emerge directly as a major preoccupa-tion of the exodus narrative, it does surface from time to time. When Yahweh speaks to Moses in the wilderness (3:6), he introduces himself as the God of Abraham, Isaac, and Jacob. Furthermore, he announces that he has come to rescue Israel and take them to a good land. Thus to the extent that the story of the exodus is read in the context of the larger nar-rative about Israel, the situation of the people in Egypt may be seen as a difficulty that Yahweh must overcome in order to carry out his promise.

Once the difficult situation has been expressed in chapter 1, the rescue sequence has begun, and the rest of the story deals with the rescue itself. As we have seen in previous examples, it is not unusual for a rescue sequence to contain an explicit appeal for help that alerts the potential rescuer to a need requiring attention. An appeal is found in 2:23–25, where it is reported that the people cried out because of their labor and that God heard their groaning and remembered the covenant with the fathers. This section is usually and reasonably taken to belong to P on the grounds of vocabulary and content. In terms of rescue sequences, it is quite appropriate to have an official appeal for help at this point in the action. In the present version of the story, however, the birth of Moses already appears to be a first step in Yahweh's response to the crisis even before any appeal is made. We will return to this problem in a moment.

Following the appeal for help (2:23–25), Yahweh meets Moses at the burning bush. Introducing himself as the God of the Fathers, Yahweh declares that he has come down to rescue his people from Egypt and to bring them up to a rich and fertile land (3:8). This declaration identifies two goals: the intention to rescue and the intention to lead the people to new land. The first declared aim is achieved in Exodus 13 and 14, where the rescue from Egypt is recounted. The second does not happen until later in the biblical narrative tradition when the conquest is narrated in the book of Joshua. Since both these declarations of intention come from a deity, they are something like the beginnings of announcement sequences in that they point ahead to a fulfillment. One could conceivably treat them as such; but, having noted this possibility, I will not pursue the matter further.

In appearing to Moses, Yahweh has already taken the first step in the rescue: the selection of an agent to act on his behalf. A rescue sequence often involves the selection of a person to act as agent for the deity, as may be seen in the stories of the judges, where, for example, Yahweh chooses Gideon to save the people from the Midianites. In the exodus story, 3:1–4:17 are devoted to this kind of selection. Yahweh meets Moses and sets him a task. He is to go take the people out of Egypt (3:10). This forms an achievement sequence (*task/accomplished*). Yahweh will accomplish his intention to rescue Israel through his agent Moses.

But, as I have already noted, long before the dramatic appearance to Moses, the rescue had been quietly set in motion. The early story of Moses from birth to marriage (2:1–22) is very much part of the selection of Yahweh's agent. This phase of the story, however, proceeds without any divine intervention or even any comment by the narrator that Yahweh is working behind the scenes. This absence of divine intrusion stands in sharp contrast to Yahweh's encounter with Moses in the wilderness, and indeed in most of the Exodus account, where divine intervention is unmistakable and prominent. While nothing is said about Yahweh's presence in the life of Moses before the appearance at the burning bush, one may assume it on the basis of Yahweh's continuous presence in the rest of the story.

Once Moses has been selected as agent and the intention of rescue declared, one expects to learn more about how Yahweh plans to carry it out. What are the specific instructions for the task? The action becomes rather complex at this point because a number of announcements and instructions are issued. I will limit myself to enumerating a few salient features.

(1) The journey for three days. Instructions are given to Moses to go with the elders to Pharaoh and ask permission to make a three-day journey into the wilderness in order to sacrifice to Yahweh (3:18). This appears to be a deceptive ploy to enable the Israelites to escape. The

request implies that Pharaoh might be prepared to allow the people to go for three days, if they were planning to return, whereas under no circumstances would he allow them to leave for good. A deception is often used in stories where the person trying to gain something is weak and does not possess the power to obtain what is needed in any other way. Deception often functions in stories where little or no explicit divine intervention occurs, as for example in the story of Ehud (Judges 3) or Tamar (Genesis 38). In such stories the action usually operates at the human level. Here in Exodus the pretense of leaving the country to worship Yahweh in the wilderness continues throughout the plague narratives; it is explicitly mentioned in most of them, as though permission to go on a three-day journey remains a serious issue in these confrontations. When the people are finally given permission to leave, it is less clear what role the deception plays in enabling them to escape, even though Pharaoh still seems to be under the impression that he is allowing the people to go to worship Yahweh as they had requested (12:31). One might deduce that the deception is implemented and successful, except that it is only part of what goes on to secure the rescue.

(2) The use of force by means of the plagues. Alongside the strategy of a three-day journey, another course of action can be distinguished. Directly following the instruction about the deception (3:18), the deity concludes that Pharaoh will not grant permission unless he is forced (3:19–20). Yahweh then declares that he will strike him with all his miracles, after which Pharaoh will allow the people to go. The use of force becomes a central element in the proceedings. This suggests a contest between two powerful individuals in which increasing force must be used by one in order to compel the other to acquiesce. Indeed, ten plagues are introduced, and it is only the last that produces the desired result. The appearance of a contest of power is strongest at the beginning of the plagues, when Pharaoh's magicians match the miracles performed by Moses. Power is pitted against power. After the magicians drop out of the picture, the struggle shifts to a contest of wills in which escalating force is used against Pharaoh, whose only weapon is stubborn refusal.

(3) The hardening of Pharaoh's heart. In Exod 4:21 another important announcement is made relating to how the rescue will occur. Moses is told that, when he goes to Pharaoh and performs all the signs given him, Yahweh will harden Pharaoh's heart so that he will not send the people out. This is only the first of several references to Yahweh's hardening Pharaoh's heart, all of which adds further complexity to the rescue. According to this view of what is happening, Pharaoh is simply and

purely a victim of a much greater power. The rescue will occur when Yahweh wishes and how Yahweh wishes. Pharaoh is in no position to influence the outcome one way or another. In 4:22–23, directly following the statement about hardening Pharaoh's heart, Yahweh declares that, because Pharaoh has refused to let Yahweh's first-born go, Yahweh will kill the first-born of Pharaoh. Pharaoh is held responsible for his refusal even though he has no choice but to refuse.

These three salient strands form a remarkable combination as they run side by side through the narrative. They imply different strategies in the process of the rescue: a deception at the human level, a contest of power or wills involving divine intervention that mixes the divine and human, and the use of divine power on a human victim who is rendered totally helpless. While these views appear to be alternate perceptions of how the rescue will take place, the present narrative simply interweaves them. It will be important to trace these strands in more detail through the rest of the story.

Exodus 5 depicts the first confrontation with Pharaoh. The deception does not work, and, as a result, the people find themselves worse off, as Pharoah makes their work even more difficult. The people reproach Moses who in turn reproaches Yahweh (5:21–23). The reproach may add another layer to the rescue story, and I only make this as a suggestion. It may imply that another difficult situation has been introduced, this time a difficulty for Yahweh. Both Moses and the people have now reproached him for not rescuing them as he said he would, along with the added problem that the situation has become worse for the people and Moses. A reason for suggesting that this reproach to Yahweh may function as a difficulty may be found in the fact that, at the end of the story (14:31), it is remarked that the people believed in Yahweh and in Moses his servant. I have discussed a similar situation in example 3(c) of Chapter Two above, the story of Elijah and the sick boy (1 Kgs 17:17–24). If my suggestion about Exodus 5 is correct, a fourth strand may be functioning within the rescue involving Yahweh's need to vindicate himself after his apparent failure. I will let this remain a suggestion.

Just a brief comment on 6:1–7:14, which is commonly assigned to P by critics and may be a variant of the selection story in chaps. 3–4. As it stands now, however, it restates a number of issues already introduced into the story. Because this section follows the first encounter of Moses with Pharaoh and its unfortunate outcome, in the present form of the story the repetition serves to reaffirm what Yahweh plans to do. Yahweh announces that he will take the people out and instructs Moses to pass on his words to Pharaoh. With regard to the means by which rescue is to be accomplished, which have already been introduced into the story, it is interesting to note that deception is not mentioned, but Yahweh's plan to harden Pharaoh's heart is.

The description of the first nine plagues runs from 7:14 to the end of chap. 10, over three and a half chapters (see Van Seters, 1986 for a discussion of origin and nature). Here, I only wish to identify more specifically the strands just identified, since they can be traced through the plague stories. The deception remains an issue, as shown by the negotiations surrounding the eighth and ninth plagues. Even at the time of the eighth plague (locusts), a discussion takes place as to whether or not the children need to go, and Moses claims all must go for the festival (10:9). In the same chapter but in connection with the ninth plague (darkness) Pharaoh offers to allow the people to go but insists that the animals must stay. Moses counters that they are needed for sacrifices.

The use of divine force to bend Pharaoh's will is evident in the relentless application of the plagues. The hardening of Pharaoh's heart is mentioned frequently. Sometimes it is said that Pharaoh hardens his own heart (8:15), as though he were stubbornly resisting the displays of divine power. Yet at other times it is said that Yahweh hardens Pharaoh's heart (9:12), as though Yahweh wished to manipulate the king's reaction to the plagues, and indeed a reason is given for this. In 9:16 it is noted that Pharaoh is allowed to survive so that he might see Yahweh's strength and, more importantly, so that Yahweh's name might be recounted in all the land (or all the earth). A similar comment in 10:1–2 indicates that Yahweh hardens Pharaoh's heart in order that, having seen remarkable signs (the plagues), the people would recount these happenings to future generations. Here, the signs are directed toward the people of Israel.

The last plague merits closer attention. Exod 11:1 introduces the plague and takes the form of an announcement sequence (*announcement /happened*). The announcement declares that Yahweh will bring this last plague on Pharaoh, who will then send the people out. Another announcement follows and states more precisely how this will happen (vv. 4–8): the first born of the Egyptians will die, and the Egyptians will send the people of Israel on their way. When Moses has made this announcement to Pharaoh and has instructed the people to make their preparations, his task has virtually come to an end, and with it the achievement sequence started in (3:18). All the strategies (the deception, the application of force to Pharaoh, and the hardening of his heart) have come into play. The next chapter reports that the announced events happen (12:29–32), thus completing the announcement sequence begun in 11:1. The Egyptians give permission for all the people to go to serve Yahweh. In fact, the Egyptians are in such a state of fear that they press the Israelites to be on their way.

The main rescue sequence has now been completed. The original difficulty, the forced labor in Egypt, has been resolved, and the people have been rescued. But the story continues for one further episode.

The story of the miracle at the sea (13:17–14:31) has a curious structure with respect to narrative sequences. Two major sequences run side by side and become intertwined. I will support this suggestion by identifying what I think are the main outlines of the two sequences. This section of text is a complicated one in which source critics have found J and P as well as some E. Certainly the kinds of tensions we find in the text suggest that different traditions have come together. One may cite here the famous example of the waters of the sea in 14:21. Within this one verse, the waters are pictured on the one hand as being split instantaneously at a single point in time and on the other hand as being blown away by a wind during the night, a period of several hours. In addition, the panic of the Egyptians in the camp (14:24) is also a puzzling element in the action.

Once the people are on their way (13:17), the narrator reports that God leads them around by the sea in order to avoid the territory of the Philistines lest they become afraid at the prospect of battle and return to Egypt. It is also pointed out that they are led by the pillar of cloud by day and the pillar of fire by night.

Exodus 14 opens with a speech of Yahweh containing an instruction and an announcement. First, the people are instructed to return and camp by the sea. This is done, it is explained, in order that Pharaoh will think that the people are trapped in the wilderness. Then Yahweh announces that he will harden Pharaoh's heart so that he will pursue the Israelites. By means of this, Yahweh will triumph gloriously over Pharaoh, and Egypt will know "that I am Yahweh" (14:4). From these verses it appears that the story about the miracle at the sea is governed by an announcement sequence (*announcement/happened*): Yahweh declares that he will gain glory over Pharaoh, and he accomplishes this in two stages, hardening Pharaoh's heart so that he pursues Israel and then opening and closing the waters.

ANNOUNCEMENT ⟶		HAPPENED
harden heart		hardens heart to pursue (v. 8)
gain glory	opens waters	closes waters
(v. 4)	(v.21)	(vv. 27–28)

Yahweh has decided to humiliate Pharaoh in order to make it perfectly clear to Egypt who Yahweh is. In this announcement sequence Yahweh is totally in charge. He declares in advance what he will do, and then he brings it to pass. Pharaoh is a victim. He may think that he is pursuing the Israelites in order to destroy them, but in reality he is being manipulated into meeting his fate. In this scenario the Israelites are neither at risk nor in any danger. They are simply the bait.

As this series of events unfolds in the narrative, another line of action can be discerned. In v. 5 it is reported that the king of Egypt learned of the flight of the people and had a change of mind. Regretting the action he had taken in letting them go, he leads his army in pursuit. When Pharaoh comes within sight of the Israelites, they cry out to Yahweh in the face of this danger. They appear to be genuinely terrified in the face of a real threat. Their first action is to lay the charge that Moses has committed a serious error by undertaking this fatal venture. In reply, Moses calmly states that they should not fear but watch for Yahweh's rescue. The Egyptians are finished. Yahweh will fight for his people. These aspects of the story (the dangerous situation created by the presence of the Egyptian army, the fear of the people, and the cry to the deity) all represent the kind of dangerous situation often found in rescue sequences (*difficulty/rescue*).

The rescue itself takes the form of an embedded announcement sequence.

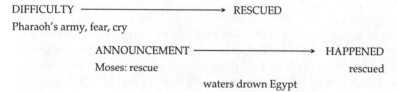

All that Moses said happens, and at the end of the story it is explicitly stated (14:30) that Yahweh has rescued the people from the Egyptians. This sequence seems to take the threat of Pharaoh seriously. He presents a real danger from which Yahweh needs to rescue the people. From this point of view Pharaoh is more opponent than victim, even though in the end he has no chance against Yahweh.

In summary, this final episode in the exodus narrative contains two intertwined action sequences (announcement and rescue). They stand in certain tension with each other because they portray the action differently. In the announcement sequence the fate of the Egyptians is sealed from the start and the tension consists in watching the announced events unfold. In the rescue sequence, a real threat to a small and vulnerable group fleeing from a powerful army leads to a dramatic intervention to save them. Nevertheless, the two interwoven sequences still represent two versions of the same set of events. For example, the sea plays a role in both, whether this is an immediate splitting to form two walls of water or whether this is an all-night action of the wind to move the waters (v. 21). It might be added that Yahweh's looking down from the cloud to panic the Egyptian camp might even introduce a third view of the crucial act of rescue.

In his discussion of Exod 13:17–14:31, Brevard Childs touches on many of the issues I have been discussing. In his commentary on Exodus generally, Childs has sought not only to identify the various sources and traditions that may lie behind the text but also to recognize that the text has attained a final form that is worthy of attention. As far as sources are concerned, he identifies elements from the traditional sources J, E, and P and has no difficulty in treating the exodus account as a composite of these three sources (1974:218–21). But having noted this, Childs then makes a serious effort to deal with the final text. He remarks that "the final literary production has an integrity of its own which must not only be recognized, but studied with the same intensity as one devotes to the earlier stages" (224). Childs explores the "combined witness" of the final text in terms of two conflicting plans, Yahweh's plan and Pharaoh's plan, which start out as a struggle for supremacy. At the announcement about hardening Pharaoh's heart, however, Pharaoh's plan becomes absorbed within Yahweh's. From here on, the divine plan works itself out on two levels. First, the plan is announced to Moses and takes on the form of an announcement-fulfillment pattern. Second, "Yahweh acts directly against the Egyptians in a way not related to Moses' mediation" (227).

My own perception takes a different tack. Looking at Exodus 1–14 as a whole, my analysis has suggested that this text consists of a lengthy rescue sequence (1:1–12:36) followed by a further episode (13:17–14:31), combining an announcement sequence and a rescue sequence. The presence of different sources has resulted in a rather complicated text with many kinds of tensions. Certain kinds of tensions lead to a blurring, in which usually details conflict or small gaps are apparent. Perhaps the different descriptions of what happens to the waters at the crossing of the sea may represent this kind of blurring. Yahweh makes the waters move all night by means of a strong east wind, but it is also said that the waters are immediately divided. Even though two distinct pictures are presented, the action of the waters, whatever it is, involves being moved so that the people can cross. Since the same effect is achieved either way, the story can continue without a major disjunction.

There are also tensions of the sort I have called shimmering. An example of this would be the major tension in Exod 1:1–12:36 with regard to how the rescue is accomplished—by a deception, by the use of force, and by the hardening of Pharaoh's heart. Similarly, there is the example of 13:17–14:31, where two different sequences are intertwined reflecting two different perceptions of the action: the announcement sequence in which Pharaoh's destruction is achieved by a trick, and the rescue sequence in which Israel is rescued from the threat of Pharaoh's army. In these examples a reader is shifted back and forth from one perception to the other with no clue in the story as to how the tension is to be resolved, or even whether it is to be resolved. Many of the tensions stem from the sources and represent a shifting back and forth from one narrator to another, so that readers are invited by each to view the action in a different way. The intertwining of different sequences in the text implies that the different perceptions legitimately belong to the tradition, in fact make up the tradition. All the major sequences of the Exodus involve divine action. In a way the presence of different perceptions can be understood as an exploration of the question of divine presence and activity in the human sphere. Since these perceptions are left to counter one another, no single perception can dominate. Each questions and qualifies the other.

2. *The Joseph Story (Gen 37–50)*. The term "Joseph story" will be used in a very general sense to refer to the material that runs from Genesis 37, when Joseph first appears on the scene, right up to Genesis 50, where his death is reported. These chapters mark the boundaries of what I have in the discussion of the judges above called a life story pattern. While this pattern does mark a beginning and an ending, it was not identified as a sequence. Joseph plays an important role through most of these chapters, even though other things seem to be going on alongside what happens to Joseph; Joseph's life story is a major factor in holding these chapters together. There has been some discussion about sources in the Joseph story (see recently Schmidt), although the tensions in the text here seem far less evident than in the Exodus story. The Joseph story has attracted the attention of a number of scholars taking a literary approach to biblical narrative who have investigated issues like plot and characterization. I will return to the work of some of these scholars below.

What sequences can be identified in Genesis 37–50? The very first chapter depicts some events that raise expectations about what will happen later on in the story. First of all, Joseph has two dreams about the future. Both of these suggest that Joseph will gain a position of authority so that his brothers (in the first dream) and then his brothers along with his mother and father (in the second dream) will recognize his status by bowing down to him. These dreams appear to come true, but it is not clear in the ensuing story at what exact point the realizations of the events forecast in the dreams occur. The narrator comments on these dreams only once after chap. 37, when the ten brothers first arrive in Egypt to buy grain (42:9). As they enter and bow, it is noted that Joseph remembers his dreams. This does not strictly fulfill the first dream since Benjamin is missing. Later, when Benjamin is brought, it is reported (43:26 and 28) that the brothers bow down before Joseph. This at least realizes what the first dream announced, if the brother's act of bowing is the issue rather than the general idea of Joseph's wielding power over them. But as far as the second dream is concerned, there is no scene in which the parents along with the brothers bow down. On his deathbed the father bows to Joseph, but nothing is said about the mother doing so. (In the larger context, the mother has died; Gen 35:18–19.) At any rate, Joseph does achieve a position of authority and his family eventually does come under his direct authority when they arrive in Egypt. Perhaps this is all that is necessary to establish the fulfillment of the dreams.

Even though there is some uncertainty about the dreams and their fulfillment, they seem to point to an important line of action. If we take both dreams together to mean simply that Joseph would rise to power and that the family would come under his authority, then we might posit an announcement sequence that begins with what was announced in the dreams and then comes true in stages, first with respect to the brothers when they arrive with Benjamin and then with regard to the parents when they arrive at a later point. If one wished to identify a separate announcement sequence for each dream and make the act of bowing the sign of fulfillment, this could be worked out for the first dream more successfully than for the second.

A second event in Genesis 37 that points ahead, arousing expectations, consists of the action taken against Joseph by his brothers. As a result of their hostile action, Joseph is taken to Egypt and thus separated from his father. This misfortune is eventually set right when Joseph rises to a powerful post in Egypt and is reunited with his father (46:29). The movement leading from misfortune to a restoration of good fortune can be construed as a rescue sequence. It was noted earlier in the general discussion of sequences that two types of rescue sequences could be distinguished: those in which a rescuer (usually the deity or an agent of the deity) delivers the victim, and those in which the victim takes action on his or her own behalf to escape from difficulty, as does Tamar in Genesis 38.

The movement from Joseph's misfortune to his rise to power can be construed as a rescue sequence. Its definition remains somewhat ambiguous, however, since some characteristics of both types of rescue sequence are present. From one angle, it appears that Yahweh does have a hand in rescuing Joseph. At one stage, the text states explicitly that Yahweh has assisted Joseph (39:2,21,23), although direct intervention is not implied. The remarks in these verses are directed to the reader by the narrator, but it is not said that Joseph is aware of this divine activity. Beyond these comments, however, no other signs of divine intervention emerge in the section of the story recounting Joseph's rise to power in Egypt. Furthermore, Joseph remains passive throughout the movement toward restoration, as though he is neither guiding nor controlling the course of events. He sets no goals. Nor does he speak as though he knows where he is heading. One could then assume that Yahweh is behind everything and take this to be a rescue sequence of the *difficulty/rescued* type in which the ultimate rescuer is the deity.

On the other hand, Joseph possesses immense ability that is recognized wherever he goes, much to his advantage. He has the power to interpret dreams, a gift that eventually leads to his appointment in Pharaoh's court. On the surface, at least, Joseph has found his own way out of his difficulty by using his gifts in administration and interpreting dreams. Since there is no clearly identified rescuer who plays an explicit role in Joseph's escape from his difficult situation, one might consider this a rescue sequence of the second type just mentioned, a *difficulty/escaped* sequence in which the victim arranges for his or her own escape or rescue. Propp (36–37) has described this kind of movement as that of a victim hero who suffers misfortune and separation from his family but is able to correct the situation. Thus, features of both types of rescue sequences remain in tension and so therefore does ambiguity.

The third event in Genesis 37 that looks ahead and creates expectation consists of the hostile action taken by the brothers against Joseph. Here as well, two possibilities emerge. If the action of the brothers is seen as a crime against the deity, it is conceivable that we have the beginning of a punishment sequence of the type *wrong/punished*. If, on the other hand, the act is understood to be directed against Joseph alone, we may have the beginning of a punishment sequence of the type *injury/avenged*. The difficulty with either proposal is that nothing happens that can be identified unequivocally as a divine punishment, nor does any clear act of revenge occur on the part of Joseph. Nevertheless, indications exist in the narrative that the action is to be understood as a wrong or injury. With regard to divine punishment, Reuben interprets the charge against the brothers that they are spies as retribution for killing (so he thinks) Joseph (42:22, see also 39:22). With regard to revenge, it is noted when their father dies that the brothers fear Joseph will pay them back for what they did to him (50:15). One might also interpret the difficulties Joseph creates for his brothers when they appear before him in Egypt as a measure of revenge for what they did to him, although nothing is said explicitly to this effect. Nor does the comment of the brothers later in the story suggest that revenge has been exacted (50:15) since they are still expecting it. Perhaps the difficulties created for the brothers is a testing that serves to demonstrate that their original act against Joseph does not in fact represent their true character. Here again the matter remains ambiguous. Since the brothers in this story represent the future people, any punishment must be limited, or even blurred, and reconciliation must ultimately take place.

What are we to make of all these possibilities? None of the potential sequences just delineated is free from ambiguity, nor indeed is their relationship to each other entirely clear. However, two main movements seem to stand out: Joseph's rise to power in Egypt and the rescue of the family of Jacob from famine.

The rise of Joseph from a lowly rank among his brothers to the position of ruler over them is announced by the dreams, and it comes to pass. The central action in this movement seems to be the announcement sequence initiated by the dreams (*announcement/happened*). This announcement sequence can account for the action in the Joseph story up until his achievement of power. Nevertheless, within this announcement sequence there also appears to be a rescue sequence, apparently with the double aspect of human escape and divine rescue. On the one hand, Joseph escapes because of his talent and ability (*difficulty/escaped*). On the other hand, a role for Yahweh is explicitly mentioned in Genesis 39, and this suggests a rescue arranged and carried out quietly by Yahweh (*difficulty/rescued*). But, of course, from the perspective of the announcement made in the dreams, the misfortune is essential in order that a rise to power can take place. Finally, the punishment sequence, be it divine punishment or human revenge, is related to both the rescue sequence and the announcement sequence. The misfortune into which Joseph falls is caused by the brothers in reaction to the dreams, which deeply offend them. They can be held accountable by Yahweh (*wrong/punished*). More narrowly, the action may be interpreted as simply an injury to Joseph that he repays to some degree with his harsh treatment of the brothers when they stand before him in Egypt (*injury/avenged*). Here again, with regard to the announcement of the dreams, the attempt of the brothers to remove any possibility of the dreams coming true is exactly the first step needed in order to bring them to fulfillment. Thus, the announcement sequence about the dreams intimates that other sequences are intertwined with it. This in turn introduces further perspectives on the action going on.

The other main action is the rescue from famine, although it does not emerge clearly until well into the story. When Joseph finally reveals himself to his brothers, he says to them that they should not be concerned about what they did to him because God had sent him ahead in order to preserve a group of survivors in the face of the great seven-year famine (45:4–9). This statement suggests that the whole Joseph story up to this point must be read in a different light. Joseph's dreams, his misfortune along with his rise to power, and the actions of the brothers have all been part of a plan to rescue the family of Jacob from starvation and death in the face of a coming famine. In terms of the sequences discussed so far, the famine has served primarily to enable Joseph to rise to power by means of his success in interpreting the dreams about the coming disaster and his apparent ability to take the lead in meeting the crisis. Now, however, according to the words of Joseph in 45:4–9, the famine represents a threat to the survival of the family of Jacob from which they need to be rescued. From this angle, Joseph sees his trip to Egypt primarily for the benefit of his family. He is to be their rescuer. The famine becomes a threat to Jacob and his family.

It is clear then that Joseph's words to his brothers (45:4–9) indicate that another rescue sequence, this time concerning Jacob's family, has been in motion within the story. If so, the difficult situation is clear: the famine announced in Pharaoh's dreams has come to Egypt and spread to neighboring countries (41:57). Jacob and his family stand in danger. He sends the brothers, except Benjamin, to Egypt to buy grain "so that we might live and not die" (42:2, also later Judah, 43:8). Now it becomes apparent in Joseph's speech to the brothers (45:4–5) that he is God's agent, provided long in advance to rescue Jacob and his family from death.

Like Moses, Joseph is a rescuer of Israel acting on behalf of the deity; but, of course, their stories are quite different. In the story of Moses, the crisis already exists (Exodus 1) so that one can readily see that the birth of Moses and his escape from death in Exodus 2 prepare the way for his later role in the rescue of the people. This role gains confirmation when, as a refugee, he is confronted by the deity, formally assigned the task of rescue, and armed with instructions and signs. In contrast to Moses, Joseph is never confronted by the deity or formally assigned a task. In fact, Joseph gives no sign that he is aware of his role as rescuer until the speech to the brothers. Nor is it ever explained how and when he discovered his part in the rescue. Most curious of all, the hidden preparation of Joseph, including his selection, his preparation, and placement in a situation of power, all precede the difficult situation and quietly anticipate it. Once the crisis comes, Joseph is already in a position to take appropriate action to save his family by inviting them to Egypt, which, due to his wise supervision, is insulated from the worst of the effects of the famine.

This rescue sequence concerning Jacob/Israel and his family has close links with other larger narrative frameworks within which the Joseph story is set. For example, it fits within the framework of the life of Joseph. It also fits within the life of Jacob, which overlaps with the life story of Joseph, seeing that the death of Jacob is not reported until the end of Genesis 49. Then too, since Jacob/Israel and his sons represent the future Israel, the rescue story becomes part of the story of the promise that began with Abraham. From the perspective of these broader narrative frameworks, the rescue element in the Joseph story takes on paramount importance since the very existence of the future people of Israel is at stake. The more one gives prominence to the action of the rescue, the more the first part of the Joseph story with its closely intertwined sequences of announcement, rescue, and punishment, becomes subordinated to and absorbed into it so that it functions in a way similar to the birth and call of Moses in the rescue story in Exodus.

Nevertheless, the narrative concerning Joseph's dreams, the misfortune, and the brothers seems to resist simply being absorbed into and dominated by the larger story of the rescue of the people. For one thing, it makes such a good story that it stands out from the major rescue story and calls for attention on its own. Then too, as we have noted, the subordinate role of this segment about the rise of Joseph to power is not signalled until the comment of Joseph in Genesis 45, which introduces a shift of perspective and invites a rereading of the misfortune account in a new light. To go back and read the misfortune story in a new light does not do away with it by restructuring it within the rescue story. Rather, since the story of the rise to power comes before the main rescue sequence begins, rereading in light of the rescue scheme actually adds further strength and independence to the narrative relating Joseph's rise to power.

What we have, then, is a merging of an attractive story about Joseph's rise to power with an important rescue story that is critical for the future of the people of Israel. The merger is only partial, however, because the two stories remain in tension with each other. This may account for the fact pointed out above, that the sequences related to dreams, the escape of Joseph, and the wrong of the brothers do not come to clear and unambiguous endings but tend to become diffused through the rest of the material in the Joseph account. When I speak of merging here, I am only referring to how sequences are related to each other in the text. It may well be, historically speaking, that different traditions have been brought together, thus producing different perspectives in the text. In the present Joseph story, the tension between the two parts sets two perspectives in a balance so that the story about the misfortune and rise of Joseph and the story about the rescue of the people can be played off against each other with neither losing its force. Since the two parts have been merged and blended together, they depend on each other, but to different degrees. The rescue story requires that Joseph be in power in Egypt at the right time. It therefore needs the sequences that recount Joseph's escape from misfortune, now reinterpreted as a secret preparation for the rescue. The story of Joseph's rise to power can almost stand alone except that, as I have said, the sequences we identified do not come to clear endings all at once but seem to disperse throughout the larger story.

The Joseph story has appealed to many readers and critics over the years, and it has engaged several recent commentators with an interest in the study of narrative. Perhaps this is so because the Joseph story, with its complexity of plot, general lack of direct divine intervention, and apparent interest in characters and human relationships, comes closer than most biblical narrative to the realistic novel of the western tradition. It may be pertinent, then, to take account of some of the ways recent writers have dealt with this narrative text. A remarkable variety of approaches exists, and my selection has been to some degree random. Nevertheless, it gives, I think, a good sense of the range of the approaches that have surfaced. The authors concerned display interest in two directions: action and character. Some pursue both. I will mention first writers who have sought to describe movement or action, and then I will turn to those who talk about character.

While I have concentrated on the movement of specific kinds of action from their beginnings to their conclusions, this is by no means the only kind of movement going on in stories. For example, Hugh White (1985) finds the key to the narrative in a recognition of the tension between the direct discourse of the characters and the indirect discourse of the narrator, or the narrative framework. In his view, the narrative closure of the plot is set against the dynamic openness of the dialogical discourse of the characters. White argues that the "closed internal logic" of the narrative framework of the Joseph story is "consumed" by, or subordinated to, the "open logic of spoken discourse" (67) so that the central tension of the plot becomes the broken communication between the brothers. This problem (37:1–4) is resolved by the reunion of the brothers with Joseph (45:15) and reaffirmed at the end of the story (50:21), where resolution is accomplished by means of direct discourse (66).

Another kind of movement has been identified by Robert Alter (1981), who argues that the central action in the Joseph story lies in the contrast between true knowledge and false knowledge. All the characters start out with varying degrees of ignorance and move to greater knowledge of themselves, each other, and the ways of God. The two examples of White and Alter illustrate that narrative is exceedingly complex and that one may well expect different kinds of movement to take place at different levels of the text. In limiting myself to tracing narrative action in particular ways, I remain open to consider other descriptions of movement in stories.

Other scholars, who have pursued the question of movement more directly in terms of action or plot, touch more nearly on my discussion of action in terms of sequences. One of the most detailed analyses of action may be found in Robert Longacre's study of the Joseph story (1989). Here he resumes the kind of discourse analysis he has applied to the flood story (1979; see my brief comments, Culley, 1985a:169–70). He describes the action in the main part of the Joseph story (Genesis 37, 38–48) in terms of ten major episodes (which in turn are frequently composed of smaller episodes). The first four episodes rise toward three central episodes: peak (climax), chap. 41; interpeak, chap. 42; and peak' (denouement), chap. 43–45. The action falls again to a close through three post peak episodes. He summarizes the macrostructure of this section in the following sentence: "Joseph's brothers, meaning to harm him, sold him into Egypt, but in reality God sent him there so that he could save Jacob's family and many others from starvation."

Longacre recognizes two main movements in the story, the first embedded in the second: the brothers selling Joseph into Egypt, and the rescue of the family—as well as others—from the famine. My own analysis agrees with the basic outline of the rescue story within which is the descent to Egypt. I would, however, find more tension between the embedded account of Joseph's rise to power in Egypt and the rescue of Jacob. Longacre analyzes the action by tracking various kinds of surface markers in the text. My description of the sequences is based not on surface marking but on shared patterns among compared texts. At this point I see no simple way to integrate the two approaches.

In his article on Joseph, Judah and Jacob (1982), James Ackerman's description of plot centers on features of doubling. For example, a denouement seems to come in Genesis 42, where the brothers bow down to Joseph as the dreams had indicated they would. In my view more needs to happen and many loose ends must be tied before the dreams can be understood to be truly fulfilled. After chap. 42 another plot doubling ensues in which the brothers suffer retribution for their crime at the hands of Joseph. They must, in effect, perform a re-enactment of their crime by returning home to their father without Benjamin and, indeed, face the temptation to lie their way out of this one as well. Ackerman agrees that the main theme of the story may well be the rescue of the family through Joseph, but he holds that the reconciliation of the brothers stands very close to this as a sub-theme, so that the story cannot end until the reconciliation occurs. This will involve the father and the fulfillment of the second dream. Thus, while Ackerman traces the action in his own way, he also recognizes two movements, one subordinated to the other: an action about Joseph and his brothers, and an action about a rescue, although this sub-theme runs alongside and then continues beyond the main one.

George Coats (1983) calls Genesis 37–50 the Jacob saga and describes it as a redactional framework on the subject of Jacob and his sons. Within this framework—in fact making up most of it—is the Joseph story, a novella, a unit with a plot (crisis to resolution) and a unity of action throughout the whole. For Coats, the major crisis in the Joseph story is the tension between Joseph and his brothers; the plot, therefore, moves from alienation to reconciliation. The plot reaches its climax when the family is brought together and the brothers' deception is neutralized. Coats, too, distinguishes two movements; but for him the story of Joseph and his brothers becomes central as a novella while the rescue story remains in the redactional framework.

Humphreys (1988) takes the whole Joseph story as a novella and devotes a chapter to the description of its plot. According to Humphreys, the plot of a novella follows a trajectory that begins with a complication or tension, has a middle that entails further complications, rises to a climax resolving the tension, and ends with a denouement in which complications disappear (22). Humphreys (23) judges the basic complication of the Joseph story to be "a family split by hatred and seemingly intent on its own destruction." In his reading a single plot about the family situation contains and orders all the material in the story.

Finally, J. Robin King sets the Joseph story in the context of some stories from the ancient Near East. This is of particular interest because the author has developed his approach from the work of Propp. King's analysis of Near Eastern tales yields a narrative sequence of ten steps that, he claims, underlies a certain type of life story in the ancient Near East:

> a hero, living in an initial situation of privilege (because of his initial patron), is forced to flee from it as a result of a threat against him; in exile he receives support; and with the assistance of a divine helper he is able to return and be reconciled with his former community, there to live out a life in harmony with it. . . . (585–86)

King suggests that this sequence can be found in the stories of Moses and David, which he discusses briefly, but especially in the Joseph story. The Joseph story, it is argued, follows this general outline. Joseph goes into exile in Egypt; there is a repetition of the exile experience when he is thrown into jail. King suggests that this is an instance of the same sequence being repeated, one (the familial sequence) being embedded within the other (the Egyptian sequence).

King's use of Propp and his analysis of the Joseph story have turned out quite differently from mine. It does seem that the Joseph story, when placed alongside other Near Eastern texts, bears some similarity to them in terms of the common pattern outlined above. I, however, have taken a different tack. Using Propp much more indirectly, I have sought to uncover patterns by linking the Joseph story with a wide range of stories in biblical narrative, especially setting it beside the rescue story of the Exodus. Accordingly, my results have been different.

All the above-mentioned interpreters of the Joseph story except Humphreys have identified two movements in the narrative; but they have treated the relationship between the movements in various ways, subordinating Joseph in Egypt to the rescue or subordinating the rescue to the descent to Egypt. I have chosen to allow a certain tension to remain so that it is possible to read the text in different ways, emphasizing the descent to Egypt story in one reading but highlighting the rescue in another, especially when the surrounding material in the Pentateuch is brought into consideration. A reader may take advantage of both possibilities.

It must also be admitted that my own analysis of sequences omits a number of issues. I do not identify a sequence related to the tension within the family and its healing, though I would agree that this theme is important. The family is at odds, or at least the brothers have taken hostile action against Joseph and lied to their father. In the end, all is out in the open and reconciliation has taken place. In my analysis, the tension in the family and its reconciliation do not appear to form a separate sequence but belong rather to actions related to the sequences I have identified.

Now, the question of character. As I explained earlier, I have chosen in this study to concentrate on action and leave out the whole matter of the participants. However, the Joseph story in particular invites a consideration of character, and, indeed, many of the scholars discussed above have shown a keen interest in this subject. A few comments on the participants are therefore in order.

It is evident that the treatment of character in biblical narrative presents a number of difficulties. Characters are rarely described in any detail either with regard to external appearance or inner thoughts and motivations. We do not know what the characters looked like, apart from striking features, like Absalom's long hair, that are mentioned from time to time. Nor are we often told explicitly what participants think or why they act the way they do. Individuals act and speak but beyond this we are seldom told much more. The minimal information given about characters stands in contrast to the much greater amount of information that is usually provided, say, by the novel in western literature. The question is: should we read biblical narrative as though the minimal description of characters is a device of understatement that says little but implies more? If so, readers will need to pick up the textual clues in order to fill in the gaps. An alternate way of responding to the minimal description of character in biblical narrative is to assume that the spaces need not be filled. Let the participants remain defined only in outline form. I think both options are legitimate.

Some recent studies have sought to build on clues in the text in order to create a fuller understanding of character. For example, Robert Alter contrasts the young Joseph with the mature Joseph and proposes that both events and Joseph's manipulations unite to lead the brothers to self knowledge. In Joseph's weeping Alter sees an emotional process in the hero in which years of anger begin to dissolve (1981:168). Similarly, in a stimulating article, James Ackerman discerns a process of learning and growth that works itself out in Joseph, the brothers, and Jacob. For example, it is argued that Joseph learns from Judah's last speech about risking, offering, and suffering. For Alter and Ackerman, then, what happens inside characters is important for the action of the story and may even reflect what the story is all about.

A minimal reading of characters, on the other hand, might mean treating them largely in terms of their roles in action sequences. In this case it may be useful to offer a few comments on the participants in the Joseph story from such a perspective. First, Joseph. As far as action sequences are concerned, the character of Joseph can be viewed in at least three ways. In the early chapters, Joseph is a victim hero who manages to escape and rise to the top through his ability to interpret dreams and administer well, even though he is also seen to some extent as a victim rescued by the deity. Joseph is also the agent of the deity, chosen and prepared beforehand to rescue the people from the great famine. In this role he is a rescuer and a leader similar in this regard to the figure of Moses. The two roles of victim hero and rescuer combine but remain in tension. The third way in which Joseph's role can be viewed is at the life story level. At this level he is something of a parallel to Abraham, Isaac, and Jacob, although he is not a patriarch who receives the divine promise.

The brothers are also participants in the Joseph story. For purposes of this brief discussion, the brothers may be taken to play a single role. At the beginning, the brothers are wrongdoers—at least they finally perceive themselves as such. They are punished, but only to the extent that Joseph deals harshly with them, if this may be taken as punishment. In the rescue story, they are the ones, along with their father (and mother?—see above), who are threatened with extinction and rescued. The rescue is for their sake as the future Israel. Their role as villains is blended with their role as victims. In the rescue perspective, their action against Joseph is essential because it gets Joseph to Egypt, where he can rise to power. From this point of view, they are not really wrongdoers.

Jacob, too, has more than one role. He is a father who loses a son and gets him back. But, along with the brothers, he is a victim who is rescued. Of course, he is also Jacob/Israel and has a life story as one of the patriarchs. His story seems to be largely completed when the Joseph story begins, although to the extent that the Joseph story is a rescue of Jacob and his family, the future Israel, the rescue is an important part of his life story.

The role of the deity is not an easy one to define. In the main story about the rescue of the people, the deity is the rescuer. Nevertheless, the deity, who had decided to cause the famine, planned the rescue well in advance of the announcement of the famine. In the segment about Joseph's misfortune and good fortune, Yahweh is identified at one point (Genesis 39) as one who is "with Joseph"; otherwise little place is given to divine activity. Joseph attributes the message of Pharaoh's dreams to the deity (41:25), and Pharaoh credits Joseph's ability in interpretation to the deity (41:38–39). On the other hand, the source of Joseph's original dreams is not given, nor is it explained why things happen to him the way they do, except for the comment in Genesis 39 just mentioned. As in many folktales a kind of narrative logic seems to be operating according to which victim heroes end up successful and wrongdoers are always caught. This may be understood as fate, fortune, or happy coincidence, according to whatever it is that causes the right things to happen at the right time. To be sure, in Hebrew tradition the God of Israel normally makes things happen the way they should, and circumstances are rarely attributed to fate or happy coincidence. While Yahweh's role as the rescuer of Joseph and the people seems to be strongly affirmed, the fact that some room remains for unexplained and unattributed occurrences leaves the question of Joseph's escape slightly open.

I have in this discussion sought to define character simply in terms of the roles participants play in action sequences. Understanding character in this way implies that participants in the Joseph story, and many of the other stories I have discussed in this chapter, do not move very far toward becoming central to the narrative by motivating and governing action. My description of characters is largely consistent with the role or roles they play in action sequences. Joseph fills the role of the victim hero in an escape sequence and the agent of the deity in a rescue sequence. Some of the complexity in character develops when these two roles are conjoined as Genesis 37–50 is read through as a single narrative.

Concluding Comments

This study is offered as a contribution to the ongoing discussion of biblical narrative. It will be a limited contribution because it has investigated only one feature of narrative, action, and proposed only one way of treating this feature, examining examples of certain kinds of repeated and varied patterns in biblical narrative that I have called sequences. Nevertheless, since action in biblical narrative has been little studied, my investigation may prove useful. Certainly, in my view, Chapters Two and Three suggest that examining sequences may be a helpful and interesting way of tracking action in biblical narrative. There it was noted how different kinds of sequences were joined together in stories and in groups of stories in various ways, by adding one sequence to another in succession (sometimes with overlapping), by embedding one inside the other, or by setting two side-by-side so that they run concurrently (sometimes intertwined). From the perspective of this kind of analysis, sequences almost seem to be building blocks of narrative action.

It is important to recognize repeated patterns; but because I wanted to avoid simply reducing stories to abstract patterns, I tried as well to note how sequences vary, how at the level of the individual occurrence of a sequence, say a punishment sequence, each instance is different with its own elaborations and emphases. Thus, keeping track of repeated sequences and their variations means reading the narrative material at two levels, at the level of the patterns shared by several stories and at the level of the individual story, which develops the common patterns in specific ways. It was noted that an ancient witness, the book of Judges, seems to invite this kind of approach.

Studying sequences and their variations is particularly useful in dealing with a traditional and composite text like the Bible because it enables us, at least with regard to action, to examine both similarity and difference. Repeated patterns encourage a sense of coherence and closure. Varied patterns favor a sense of multiformity and openness. With regard to coherence, the repeated sequences function both syntagmatically and paradigmatically. Syntagmatically, sequences are strung together, marking the forward movement of the narrative material as it recounts the history of Israel. Sequences sometimes stretch over long sections of text and tie stories and episodes together. An example of this on a small scale was seen in the narratives about the conquest, where an announcement sequence binds several chapters together. At the beginning of the book of Joshua, Yahweh announces that the land will be given to the Israelites, and this happens in Josh 11:23. Even within this material, some sequences cross over from one story to another providing further coherence.

Paradigmatically, sequences hold the narrative material together in another way. The very repetition of the same sequences (the iteration of the themes of rescue, punishment, achievement, and announcement, for example) provides a redundancy that fosters a sense of the coherence of biblical narrative. For example, rescue sequences appear throughout the narrative material and function at different levels, whether in very short accounts like some prophet stories, or in stories like that of Ehud, or in longer, more complex stories like the exodus account.

A sense of difference is highlighted by the variations of the sequences. An interesting example of this was found in the group of punishment stories discussed at the beginning of Chapter Three. The theme of punishment was repeated again and again in each story, which seemed to affirm and establish the idea that wrong leads to punishment. On the other hand, the specific examples of these sequences express variations that seemed to complicate the notion of punishment and work against any simple notion of it (see further Culley, 1990, and the comments of Greenstein, 1989a:61–64).

There is also the phenomenon that I described as shimmering. I used this term to describe two sequences running side-by-side in the same story that give different perspectives on the same action so that readers are invited to shift back and forth between the two. In this case, some of the differences may be due to the traditional and composite nature of the text. However, instead of viewing the sources separately, I tried to read them as part of one text. Shimmering was noted in the story of the capture of Ai, where the victory seems to depend both on a human stratagem and a divine intervention. It was also seen in the account of the victory at the sea at the end of the exodus story, where a rescue sequence involving escape from a powerful pursuer is interwoven with a sequence entailing the entrapment of a helpless victim by Yahweh. Another kind of shifting between different narrative possibilities was seen in the Joseph story. Joseph's rise to power could be subordinated to the rescue story of the family of Jacob. On the other hand, the story of Joseph's rise is so interesting in and of itself that it seems to resist being subordinated. In a way this amounts to reading at different levels of the narrative tradition: a more restricted one, where attention is on the adventures of Joseph, and another more extensive one, which includes the broader history of the people of Israel.

Six kinds of sequences were identified and studied: punishment, rescue, achievement, reward, announcement, and prohibition. It was not claimed that this list is exhaustive. Of these, rescue and punishment sequences seem to be the most common, reward sequences rather rare. As the variations of a given sequence were examined it was seen that the basic movement of sequences (for example, wrong to punishment) could be elaborated in various ways. In punishment sequences, and this can be seen in the examples introduced in the first section of Chapter Three, one important elaboration consists of the use an agent (a prophet) to act on behalf of the deity. This may involve a confrontation with the guilty party and a declaration of guilt, sometimes getting the wrongdoers to declare their own guilt by use of a deception. A punishment sequence may also be elaborated by having the guilty party make an appeal for a reduced punishment, that is then granted. Rescue sequences may also be elaborated by having an agent, like Moses, carry out the rescue and by adding an account of the selection of the agent, as in the stories of Gideon and Moses.

The introductory chapter was intended to be an orientation to the study of sequences and designed to give some indication of the understanding of text and literary criticism that lies behind this particular examination of narrative patterns. While I expressed a desire to be open to directing different kinds of questions to the text (historical, literary, and religious), I did not do much to raise historical questions, say about historical or social context, although I did hint at how I would proceed in addressing the religious dimension. I proposed that, for the purposes of this study, the body of biblical narrative would be treated like a text that is traditional and composite as well as religious. Thus, sequences were examined in terms of their presence in a traditional and composite text, and this allowed some exploration of what makes a text complex and rich. While I am still not clear how best to describe this kind of text or even how to suggest it be read, I am encouraged by the analysis of specific biblical texts in Chapter Three to think that there are some advantages in attempting to read the narrative material as a whole and some of the stories in it as traditional composites.

While sequences were treated primarily as narrative patterns within the text, they were at the same time described in terms of the kind of action they expressed, such as rescue or punishment, two sequences that were frequently encountered. Where did these specific themes of rescue and punishment come from? Perhaps they go back to patterns produced in oral tradition, or perhaps they emerged in the work of scribes who organized the traditions (see Ben-Amos, who prefers the latter). I have simply used the word traditional to cover both modes. In any event, the patterns seemed to have been important in ancient Israel, even if this were a later stage. As patterns in the Bible, they become part of the world of this text. In this capacity, they play a role in the vision of reality adopted by the religious communities who gather around this text. It is certainly clear that themes of punishment and rescue have an important place in biblical literature other than narrative. In the prophetic writings, punishment is a consuming concern of the pre-exilic prophets. While rescue is also present in significant ways in the writings of these prophets, it is in Second Isaiah that the theme of rescue takes over. The relationship between the divine and the human is also part of this larger picture, although I raised questions about it from time to time. It was not a question of finding anything new on this topic but rather of noticing how the study of sequences and variations provides a useful framework within which to consider this relationship. One can find no better examples of the contrast between the direct and indirect action of the deity than in the two rescue stories with which we concluded Chapter Three, the exodus and the story of Joseph.

Works Consulted

Ackerman, James S.
    1982   "Joseph, Judah, and Jacob." Pp. 85–113 in *Literary Interpretations of Biblical Narratives. Volume II.* Ed. Kenneth R.R. Gros Louis, with James Ackerman. Nashville: Abingdon.

Aitken, Kenneth T.
    1984   "The Wooing of Rebekah: A Study in the Development of the Tradition." *JSOT* 30:3–23.

Albright, William Foxwell
    1964   *History, Archaeology and Christian Humanism.* New York: McGraw-Hill.

Alonso Schökel, Luis
    1961   "Erzählkunst im Buche der Richter." *Bib* 42:143–72.

Alter, Robert
    1981   *The Art of Biblical Narrative.* New York: Basic Books.
    1983   "How Convention Helps Us Read: The Case of the Bible's Annunciation Type-Scene." *Prooftexts* 3:115–30.

Alter, Robert, and Frank Kermode
    1987   *The Literary Guide to the Bible.* Cambridge: Belnap, Harvard University Press.

Amit, Yairah
    1987   "The Dual Causality Principle and its Effects on Biblical Literature." *VT* 37:385–400.

Anderson, Bernard W.
    1978   "From Analysis to Synthesis: The Interpretation of Genesis 1–11."
          JBL 97:23–39.

Atkins, G. Douglas, and Laura Morrow, eds.
    1989   *Contemporary Literary Theory*. Amherst: University of Massachusetts
          Press.

Auld, A. Graeme
    1989   "Gideon: Hacking at the Heart of the Old Testament." *VT* 39:257–67.

Bal, Mieke
    1987   *Lethal Love: Feminist Literary Readings of Biblical Love Stories*. Indiana
          Studies in Biblical Literature. Bloomington: Indiana University
          Press.
    1988   *Murder and Difference: Gender, Genre, and Scholarship on Sisera's Death*.
          Indiana Studies in Biblical Literature. Bloomington: Indiana
          University Press.

Bar-Efrat, Shimon
    1989   *Narrative Art in the Bible*. Bible and Literature Series 17. Sheffield:
          Almond. (Hebrew 1984, 2d ed.)

Barr, James
    1973   *The Bible in the Modern World*. New York: Harper and Row.
    1980a   "Story and History in Biblical Theology." Pp. 1–17 in *The Scope and*
          Authority of the Bible. Philadelphia: Westminster.
    1980b   "The Bible as a Document of Believing Communities." Pp. 111–33 in
          The Scope and Authority of the Bible. Philadelphia: Westminster.
    1981   "Some thoughts on Narrative, Myth, and Incarnation." Pp. 14–23 in
          God Incarnate: Story and Belief. Ed. A.E. Harvey. London: SPCK.
    1983   *Holy Scripture: Canon, Authority, Criticism*. Philadelphia: Westmin-
          ster.

Barton, John
    1984   *Reading the Old Testament: Method in Biblical Study*. London: Darton,
          Longman and Todd.

Ben-Amos, Dan
    1990   "Comments on Robert C. Culley's 'Five Tales of Punishment in the
          Book of Numbers'." Pp. 35–45 in *Text and Tradition: The Hebrew Bible*
          and Folklore. Ed. Susan Niditch. Semeia Studies. Atlanta: Scholars.

Berlin, Adele
    1983   *Poetics and Interpretation of Biblical Narrative*. Bible and Literature
          Series 9. Sheffield: Almond.

Blum, Erhard
    1984   *Die Komposition der Vätergeschichte*. WMANT 57. Neukirchen-Vluyn:
          Neukirchener Verlag.

1990 *Studien zur Komposition des Pentateuch.* BZAW 189. Berlin: Walter de Gruyter.

Boling, Robert G.
1975 *Judges.* AB 6A. Garden City, NY: Doubleday.

Boling, Robert G., and G. Ernest Wright
1982 *Joshua.* AB 6. Garden City, NY: Doubleday.

Brettler, Marc
1989 "The Book of Judges: Literature and Politics." *JBL* 108:395–418.

Chatman, Seymour
1978 *Story and Discourse: Narrative Structure in Fiction and Film.* Ithica and London: Cornell University Press.

Childs, Brevard S.
1964 "Interpretation in Faith: The Theological Responsibility of an Old Testamtent Commentary." *Int* 18:432–49.
1974 *The Book of Exodus: A Criticial, Theological Commentary.* OTL. Philadelphia: Westminster.
1979 *Introduction to Old Testament as Scripture.* Philadelphia: Fortress.
1977 "The Sensus Literalis of Scripture: An Ancient and Modern Problem." Pp. 80–93 in *Beiträge zur Alttestamentlichen Theologie: Festschrift für Walther Zimmerli zum 70. Geburtstag.* Ed. Herbert Donner, Robert Hahnhart and Rudolph Smend. Göttingen: Vandenhoeck & Ruprecht.
1986 *Old Testament Theology in a Canonical Context.* Philadelphia: Fortress.

Clines, David J. A.
1978 *The Theme of the Pentateuch.* JSOTSup 10. Sheffield: JSOT.
1980 "Story and Poem: The Old Testament as Literature and as Scripture." *Int* 34:115–27.

Coats, George W.
1968 *The Rebellion in the Wilderness.* Nashville: Abingdon.
1983 *Genesis: With an Introduction to Narrative Literature.* The Forms of the Old Testament Literature 1. Grand Rapids: Eerdmans.
1988 *Moses: Heroic Man, Man of God.* JSOTSup 57. Sheffield: Sheffield Academic.

Collins, Adela Yarbro
1985 *Feminist Perspectives on Biblical Scholarship.* Biblical Scholarship in North America 10. Chico, CA: Scholars.

Conroy, Charles
1978 *Absalom Absalom!* AnBib 81. Rome: Biblical Institute.

Crenshaw, James
1977 *Samson: A Secret Betrayed, a Vow Ignored.* Atlanta: John Knox.

Culley, Robert C.

1963   "An Approach to the Problem of Oral Tradition." *VT* 13:113–25.

1967   *Oral Formulaic Language in the Biblical Psalms*. Near and Middle East Series 4. Toronto: University of Toronto Press.

1972a   "Oral Tradition and Historicity." Pp. 12–28 in *Studies on the Ancient Palestinian World*. Ed. J. W. Wevers and D. B. Redford. Toronto Texts and Studies. Toronto: University of Toronto Press.

1972b   "Some Comments on Structural Analysis and Biblical Studies." Pp. 129–42 in *Congress Volume: Uppsala, 1971*. VTSup 22. Leiden: Brill.

1974   "Structural Analysis: Is It Done with Mirrors?" *Int* 28:165–81.

1975   "Themes and Variations in Three Groups of Old Testament Narratives." *Semeia* 3:3–13.

1976a   "Oral Tradition and Old Testament Studies." *Semeia* 5:1–33.

1976b   *Studies in the Structure of Hebrew Narrative*. Semeia Supplements. Philadelphia: Fortress; Missoula, MT: Scholars.

1978   "Analyse alttestamentlicher Erzählungen—Erträge der jüngsten Methodendiscussion." *Biblische Notizen* 6:27–39.

1980a   "Punishment Stories in the Legends of the Prophets." Pp. 167–81 in *Orientation By Disorientation: Studies in Literary Criticism Presented in Honor of William A. Beardslee*. Ed. Richard A. Spencer. PTMS 35. Pittsburgh: Pickwick.

1980b   "Action Sequences in Gen 2–3." *Semeia* 18:25–33.

1985a   "Exploring New Directions." Pp. 167–200 in *The Old Testament and Its Modern Interpreters*. Ed. Douglas A. Knight and Gene M. Tucker. Philadelphia: Fortress; Chico, CA: Scholars.

1985b   "Stories of the Conquest: Joshua 2, 6, 7, and 8." *Hebrew Annual Review* 8:25–44.

1986   "Oral Tradition and Biblical Studies." *Oral Tradition* 1:30–65.

1990   "Five Tales of Punishment in the Book of Numbers." Pp. 25–34 in *Text and Tradition: The Hebrew Bible and Folklore*. Ed. Susan Niditch. Semeia Studies. Atlanta: Scholars.

Damrosch, David

1987   *The Narrative Covenant: Transformations of Genre in the Growth of Biblical Literature*. San Francisco: Harper & Row.

Detweiler, Robert

1985   "What is a Sacred Text?" *Semeia* 31:213–30.

Driver, S. R.

1956   *An Introduction to the Literature of the Old Testament*. New York: Meridian Books.

Emerton, J. A.

1987   "An Examination of Some Attempts to Defend the Unity of the Flood Narrative in Genesis. Part I." *VT* 37:401–20.

1988   "An Examination of Some Attempts to Defend the Unity of the
        Flood Narrative in Genesis. Part II." *VT* 38:1–21.

Exum, J. Cheryl, and J. William Whedbee
1984   "Isaac, Samson, and Saul: Relfections on the Comic and Tragic
        Visions." *Semeia* 32:5–40.

Fewell, Danna Nolan
1987   "Feminist Reading of the Hebrew Bible: Affirmation, Resistance and
        Transformation." *JSOT* 39:77–87.

Flanagan, James W.
1985   "History as Hologram: Integrating Literary, Archaeological and
        Comparative Sociological Evidence." Pp. 291–314 in *SBL Seminar
        Papers*. Ed. Kent Harold Richards. Atlanta: Scholars.

Floss, Johannes P.
1982   *Kunden oder Kundschafter?* ATAT 16. St. Ottilien: EOS.

Fokkelman, J. P.
1981   *Narrative Art and Poetry in the Books of Samuel, Vol. 1*. King David (II
        Sam. 9–20 & I Kings 1–2). Assen/Amsterdam: Van Gorcum.

Ford, D. F.
1979   "Barth's Interpretation of the Bible." Pp. 55–87 in *Karl Barth: Studies
        of his Theological Method*. Ed. S. W. Sykes. Oxford: Clarendon.

Fowler, Robert M.
1985   "Who Is "the Reader" in Reader Response Criticism?" *Semeia* 31:5–
        23.
1989   "Postmodern Biblical Criticism." *Forum* 5:3–30.

Frei, Hans
1974   *The Eclipse of Biblical Narrative*. New Haven: Yale University Press.
1986   "'Literal Reading' of Biblical Narrative in Christian Tradition." Pp.
        36–77 in *The Bible and the Narrative Tradition*. Ed. Frank McConnell.
        New York and Oxford: Oxford University Press.

Frye, Northrop
1963   *The Educated Imagination*. Toronto: Canadian Broadcasting Corpora-
        tion.
1982   *The Great Code: The Bible and Literature*. Toronto: Academic.

Gottwald, Norman K.
1979   *The Tribes of Yahweh*. Maryknoll, NY: Orbis Books.
1983   "Sociological Method in the Study of Ancient Israel." Pp. 26–37 in
        The Bible and Liberation. Ed. Norman K. Gottwald. Maryknoll, NY:
        Orbis.
1985   *The Hebrew Bible: A Socio-Literary Introduction*. Philadelphia: Fortress.

Greenstein, Edward L.

1982 "An Equivocal Reading of the Sale of Joseph." Pp. 114–25 in *Literary Interpretations of Biblical Narrative. Volume II.* Ed. Kenneth R. R. Gros Louis with James Ackerman. Nashville: Abingdon.

1988 "On the Genesis of Biblical Prose Narrative." *Prooftexts* 8:347–63.

1989a "Deconstruction and Biblical Narrative." *Prooftexts* 9:43–71.

1989b *Essays on Biblical Method and Translation.* BJS. Atlanta: Scholars.

1990 "The Formation of the Biblical Narrative Corpus." *AJS Review* 15:151–78.

Grimes, Joseph E.

1975 *The Thread of Discourse.* Janua Linguarum, Series Minor, 207. The Hague: Mouton.

Groupe d'Entrevernes

1977 *Analyse sémiotique des textes.* Lyon: Presses Universitaires de Lyon.

Gülich, Elizabeth, and Wolfgang Raible

1977 *Linguistische Textmodelle.* Uni-Taschebücher 130. Munich: Wilhelm Fink.

Gunkel, Hermann

1963 *Die israelitische Literatur.* Darmstadt: Wissenschaftliche Buchgesellschaft. Reprint from Kultur des Gegenwart I/7. 1925.

1964 *Genesis, übersetzt und erklärt.* Göttingen: Vandenhoeck & Ruprecht. 6th ed. Reprint of 3rd. 1910.

Gunn, D. M.

1978 *The Story of King David: Genre and Interpretation.* JSOTSup 6. Sheffield: JSOT.

1980 *The Fate of King Saul: An Interpretation of a Biblical Story.* JSOTSup 14. Sheffield: JSOT.

1982 "The 'Hardening of Pharoah's Heart': Plot, Character and Theology in Exodus 1–14." Pp. 72–96 in *Art and Meaning: Rhetoric in Biblical Literature.* Ed. David J. A. Clines, David M. Gunn, and Alan J. Hauser. Sheffield: JSOT.

1987 "New Directions in the Study of Biblical Hebrew Narrative." *JSOT* 39:65–75.

Hendel, Ronald S.

1987 *The Epic of the Patriarch: The Jacob Cycle and the Narrative Traditions of Canaan and Israel.* HSM 42. Atlanta: Scholars.

Humphreys, W. Lee

1988 *Joseph and His Family: A Literary Study.* Columbia: University of South Carolina Press.

Hutcheon, Linda

1989 *The Politics of Postmodernism.* New Accents. London: Routledge.

Jackson, Jared J., and Martin Kessler, eds.
1974 *Rhetorical Criticism: Essays in Honor of James Muilenburg.* PTMS 1. Pittsburgh: Pickwick.

Jason, Heda
1977 *Ethnopoetry: Form, Content, Function.* Bonn: Linguistica Biblica.

Jobling, David
1986 *The Sense of Biblical Narrative: Structural Analyses in the Hebrew Bible.* II. JSOTSup 39. Sheffield: Sheffield Academic.

Josipovici, Gabriel
1988 *The Book of God.* New Haven: Yale University Press.

King, J. Robin
1987 "The Joseph Story and Divine Politics: A Comparative Study of a Biographic Formula from the Ancient Near East." *JBL* 106:577–94.

Klatt, Werner
1969 *Herman Gunkel.* Göttingen: Vandenhoeck & Ruprecht.

Klein, Lillian R.
1980 *The Triumph of Irony in the Book of Judges.* Bible and Literature Series 14. Sheffield: Almond.

Knight, Douglas A.
1982 *Julius Wellhausen and His Prolegomena to the History of Israel. Semeia* 25. Chico, CA: Scholars.

Leach, Edmund
1969 *Genesis as Myth and Other Essays.* London: Jonathan Cape.

Lévi-Strauss, Claude
1967 "The Structural Study of Myth." Pp. 202–27 in *Structural Anthropology.* Trans. C. Jacobson and B. G. Schoepf. Garden City, NY: Anchor.

Long, Burke O.
1973 "2 Kings iii and Genres of Prophetic Narrative." *VT* 23: 337–48.
1984 *1 Kings; with an Introduction to Historical Literature.* The Forms of the Old Testament Literature 11. Grand Rapids: Eerdmans.

Longacre, Robert E.
1979 "The Discourse Structure of the Flood Narrative." *JAAR* 47 SupB:89–133.
1989 *Joseph: A Story of Divine Providence: A Text Theoretical and Textlinguistic Analysis of Genesis 37 and 39–48.* Winona Lake: Eisenbrauns.

Lord, Albert B.
1960 *The Singer of Tales.* Harvard Studies in Comparative Literature 24. Cambridge: Harvard University Press.

McCarter, P. Kyle
    1980   *I Samuel.* AB 8. Garden City, NY: Doubleday.
    1984   *II Samuel.* AB 9. Garden City, NY: Doubleday.

McEvenue, Sean E.
    1971   *The Narrative Style of the Priestly Writer.* AnBib 50. Rome: Biblical
              Institute.

Malina, Bruce J.
    1982   "The Social Sciences and Biblical Interpretation." *Int* 37:229–42.

Milne, Pamela J.
    1988   *Vladimir Propp and the Study of Structure in Hebrew Biblical Narrative.*
              Bible and Literature Series 13. Sheffield: Almond.
    1989   "The Patriarchal Stamp of Scripture: The Implications of Structural-
              ist Analyses for Feminist Hermeneutics." *JFSR* 5:17–34.

Miscall, Peter D.
    1986   *1 Samuel: A Literary Reading.* Indiana Studies in Biblical Literature.
              Bloomington: Indiana University Press.

Moore, Stephen D.
    1989   "Postmodernism and Biblical Studies: A Response to Robert
              Fowler." *Forum* 5:36–41.

Neusner, Jacob
    1983   "I. Introduction: Metaphor and Exegesis." *Semeia* 27:39–44.

Niditch, Susan
    1987   *Underdogs and Tricksters: A Prelude to Biblical Folklore.* San Francisco:
              Harper & Row.

Noth, Martin
    1968   *Numbers: A Commentary.* OTL. Philadelphia: Westminster.
    1972   *A History of the Pentateuchal Traditions.* Trans. with an introduction
              by B. W. Anderson. Englewood Cliffs, NJ: Prentice-Hall. (German
              1948.)
    1981   *The Deuteronomic History.* Sheffield: JSOT.

Oeming, Manfred
    1986   "Naboth, der Jesreeliter: Untersuchungen zu den theologischen
              Motiven der Überlieferungsgeschichte von I Reg 21." *ZAW* 98:363–
              82.

Ong, Walter J.
    1982   *Orality and Literacy: The Technologizing of the Word.* New York:
              Methuen.

Overholt, Thomas W.
    1986   *Prophecy in Cross-Cultural Perspective.* SBL Sources for Biblical Study
              17. Atlanta: Scholars.

Phillips, Gary A., ed.

1990   *Poststructural Criticism and the Bible: Text \ History \ Discourse. Semeia* 51. Atlanta: Scholars.

Polzin, Robert M.

1980   *Moses and the Deuteronomist: A Literary Study of the Deuteronomistic History. Part One: Deuteronomy, Joshua, Judges.* New York: Seabury.

1989   *Samuel and the Deuteronomist: A Literary Study of the Deuteronomistic History: 1 Samuel.* San Francisco: Harper & Row.

Propp, Vladimir

1968   *Morphology of the Folktale.* 2d ed. Austin: University of Texas Press.

Pury, Albert de

1975   *Promesse divine et légende cultuelle dans le cycle de Jacob.* 2 vols. Etudes bibliques. Paris: J. Gabalda.

Richter, Wolfgang

1971   *Exegese als Literaturwissenschaft.* Göttingen: Vandenhoeck & Ruprecht.

Ricoeur, Paul

1981   "The Hermeneutical Function of Distanciation." Pp. 131–44 in *Paul Ricoeur: Hermeneutics and the Human Sciences.* Ed. and trans. John B. Thompson. Cambridge: Cambridge University Press.

1984-88   *Time and Narrative.* 3 vols. Trans. Kathleen McLaughlin and David Pellauer. Chicago: University of Chicago Press.

Rimmon-Kenan, Shlomith

1983   *Narrative Fiction: Contemporary Poetics.* London: Methuen.

Robertson, David

1977   *The Old Testament and the Literary Critic.* Guides to Biblical Scholarship: Old Testament Series. Philadelphia: Fortress.

Rofé, Alexander

1988a   *The Prophetical Stories.* Jerusalem: Magnes.

1988b   "The Vineyard of Naboth: The Origin and Message of the Story." *VT* 38:89–104.

Rosenberg, Joel

1986   *King and Kin: Political Allegory in the Hebrew Bible.* Indiana Studies in Biblical Literature. Bloomington: Indiana University Press.

Salusinszky, Imre

1987   *Criticism in Society.* New York: Methuen.

Sanders, James A.

1984   *Canon and Community.* Philadelphia: Fortress.

Schmidt, Ludwig
    1986   *Literarische Studien zur Josephgeschichte.* Pp. 121–297 in BZAW 167.
            Berlin: Walter de Gruyter.

Schmidt, Werner H.
    1974   *Exodus.* BK 2. Neukirchen-Vluyn: Neukirchener Verlag.

Scholes, Robert, and Robert Kellogg
    1966   *The Nature of Narrative.* New York: Oxford University Press.

Sheppard, Gerald T.
    1982   "Hearing the Voice of the Same God through Historically Dissimilar
            Traditions." *Int* 36:21–33.

Ska, Jean Louis
    1986   *Le passage de la mer: étude de la construction, du style et de la symbolique
            d'Ex 14,1–3.* AnBib 109. Rome: Biblical Institute.

Soggin, S. Alberto
    1987   *Judges: A Commentary.* 2d ed. London: SCM.

Stendahl, Krister
    1962   "Biblical Theology, Contemporary." Pp. 418–32 in *IDB.* Vol. 1.

Sternberg, Meir
    1985   *The Poetics of Biblical Narrative: Ideological Literature and the Drama of
            Reading.* Bloomington: Indiana University Press.

Stipp, Hermann-Josef
    1987   *Elischa—Propheten—Gottesmänner?* ATAT 24. St. Ottilien: EOS.

Thompkins, Jane P., ed.
    1980   *Reader-Response Criticism: From Formalism to Post-Structuralism.*
            Baltimore: Johns Hopkins University Press.

Thompson, Thomas L.
    1987   *The Origin Tradition of Ancient Israel: 1. The Literary Formation of
            Genesis and Exodus 1–23.* JSOTSup 55. Sheffield: Sheffield Academic.

Tigay, Jeffrey H., ed.
    1985   *Empirical Models for Biblical Criticism.* Philadelphia: University of
            Pennsylvania Press.

Van Seters, John
    1975   *Abraham in History and Tradition.* New Haven: Yale University Press.
    1983   *In Search of History: Historiography in the Ancient World and the Origins
            of Biblical History.* New Haven: Yale University Press.
    1986   "The Yahwist as Historian." Pp. 37–55 in *SBL Seminar Papers.* Ed.
            Kent Harold Richards. Atlanta: Scholars.
    1987   *Der Jahwist als Historiker.* TS 134. Zürich: Theologischer Verlag.

Van Winkle, D. W.
1989 "1 Kings XIII: True and False Prophecy." *VT* 39:31–43.

Veyne, Paul
1988 *Did the Greeks Believe in their Myths?* Trans. Paula Wissing. Chicago: University of Chicago Press.

Walsh, Jerome T.
1989 "The Contexts of 1 Kings XIII." *VT* 39:355–70.

Weimar, Peter
1977 *Untersuchungen zur Redactionsgeschichte des Pentateuch.* BZAW 146. Berlin: Walter de Gruyter.

Weiss, Meir
1984 *The Bible from Within: The Method of Total Interpretation.* Jerusalem: Magnes.

Wellhausen, Julius
1957 *Prolegomena to the History of Ancient Israel.* New York: Meridian.

Westermann, Claus
1980 *The Promises to the Fathers.* Trans. David E. Green. Philadelphia: Fortress. (German: 1976.)
1981 *Genesis.* BKAT 1/2. Neukirchen-Vluyn: Neukirchener Verlag.
1984 *Genesis 1–11: A Commentary.* Trans. John J. Scullion. Minneapolis: Augsburg. (German: 1974.)
1985 *Genesis 12–36: A Commentary.* Trans. John J. Scullion. Minneapolis: Augsburg. (German: 1981.)
1986 *Genesis 37–50: A Commentary.* Trans. John J. Scullion. Minneapolis: Augsburg. (German: 1983.)

White, Hugh C.
1985 "The Joseph Story: A Narrative Which Consumes Its Content." *Semeia* 31:49–69.

Whybray, R.N.,
1987 *The Making of the Pentateuch: A Methodological Study.* JSOTSup 53. Sheffield: Sheffield Academic.

Wilcoxen, Jay
1968 "Narrative Structure and Cult Legend: A Study of Joshua 1–6." Pp. 43–70 in *Transitions in Biblical Scholarship.* Ed. J. Coert Rylaarsdam. Chicago: University of Chicago Press.

Wilson, Robert R.
1984 *Sociological Approaches to the Old Testament.* Philadelphia: Fortress.

Zakovitch, Yair
  1984   "The Tales of Naboth's Vineyard, I Kings 21." Pp. 379–405 in Meir
            Weiss, *The Bible from Within: The Method of Total Interpretation.*
            Jerusalem: Magnes.
  1990   "Humor and Theology or the Successful Failure of Israelite Intelli-
            gence: A Literary-Folkloric Approach to Joshua 2." Pp. 75–98 in *Text
            and Tradition: The Hebrew Bible and Folklore.* Ed. Susan Niditch.
            Semeia Studies. Atlanta: Scholars.

Index of Biblical Citations

Index of Authors